Block Time

A Memoir

Harry Anderson

outskirts
press

Outskirts Press, Inc.
http://www.outskirtspress.com

ISBN: 978-1-9772-2946-5

PRINTED IN THE UNITED STATES OF AMERICA

Our memory is a more perfect world than the universe: it gives back life to those who no longer exist.

Guy deMaupassant

With you in mind and heart, I sew with words
this story quilt,
my children

TABLE OF CONTENTS

A WORD FROM THE QUILTER

ACCEPTING HIS CHALLENGE to create a "story quilt" – each block representing a chapter of Harry Anderson's autobiography – I have undertaken the task to interpret each chapter of *Block Time* by fashioning unique designs. His reminiscences stirred my emotions, and one by one the designs emerged.

Struck by his optimism, I have chosen a yellow fabric for the borders and sashing, thereby unifying the twenty-five blocks. Because several of the themes of the more complex stories (e.g., "Rhode Island Hospital" and "Ontonagon") are difficult to interpret, I had to be as ingenious as I could. Thus, for the Rhode Island Hospital block I have used a little-known symbol of Providence.

And as for the Ontonagon block, to depict the sunrise/sunset motif, I hand-dyed the fabric.

At all times, I have wanted each block to be just right in every which way: in its accurate symbolic depiction of an episode's theme and in its compatibility with the quilt's overall artistry. I have revised several times until the true story had emerged. My favorite ones are hand-pieced.

I can say that the process has been simple, but the execution was not. However, I have loved working on this project and am proud of the result.

Peg Facker

A WORD BEFORE MY STORY BEGINS

FOR A DOZEN or so years I have been interviewing men and women and, monthly, writing their stories for a local magazine. At last count more than a hundred of them have been published. Stories about ordinary people living quiet lives: a retired Air Force master sergeant who volunteers to assist a fourth grade teacher in an inner city school, an artist who specializes in painting nudes, a former nun who became a midwife, a horn player who for thirty years has been with the Rhode Island Philharmonic . . . and so it goes.

Common among them is their question that opens every interview: "Why are you talking with me? I've done nothing special." But with no exception every one of them, when the interview ends, gushes, "Wow! I really enjoyed that!" or something like that. I suspect that perhaps it's inherent in us the wont to tell our tales; however, modesty and other deterrents often keep that wont in check. Such has been the case with me.

Within the context of an interview, a modest and/or taciturn subject opens up *if* the interviewer asks focused questions and, most importantly, steadily demonstrates interest with body language, a word or two, and eye contact. Simply put, *if* the interviewer practices the art of listening.

Now entering the denouement of my life, I admit that I, too, wish to tell my tales, or at least some of them . . . those that put me in a lathe, so to speak, and shaped my bones and brain into the man that I am. Unlikely I'll ever be interviewed, to get my wish I must put focused questions to myself and then write out my answers. This I am about to do.

So, I will be asking myself: How and when did writing become important to you? Does Faith play a part in your life? Has schooling left lasting impressions on you? Who has influenced you, has been a mentor? What about sex? Any war stories? Your wins and losses?

I will be structuring my book along the lines of a story quilt; i.e., seeing each of the stories as a block in a quilt. (NOTE: An explanation of this comes later.) As each is written, a quilter will design a block that symbolically delineates its theme and introduces an episode. If all goes well and, if you will, the stitching together of tales and blocks reveals the essential components of my identity, then I have succeeded. Or have I? Much depends upon who does the stitching.

I was frustrated and afraid, and I was alienated.

MANTON

I DATE THIS earliest memory "January, 1935", deducing that, because I was neither walking nor talking yet, the probability of my age being fourteen months has validity. I can say then that this memory goes back 85 years and 10 months to an afternoon when guests had come to visit Mom and Dad in their second-floor tenement in the Manton section of Johnston.

I sat on the carpet beside a chair. An ankle now and then stroked my back. It was my mother's ankle. I turned my head to the left and saw knees and shoes. I turned to the right and saw more knees and shoes. I did not creep away from the security of the stroking ankle.

Above me, high sounds and low sounds blended into a drone. They came from big people. Words. The big people were making sounds that had meaning. Sounds with meaning were words. The big people were conversing.

I could not put meaning to the sounds. I had no vocabulary. I could not speak. My arms and legs went rigid. I badly wanted to speak. My mouth opened, but the gurgle was not a word. I was frustrated and afraid, and I was alienated. Never would I be like the big people. That is what scared me.

The stroking ankle did little to comfort me.

I was feeling like a real writer.

SERREL SWEET ROAD

IN 1941, WHEN I was about to turn nine, my last shred of belief in Santa Claus vanished in Dad's basement workshop where Mom had sent me to fetch potatoes from the bin. There, leaning against the foundation, was a two-wheel bicycle freshly painted a bright orange. I was no dope. Right away I knew that Dad had refurbished it for me, and I reckoned, what with Christmas but a week away, that that bicycle would be in the parlor next to the tree on Christmas morning.

And there it was off to the side of the wrapped gifts, standing smartly on its kick-stand.

"Oh, look at that!" Mom gushed. "Read the tag, Sonny."

Feigning surprise, I read it: *To Sonny from Santa*. But my glee was for real. For weeks and weeks, as I had watched Buddy and Bobby speed up and down Serrel Sweet Road on their bikes, I pained with envy. Now I could join them.

Nothing could ever top this gift, or so I had thought until Christmas of 1942 when I unwrapped a present about the size of Mom's bread box and laid eyes on a toy printing press. Gutenberg's idea of movable type had revolutionized civilization 503 years earlier. This gift – a miniature version of his invention - brought about my personal renaissance.

While tinkering with it through the winter, I hit on the idea of founding a neighborhood newspaper that I would name THE SERREL SWEET ROAD NEWS. When spring thaw came, my plans were complete. Getting an okay from Dad to set up an "office" in the crawl space under our front porch, I used much of the April school vacation to do just that. First the removal of odds and ends that Dad had tossed into the space – things like scrap lumber, yard tools with broken handles, and out grown play toys. Next, the sweeping and swishing away cobwebs. Finally, with the help of my seven year old sister, Peggy, the moving in of furniture: a plywood play table Dad had built for her to display her tea set; a discarded hassock; Mom's unwanted sewing basket; a couple of wooden crates Dad brought home from the rubber company where he worked. And the printing press.

Mastering it took much patience. To form a word, you had to pluck each of its letters molded onto 3/8″ rubber squares from a box filled with them and, using tweezers, squeeze each square into parallel groves machined into an 8″ metal drum. When a page had been formatted, you then brushed black ink onto the squares. Cranking the drum with the attached handle produced the finished product.

Peggy and I tried hard to contain our excitement, eager to get out the first edition of our newspaper. Our playmates, however, were more eager to embrace spring's pleasures than to pretend to be journalists in a dark, dank crawl space. After supper, we boys sped our bikes around the block or played pick-up baseball in the bumpy field off George Waterman Road while the girls hop-scotched in our driveway. Without their help, THE SERREL SWEET ROAD NEWS could not go to press.

TWO WEEKS BEFORE the last day of classes at Graniteville School a couple of turning points in my life happened. A copy of *The Quest*, a sixteen-page mimeographed collection of student drawings, prosody, and prose was given to each kid. A cute piece that I had written entitled "My Cat Whiskers" filled page six. To see in print something coming from my pen and my name in the by-line thrilled me.

About the same time, the school's principal – Mr. Brooks – handed me a sealed envelope and said to give it to my parents. The next day Dad came home early from work, and Mom and he drove off, giving Peggy and me orders not to leave the yard. Only once before had we been left alone at home. That was when Dad took her to Dr. Ricci to have a bad tooth pulled.

After supper that night, they sat me down in the parlor. Right off I knew they had serious business to talk about because Dad spoke first. He was the most tongue-tied man I'd ever known.

"Sonny, this afternoon we met with Mr. Brooks and two teachers." He glanced at Mom. "You tell him, Lolly."

With the same look on her face when she had read "My Cat Whiskers", Mom told me what the meeting at school was all about.

"They said such nice things about you, Sonny. How polite you are and how neat your schoolwork is. But they also said they don't know what to do with you because you're so far ahead of the rest of the class. So, they asked us what we thought about you skipping a grade. In other words, next September, instead of going into Miss Darby's fifth grade class, you'll go into Miss Jenkes's sixth grade class. Well, how do you feel about that?"

I shrugged.

"Sonny, all this is way over my head." Dad's tongue licked his lower lip, something he did whenever he was puzzled. "I don't know anything about school. I can't tell you what grade I was in when I quit and went to work in the mill. So I said to the principal you know better than us about these matters. You do what you think is best. Isn't that what I said, Lolly?"

"That's what you said. It looks like they'll skip you a grade. We're very proud of you, Sonny."

It made no difference to me what grade they put me in. My mind was on the printing press. School would end in a couple of weeks and we'd get going on the newspaper. That was all I cared about.

SIX OF US kids got together in the crawl space the first day of summer vacation: Peggy and her friends, Paula and Joey, and Buddy and Bobby, my two pals. We yammered away all morning about who was going to do what. By the time Mom called us for lunch, we each had a self-appointed job along with bragging rights to a title. Scribbled on my pad was the line-up of the staff of our newspaper:

Reporters: Margaret Anderson, Paula Burhoe, Aaron DeMoranville
Artist: Joan Risk
Circulation: Robert Scott
Editor: Harry Anderson

Mom not only grilled us cheese sandwiches but also squelched a mutiny. When Peggy whined that I was bossing everyone and ordered her to get news and she didn't know what news was, Mom put a hand to her mouth (she had bad teeth) and smiled.

"Darling, 'news' means something that happened that a lot of people don't know about but maybe would like to know."

"But I don't know about anything happening."

Miffed about her whining, with an editor's voice I said, "You're a reporter! That means you got to go out and look for it."

"I have an idea," Mom said, clapping her hands. "You know Suzy, Mrs. Fairbanks' dog? Well, Suzy just had a litter of puppies. That's news. Why don't Paula and you go down the street and take a look at them?"

"So? What am I supposed to do then?"

"You're a reporter, dummy!" I was impatient. "You gotta write a story and give it to me for the newspaper!"

Softly but firmly Mom scolded me for calling my sister that. "Remember, Sonny. She's only finished the second grade."

Joey, who was pretty good at drawing (Miss Hood always pinned her pictures on the bulletin board), shouted, "I'll go with them, Mrs. Anderson! I like puppies."

Bobby and Buddy had already run off. They said they were going to look into something. The three girls giggled as they skipped out of the house, letting the screen door whack shut behind them. Exasperated, I sat in Dad's chair in the parlor and picked up last night's rumpled *Providence Journal* to study how the front page looked. Across the top in big letters – bigger than any that came with my printing press, the head line stretched: **ROMMEL CAPTURES TOBRUK**.

Mom was on the telephone. I heard her say, "Edna? This is Laura Anderson calling. Any minute now my daughter Peggy and her two friends will be coming to see Suzy's puppies. I hope you don't mind. They're playing make-believe newspaper reporters and maybe they'll be asking you a lot of questions. So, be ready. What's that? [She laughed] Thank you, Edna. Bye."

A RAINY DAY in June cheats a kid on school vacation of outdoor fun. But I had work to do. Mom may think we were playing in the crawl space, but for me the running of a newspaper was serious business, something as real as the batch of brownies she and Peggy were making. I ran through the rain to the office that was dimmer than usual because there was no sunlight. I had to squint to read the copy that my reporters had given me.

The copy was disappointing. Not yet learning cursive penmanship, Peggy and Paula printed their story about Mrs. Fairbanks' dog. Four slanty lines of bare information: names of the four puppies, the color of their fur, and the mess they're making of the garage. Bobby's and Buddy's wasn't much better. A penciled recap of last Saturday's pick-up baseball game, scrawled on the back of a soiled, wrinkled page ripped from a calendar. I had a lot of work to do.

Step One: set the masthead. One at a time, using tweezers, I tamped into the first groove of the press's roller the twenty-two letters of the paper's name – all capitals: THE SERREL SWEET ROAD NEWS. To see how that would look printed on an 8"x11" piece of white paper, I swabbed ink onto the rubber tiles and cranked the roller. Too much ink. Blots obscured the words "SWEET" and "NEWS". Worse than that, the letters were upside down.

I slipped off my shirt and used it to wipe the tiles before inverting each one back into the groove. Gently, I gave them another coat of ink and turned the crank. Wow! The masthead came out almost perfectly! Some of the letters, though, were slightly slanted and others needed more ink.

Not until Thursday, three days later, did I typeset the first page. There were problems galore. What my reporters had given me just would not do. In my bedroom, sprawled on the floor, I fleshed out the Suzy story, and then returned to the office to lay it out. Even when the rain had stopped and more light came into the crawl space, I could hardly distinguish the vowel tiles. Then I had to reckon the spacing of the letters so that each line ended with a complete word.

From time to time, my staff stooped into the crawl space to see what I was doing. But, seeing nothing exciting, they quickly went back into the sunlight to do what kids do on a summer day.

I, however, was excited. With the squeezing into place each letter, a word was made, and the words made sentences, and the sentences became paragraphs. It was like magic! As the drum filled with tiles, I could see Suzy and her pups. I could hear their yipping, feel their fur, smell their breath. On the drum lay a story, and telling it was like taking a snap shot of the animals with the Kodak box camera that Dad had given me. But, even better, because the writing made them move, in my imagination they lived, they were for real.

When all the grooves had been filled with tiles, I had yet to tell about Mrs. Fairbanks' garden gloves getting chewed or about Suzy's biting the milkman when he petted the puppies. I was learning the importance of conciseness. I would be less wordy with the page 2 story of the pick-up baseball game.

Before going to that story, I had to see what the first page looked like in print. Carefully inking the tiles and slipping onto the ledge of the printing press a clean sheet of paper, I turned the drum , and out came my creation. Not waiting for the ink to dry, I pinched a corner of the page and scooted out and into the kitchen to show Mom page one.

"Well, well, well! So this is what you've been up to. Look, Peggy. There's your name!"

"I didn't write all that, Mommy."

To placate the girl I said, "But you gave me the facts, didn't you?

You and Paula. So, it's your story."

I was too happy to argue with her. I went to my bedroom to re-read my work. Other than a smudge or two and a couple of words with an "a" instead of an "e", the page looked good enough to keep. I decided to run off nine more copies, thinking ten in all would do. Anyway, my supply of paper and ink was low.

Mom stopped me as I quick-stepped from my room, eager to get back to the office.

"Would you mind, Sonny, if you left that page on the table so that your father can see it? I'm pretty sure he'll like it as much as I do."

Peggy knelt on a chair at the table and hunched over the page, and Mom leaned over her. I felt pretty good to see people reading it.

THE SERREL SWEET ROAD NEWS

1¢   Weather: sunny today

Editor: Harry Anderson, Jr.

SUZY HAS PUPPIES
By Peggy Anderson and Paula Burhoe

Suzy is a golden retriaver and belongs to Mrs. Fairbanks who lives in a brick house on the corner of Serrel Sweet Road and Sherwood Place. She had 4 puppies.

One puppy is all tan. Another is dark brown. The others look different. They eat only milk. It comes from Suzy. She's their mother.

Mrs. Fairbanks keeps them in her garage. She put a blanket there for them and all day long they play and sleep a lot.

The tan puppy is named Pal and the dark brown one is named Fluffy because it has a lot of fur. The different ones are called Jack and Jill.

They are very cute and like to be scratched and held.

Emboldened by the look of this page, I moved more quickly to write and set-up copy for page 2. Because I pitched for the "home team" in last Saturday's pick-up game, I could flesh out the sketchy copy Bobby and Buddy had given me, telling for instance that it was Tommy Burrows' homerun that won the game at the last minute just as Arthur Slater's father yelled for him to get home for supper.

That evening, as Mom, Peggy, and I played Chinese checkers and Dad, with a newspaper opened and crumpled on his lap, snored in his chair, I gave thought to "The Serrel Sweet Road News". Only two stories wasn't giving customers their money's worth. But nothing other than puppies and a pick-up ball game, as far as I knew, could be called news in the quiet village of Graniteville.

Coming from the cabinet RCA radio in the parlor was a bulletin: "At 0910 hours Pacific time, the First US Marine Division launched an amphibious invasion of Guadalcanal. It met with heavy Japanese fire. No casualty reports are available at this time." In a flash I had an idea for a story.

The next morning at my printing press I tamped letters into the grooves of the drum. As the lines of tiles filled them, I felt like a magician. With the spelling out of each word, Cousin Charlie's visit a week ago came back to life. It began with a touch of drama:

Charlie Anderson is a sergeant in the US Army. Last Sunday he came to see us to say good bye. He was on his way to Europe to fight the Germans. In his uniform he looked like a hero.

The whole story took up almost two pages. When I proof-read them, I was feeling like a real writer. But at the bottom of page 4 there was empty space left over, about two inches. Joey, I thought, could draw something. Maybe a B17 dropping a load of bombs.

Because she couldn't draw airplanes or because she had the soul of a dove, instead she drew a clump of lilacs. The printing press was of no use to her. So, with a tiny brush and a palette of water colors, by hand she painted those flowers in the empty space on each of the ten copies of the newspaper. Customers now would get the weather, three stories, and a nice drawing for one penny. Noting how Dad's newspaper was folded, I did the same to hold together the four sheets of paper. It was time now for Bobby to knock on neighbors' doors and ask if they wanted to buy the first issue of **THE SERREL SWEET ROAD NEWS.**

The paper sold out. With Mrs. Fairbanks' giving Bobby a nickel, we collected fifteen cents. I gave each of my staff two pennies, keeping the left over three to buy paper for the next edition. But there would be no second edition. Buddy went away to spend two weeks with his grandparents at their beach house in Scarborough. Bobby's bike's front tire tube went flat and he didn't have money to patch it. And Peggy and I came down with the mumps. By the time the six of us could get together again, summer vacation was ending and our parents were outfitting us with new shoes.

WHAT I LIKED best about skipping fifth grade was Miss Jenkes's passing out brand new geography books to her sixth graders. I caressed its smooth pages, thrilled to the clean, crisp, black print, and delighted to the smell of its newness. She would not allow us to take the books home. I looked forward to Tuesdays' geography lessons. When a book was passed to me, I quickly turned the pages to the map of Europe, found where Germany was, and imagined Cousin Charlie over there in his uniform.

Most of all, I day-dreamed of the day when I would write a book.

Sonny, you're growing up.

MILLVILLE

NOT MUCH REMAINS of Millville, Massachusetts, a five square mile speck of a town that is home to a few more than 3,000 residents. Gone is the rubber works, washed away by the flooded Blackstone River. Gone is Frank Davis' store on Central Street. Gone is the Grand Trunk Railway. Gone are all my kinsmen, many of whom rest in peace in the Wilson cemetery, just beyond St. John's Episcopal Church, which an uncle had told me was built with granite blocks in the 19th century by Millville men.

Mom and Dad married in that church and began housekeeping in a cottage on a knoll on Central Street just shy of the cemetery. It still stands as does Dad's brother's, Richard, and his wife, Alice – the last house on dead-ending Chesley Street. Mom's sister Mabel had occupied for a while the rooms over Frank Davis' store. The big Victorian on West Street, impressive because of its size, continues to lord over the humbler dwellings on this lane that twists and turns and comes to an end in Uxbridge. Dad's other brother, Fred (aka, "Uncle Punk"), and Aunt Julia lived in this Victorian house.

Down farther on West Street, withdrawn from whatever business keeps the villagers up and about, shyly sits as it has done for more than a century Grandma and Grandpa Campbell's cottage. They lived and died there. Mom took her first steps on its planked floors. In its backyard I learned how to lift a bucket of water from a well and to wipe myself with newspaper in a two-hole privy.

Although the distance from our home in Graniteville to Millville is about twenty miles, for a five-year-old boy the weekly drive – always on a Saturday – was as exiting as a rocket ride to the moon. Those drives began after the '38 hurricane had washed away the rubber mill, forcing Dad to transfer to the US Rubber plant on Valley Street in Providence and to move his family to Rhode Island, first to a tenement in Manton, then to a bungalow in Greystone, and finally to a house in Graniteville.

Until Peggy, my sister, was old enough to climb onto the back seat beside me in Dad's '34 Chevrolet, I sat alone and peered out the window, memorizing the route. Certain landmarks caught my fancy: a tilting barn with a swayed back roof; an old house shaped like none other, its upper windows shuttered save for one; a lake with petrified remains of trees sticking up; a fire tower atop a distant hill; an abandoned hay wagon off in a field.

I invented stories, and Peggy was my audience.

"See that old house? Santa Claus lives there."

"No, he doesn't."

"Yup, he does too! I saw him up there in that window. Cross my heart!"

Then, as we approached the lake with the pointy petrified trees poking through, I feigned fright and covered my eyes.

"Hide! Don't let the monster see us!"

"There's no monster."

"Yes, there is. I seen it twice. It's green and has shiny yellow eyes and . . . and it's bigger than this car. Honest!"

"Where?"

"There, in the middle of that lake."

It was Grandma's house, though, that really spooked me, especially after dark. Without electricity, a kerosene lamp had to make do. She rocked in its light in the narrow sitting room off the kitchen. The rest of us sat in the shadows on stiff, mohair cushioned chairs. The kitchen smelled of wood smoke, scrubbed linoleum, yeast and cinnamon, and the quietness cast a spell. Only the low voices of the adults, the ticking of a wind-up clock, and the creaking of her chair broke the silence. I drowsed off, as though hypnotized, sensing the presence of ghosts.

Uncle Bob, Grandma's unwed son, lodged with her. A stout man, like her and Mom, he filled a chair. Many of the chores Grandma and Uncle Bob did had to do with cooking. With no kitchen counter space, she peeled potatoes, kneaded dough, rolled out pie crust on the oilcloth-covered table. The black iron stove was his responsibility. He cleared the firebox of ashes. In the earthen-floor cellar he chopped logs into kindling and carried armfuls to the kitchen, knowing when to toss some onto the embers. A smoker of rolled cigarettes, he wheezed as he worked and whistled.

In all seasons, the stove never cooled. Whenever warm water was needed, a supply of it simmered in a large enamel pot on a back ledge. Summer breezes coming through the screen door hardly gave comfort. Drops of sweat fell from Grandma's brow and plopped onto the oilcloth, and she rolled them into the bread dough. The kitchen, however, was snug in the cold months. On Saturday visits in winter, Peggy and I sometimes made a snowman beside the outhouse, impatiently awaiting Grandma's call to come in. Stomping snow from our boots at the back door, we savored the warmth and the aroma of a batch of molasses cookies she pulled from the oven.

Only now and then I saw Grandpa Campbell because he was a trainman whose Saturday shift kept him at the throttle in the cab of a steam locomotive on its run to Boston. But when he was home, he hauled me off my feet and kissed my cheek. His white mustache tickled, and I giggled. Once, he and I walked a stretch of rails that paralleled West Street. He puffed a pipe with a curved stem, and I picked pods of milkweed and blew the gossamer seeds into the autumn air.

"Always, Sonny, when the train's about here, I pull the whistle twice so as Mary Jane, your Grandma, will know I'm passing by."

His decease, when I could still be held in Dad's arms, introduced me to death.

I could not understand that day why Dad wore a tie and Mom dressed me in my Sunday clothes or why a wreathe with a black ribbon hung on Grandma's front door or why men and women were coming and going through the front door that I never saw used before. I sat alone at the kitchen table, staring at the food spread across it: a ham, loaves of homemade bread, cakes and pies. Kindling crackled in the stove and whispering voices came from the sitting room. Over them sounded Mom's voice.

"Sonny's too young to understand. I don't think you should do that."

"Just a peek. That's all."

"Be quick about it though."

Dad took my hand and led me past the adults in the sitting room and stopped at the threshold of the front parlor, and he put his hands under my arms and lifted me. Afternoon sunlight came through the lace curtains at the two windows between which lay Grandpa in a wooden box surrounded by flowers. I knew it was Grandpa because I saw that white mustache.

For one week in the summer between third and fourth grade, I stayed with Grandma and Uncle Bob. On the second day, a Monday, as she ladled warm water into the galvanized sink and scrubbed the breakfast dishes and I wiped them and Uncle Bob stoked the embers in the big Glenwood stove, she called to him.

"Bob, we'll be needing some flour and lard if you want a slice of pie for your supper. Before the sun gets any hotter, would you go to Frank Davis' and get some?"

"Want to come with me, Sonny?"

"Tomorrow he can do that, but right now there's something I need help with."

After he had counted coins from an apothecary jar kept on the bottom shelf over the sink along with plates and platters, he limped off, letting the screen door slap shut. Grandma sidled to the ice box.

"Jeb's coming today, I suspect, with ice. This block's pretty much used up."

Albeit a big woman, she moved like a scudding cloud. Maybe she is an Indian, I thought. On a drive home from Millville I had overheard Mom's telling Dad that Grandma kept it a secret about her having Nipmuc blood.

"Sonny, I want you to fill up this pitcher and that pot on the stove for me. Think you can do that if I show you how?"

We went outside to the well house where she gave me my first lesson in pulling up a bucket of water. Seeing that I was a skinny kid yet to add inches to my height, she told me to fetch a kitchen chair.

"See that there piece of wood sticking up? That's the brake. Pull it hard toward you."

I did and got out of the way of the winch's spinning handle. Way down in the blackness of the well the bucket's splash echoed.

"Now, Sonny, with all your might crank the handle and pull up the bucket. It's heavy, I swear. Think you can do that?"

On the third try, I steadied the bucket so that it didn't tip or fall back. My arms strained until they ached, but it kept coming up and up and stopped when Grandma braked the winch.

"That's too heavy for you to bring into the house. We'll use a ladle to get the water into the pot. Anyway, Sonny, you've done yourself proud. Yes, you're growing up. From now on I'll be asking you to get the water."

Mom, Dad, and Peggy came Saturday, the last day of my vacation, to take me home. Mom squeezed me and said she very much had missed me, and Dad asked for an accounting of my week in Millville. I began with telling of me at the well and then about helping Grandma with kitchen chores and ending with a description of yesterday's visit with Uncle Fred and Aunt Julia when a real soldier shook my hand.

"Cousin Charlie was there, home from the Army. He had on a uniform with ribbons and . . . and on his sleeve were stripes. Three of them! He said he was going away to fight the Germans."

I did not tell Dad that I went to the outhouse in the dark to pee and I wasn't afraid. Neither did I tell him that Uncle Bob wanted me to put ketchup on my minced pie.

UNCLE BOB HAD his heroes. They wore chaps and spurs and Stetson hats, white ones at that. Desperados wore the black hats. He idolized them all – Roy Rogers, Gene Autry, Tom Mix, Hopalong Cassidy. I think Hopalong Cassidy was his favorite because he didn't croon in the saddle. My uncle wasn't fazed at all by being the only adult watching a Western on a Saturday afternoon in the Stadium Theatre.

We made an odd couple going down Central Street, across the bridge, and up to McNamara's pub to catch a bus into Woonsocket. In the winter he wore galoshes, a lumber jacket over overalls with suspenders and a funny looking fur hat with ear flaps. Because of a boyhood bout with polio, he limped severely. Not to embarrass him, I slowed my pace. On the bus we rarely talked or, when we did, it was about the weather or the lunch Grandma had fixed for us. On the return ride to Millville, however, he talked on and on about the movie.

"I knew Hopalong shouldn't have gone into that canyon. He should've known the villains were going to ambush him. But, yee-haw, didn't he let them have it! What did you think of that gun fight?"

Grandma's back yard slopped down to Ironstone Street. From the yard I could see the roof of the Polish Club and could hear the playing of polkas and loud laughing. Grandma forbade me to go anywhere near the place. Yet she said nothing when, after Saturday's supper, her son returned from his upstairs room wearing a white shirt and poorly knotted necktie and smelling of Old Spice and limped off into the night.

Mom always asked, "Going to the Polish Club, Bob?"

He always answered, "No place else to go on a Saturday night."

A boy cannot grasp the bedevilment of loneliness.

A GRANITE HEADSTONE with "Campbell" etched on it overlooks Central Street in Wilson's cemetery in Millville. It marks the graves of Grandma and Grandpa and Uncle Bob, who passed on alone in a nursing home. The funeral director, five paid bearers, and Pauline and I witnessed the internment. It was a January afternoon, and a moaning wind chilled us to the bone.

PEGGY AND I sprawled on an old braided rug beside the kerosene stove playing Chinese checkers, and Mom stood behind Grandma, seated in her rocking chair. She undid Grandma's bun, and the white hair cascaded down past her shoulders all the way to her waist. Grandma's eyes closed. Her lips pinched a smile. Mom's face lost its lines as she brushed and brushed the hair. She looked as she did when nursing Peggy. A boy knows nothing about saints, but in the light of the kerosene lamp she looked like the lady in the picture that hung in her bedroom.

"That's Mary, Sonny. She's baby Jesus' mother."

When we tired of playing Chinese checkers, Peggy imitated Mom by brushing her doll's hair and I, in the dim light of the lamp, squinted at a Dick Tracy big-little book, half listening to the women's conversation. I felt as though I were in a spirit world.

"Laura, won't you go into the parlor and play the piano? Some of the old songs you used to do when you was a girl?"

"Oh, Ma, I haven't touched the keys in ages."

"Sonny, ask your ma to do it."

I did and she stood, and Peggy and I followed her into the parlor. Grandma stayed in her rocking chair. Mom lit another kerosene lamp that was on a stand beside a sofa and carried it to the upright piano opposite to where Grandpa Campbell had lain in a coffin. Its keys had yellowed. On its ledge were a hymnal and some sheet music. She flipped pages of the hymnal, stopped, and began to play. The strings long ago had lost their pitch, and the tinny tone seemed to come from long ago as did everything else in the room. She hummed as she played *The Old Rugged Cross*.

"I told you, Ma, my fingers are stiff. Ma? Ma, can you hear me?"

Peggy ran to the sitting room and returned. "She's asleep."

The house itself seemed to be sleeping. I heard only the sliding of the hymnal to the edge of a page of sheet music to keep it from toppling.

"Here's Daddy's favorite song. Mine, too."

Mom leaned toward the page and hit some wrong notes. "I'm sorry," she said and started over, her thin soprano voice resonating in the quiet room. I wished Dad had come back from fishing with his brothers to hear his favorite song, *I Love You Truly*.

Mom's hands were shaking as she pressed open another piece. It fell to the carpet, and I ran to pick it up and stayed at her side to watch her fingers at the keys.

"*Whispering Hope* is another favorite, Sonny. I used to play it almost everyday when I was a little bit older than you. Can you see the words? Aren't they lovely?"

ON THE RIDE home from one of the final visits to Millville, my new sister sat between Peggy and me in the back seat. They fussed with a cardboard cut-out doll and its trousseau. Mom hummed hymns and Dad sort of bowed at the wheel, not speaking at all. What happened on Uncle Punk's porch had troubled him.

All afternoon we and most of our kin had gathered for a picnic to celebrate Cousin Charlie's homecoming. After the outdoor tables had been cleared, the adults chatted on the porch out of the blazing August sun and the cousins played tag. Peggy's whining, "I quit. It's too hot!", started the stampede. We kids dashed to the porch to beg for lemonade. The clamor stopped abruptly when Uncle Punk pointed his pipe at us and growled, "Quiet! Stop right where you are!"

In counterpoint with a somber male voce coming from a table radio, Aunts Alice and Helen sobbed. Mom had her hand on Dad's shoulder. He had his eyes fixed on his shoe laces. Uncle Bob bent to the radio, his ear nearly touching it. I had seen before his expression when a band of rustlers were about to lynch Gene Autry. Cousin Charlie, the hero of the day, said a cuss word and went to the barn out back. When no one told him to hold his tongue, I caught on. Something big was happening. Something far greater than a guy's cussing in front of women and children.

Too curious to run off with my cousins, I crouched behind a rhododendron bush, close enough to the porch to hear certain words like "incredible" and "Hiroshima".

LIKE THE 4:31 a.m. train whistling through Millville, my boyhood visits to Grandma Campbell's house on West Street passed in a rush and came to a stop when a stroke sent her to bed permanently. An ambulance transported her from Woonsocket Hospital to our house in Graniteville. My room became hers where, for a year, she lay mute and in and out of sleep every day. Often upon coming home from school, I tip-toed into that room to get my old clothes from the closet and saw Mom by the bed. She softly sang *Whispering Hope* over and over as she brushed Grandma's hair.

Then she died. Her home on West Street in Millville, Massachusetts, still stands. I did drive by it once, wanting to show my kids where my grandmother had baked me molasses cookies and had taught me how to fetch a bucket of water from a well. But I did not stop and knock on the door. I suppose because I wanted to remember it as it was, not to see its kitchen or sitting room or parlor with the eyes of a grownup. Then again, perhaps down deep I did believe in ghosts and cared not to encounter them. Not right then at any rate.

We were putting to music something unknown to us.

CONIMICUT POINT

WE GOT A gig at a gin mill in Conimicut for New Year's Eve, and we were happy about that because the owner would pay each of us ten bucks – double what the going price was in those days.

The year was 1956, arguably the last year of America's innocence. Certainly, it was the last year of innocence for us five guys who made up the band. We had recently finished college and were facing imminent military duty.

Ah – 1956! Was there ever such a year? Just a dot on the big time line. Back then church ladies feted wedding receptions in church basements and high school seniors decorated gyms for their proms; male and female danced cheek-to-cheek; kids played kick-the-can until street lights came on; a glass of beer on tap cost a nickel; and a tavern was called a "gin mill", not a "club".

But America was becoming under-nourished. The Korean imbroglio had withered the feast of celebration that had followed the triumphant end of WWII. Hungrily, America chomped on fast food. Elvis, "the king", put a new menu on the table, and we pigged out on rock and roll.

The repertoire of our band stuck with the Great American Song Book. Tunes composed by Gershwin, Rogers, Porter, Kern – melodic, dance-able stuff. Tunes that did not require a swain to shout above the music romantic professions into the ear of his dancing partner. With beer at a nickel a pop, for thirty cents a guy could get really romantic. Then, when the party became ribald, we played *I've Got a Lovely*

Bunch of Coconuts, Roll Out the Barrel, and some polkas, ending the night with *Goodnight, Irene.* That's how gigs went back then. We had fun on Saturday nights, making music and liking the adventure of drinking a couple of 'Gansetts and picking up five bucks besides.

But this gig in a Conimicut gin mill on New Year's Eve in 1956 would sully our innocence.

ONE BY ONE the five of us showed up an hour before the party began. That was our custom because you never knew what you might find in a new place. For example, once we had to lift a heavy upright piano onto the stage. Another instance, at a Grange hall we were asked who the caller was. We looked at each other and shrugged.

"Where's your caller?" the raw-boned woman in a long calico dress repeated.

"What do you mean, a 'caller'?"

Whoever had booked the gig screwed up. We had come expected to play for a hoe-down. We didn't do square dancing. Gershwin wouldn't cut the mustard. As things turned out, the country folk laughed off the gaff and had themselves a good time, dancing cheek-to-cheek.

Anyway, back to the New Year's Eve gig. As I tested the piano (only three ivories were missing, and it was just a tad flat), the proprietor came up to the stage – a big-bellied guy with bushy eyebrows. He was sweaty, nervous. He kept pulling from his wet lips a stogie as he drilled me.

"You play until midnight. Got that? And keep it at only two breaks, no more than five minutes. I got a full house comin', and they want their money's worth. Now get this straight, I paid a hundred clams to bring in four dancing girls from New York. They start their show at eleven."

Baffled by this news, I asked the proprietor what the band was supposed to do when the girls did their act. He fulminated!

"What the hell do you think? You play for them!"

"But what do we play?"

"How in hell do I know! Play music. You gotta ask them."

The room, large enough to put thirty tables close together around the dance floor, held the comfortable smell of tobacco smoke and stale beer, relics of many gone-by good times. From the kitchen in the back came the smell of garlic and sauce and frying peppers and sausage. Red and green crepe paper had been strung along the room's perimeter, and noise-makers and conical-crazy-cardboard hats decorated the tables.

As Joe set up his drums, the others put their instruments in tune with the beat up upright – Tommy on trumpet, Ed on clarinet, and the other Tommy on electric guitar. Customers straggled in. At eight on the dot we opened up the first set with our theme song, *Deep Purple*. Here we go, I thought. We sounded good. By the end of the first set waitresses were bringing drinks to the tables. There was excitement in the air. And the smell of Evening in Paris and Old Spice began to intermingle with the smell of stale beer and garlic and peppers.

Nine o'clock we took our first break. We huddled at the bar and sipped nickel beers. The proprietor came up to us. A woman joined him.

"This here's . . . what's your name?"

"Darlene."

"Look, Darlene's goin' to tell you kids what you hafta do. So, listen up and get it straight, you hear? Hey, nice crowd, ain't it?"

Darlene had to be twenty years older than we. Her hair was dyed to almost platinum, and her face – plump and rouged – shocked me. No other female I'd seen – not my mother, not my aunts, sisters, teachers, girl friends – put on all that goop.

"So, youse kids are the band? Youse damn well better know how to sight read!"

She plopped a tattered briefcase onto the bar and pulled out a sheaf of pages. "This here's the score you gotta play when us girls do our routine. Who's the piano player?" I raised my hand like a school boy and she gave me a three-inch thick pack of pages held together with an elastic. "Trombone? No trombone? That ain't good. Crap, we'll make do. There's gotta be a trumpet." Tommy reached for his pack of pages.

When everyone had his score, Darlene briefed us. What with the ruckus in the room and her New York accent, we hardly made sense of what she was telling us. We caught the gist of it, however: keep to a raunchy beat – slow and steady ("just watch our hips"). Then, at the cue ("we'll light a fire in the brazier") segue into a sexier, Latin beat. That seemed easy enough to do.

We played straight through to 10:30 before taking another break. It was a half hour before show time when we had chance to look over the scores that Darlene had handed out. I puffed when I unfolded the pack. It was like unrolling wall paper. Sheet after sheet of handwritten notes on paper smudged from lots of usage. As we made a cacophony by testing our scores, some people went to the dance floor, too far into their cups to be able to distinguish noise from music.

Just before eleven, the proprietor came on stage. There was no mike (he did not need one). Waving a stogie, he boomed: "Ladies and gentlemen! Hey, you guys over there, shut up for a minute!" Someone whistled. The customers looked around, wondering what was happening.

"Ladies and gentlemen, your attention . . . *please*! Are ya havin' a good time? [Yells and cheers.] Wait until ya see what's comin' up! I went all out and brought in an act from *New York*. Ya got that? From *New York*! Feast your eyes on these dames. They're classy, I tell ya. Come on out, ladies!" Yells and cheers.

Darlene led onto the stage three other women. They could have been identical quadruplets. She shouted to us, "Get playin'!" We did, and the four New Yorkers got their hips going.

Joe's foot caught the beat and thumped out the rhythm on his bass drum. Ed's clarinet wailed way above high C. Tommy's guitar hit the right chords at the right time. I added piano riffs to the mix. But it was the other Tommy who caught on to the eroticism of the music. His trumpet screamed and sighed. We were putting to music something unknown to us.

The dancers cavorted about the stage. And they stripped. First fell the sequined purple dresses, then the petticoats. In just panties and bras, they clicked their hips to Joe's beat. The stage went seismic, and the customers whooped and whistled.

I looked up now and then from the score and what I saw was phantasmagoric. As four nearly unclad, almost obese women gyrated this way and that, their flesh glistened with sweat and mascara seeped down their cheeks. Their breathing was mini-gales of panting.

After about eight or so minutes of this, Darlene bent down and ignited whatever fuel was in the brazier, and flames fluttered from it. Joe gave the bass drum a final big thump and segued into a Brazilian beat. Tommy's guitar picked up the changed tempo. Ed and the other Tommy found the melody line. The piano part became tricky. I leaned closer to the score and tentatively played *da-dum . . . da-dum-dum*. A few bars into this, we were making very seductive music.

The dancers put on sombreros and whirled to the brazier and, as their fingers unclipped the snaps of their bras, the stage lights went out. And the music stopped.

We were sight reading. In the dark we could not see the score. Never having played it, we couldn't fake it. Joe and Tommy bravely tried to push on, but like the last spring swamp peepers, their sounds were pathetically lonely in the dark.

I was much too embarrassed and confused to take note of what followed. The lights, of course, had come back on. The dancers had disappeared as well as their scores and the brazier. But the din in the room had not let up. [Boos and hisses.] We sat at the edge of the stage going over what had just happened.

"You two-bit jerks! You screwed up!" It was the proprietor yelling as he came toward us. "I shelled out a hundred bucks for that act, and you screwed up! Get your stuff and beat it! I ain't payin' you, you hear?"

The woman behind him – perhaps his wife – hugged his arm, trying to placate him.

"Vinnie, they're only kids. What happened wasn't their fault. You have to let them play until midnight."

He stuffed the stogie in his mouth, gave us an obscene gesture, and walked away.

"Go, go play. You're doing okay. Look, after midnight you come back to the kitchen an I'll give you some lasagna and your money."

We played polkas until a minute before twelve. A woozy woman put party hats on our heads. On the dot of twelve we played *Auld Lang Syne* and segued into *Goodnight Irene*. After putting our gear into our cars, we went to the kitchen and ate and got our ten bucks.

Light snow was dusting the parking lot when we went back to our cars. We summed up the night with steaming breath before going our separate ways.

"You know, we should've been clever and played *Dancing in the Dark* when the lights went out. The other Tommy said that, I think.

That was the last time we played together. The new year saw to that.

I was becoming a pretty good salesman.

MANSFIELD

THE LAST DAY of the second week into a summer job with Keystone Publications began in a cramped second floor room of the Grayson Building on Westminster Street in Providence at 7:45 Friday morning. Mr. Furbush, the boss, had come down from Boston to give us guys a pep talk. Word was out that our performance to date greatly displeased him. If he ended up canning us all, that would be fine with me. Had I not wanted to disappoint Dad, I would have quit after the first day on the job.

Maybe he was projecting his own lack of self-confidence upon me when, seeing a classified ad in the paper, he thought it a good idea for me to answer it. Keystone Publications wanted college students for door-to-door salesmen and ballyhooed "limitless opportunity to earn tuition money". I had just graduated from high school and would be starting college in September. I needed a job.

"You'll be meeting people, Sonny, and you'll have to speak up," he said. "You'll have to stand on your own two feet."

Mr. Furbush hired me on the spot and assigned me to Webb Latham's team. There were three teams, each made up of four kids and an adult supervisor. Webb's turned out to be an odd mix: Angelo, a choir boy type from North Providence; Arnie, an idiot savant from Cranston; Timmy, an Irish playboy of the Western World; and myself, a shy fifteen-year-old kid from Graniteville.

Webb's appearance reflected his laid back way of doing business. He seemed close to celebrating his thirtieth birthday – not too tall, balding, thin as a lap dog with a lap dog's gentle dark eyes. Although his team's success at persuading housewives to subscribe to *The Saturday Evening Post* determined how much money he took home (all of us were on commission), he showed no ire or disappointment when, at day's end, we had sold only two or three or, for that matter, no subscriptions.

Webb's daily plan of attack never varied. His crew squeezed into his blue Studebaker at 8:00 a.m. at the pick-up point on Westminster Street. Then he headed for the territory, always a densely populated place such as Fall River or Taunton where two or three deckers lined the streets, and always stopping at a roadside diner for coffee and bran muffins. After casing the neighborhood, he assigned each of us a block. Three hours later he collected us for lunch, and, as we munched our sandwiches, he verified whatever orders we had sold. For another two hours we went tenement to tenement, knocking on doors. By 4:00 p.m., Webb had us back to Westminster Street.

Mr. Furbush, unlike Webb, was not laid back. To kick off the fourth week of what he called "the summer campaign", he called all three teams together. For a half hour in his rented second floor Providence office, he tromped wall to wall, he punched the air with his fists, he wheedled, he almost sobbed. The bottom button of his shirt popped and we gawked at his stomach hair wet with sweat.

"Christ!" he roared. "You know how many sales you twelve guys made last week? Seven, that's how many. Seven lousy sales! Are you wimps or what? Next time, I'm hiring girl scouts. Damn it, one of them can sell twice as many cookies in just an hour!"

He lit a cigarette, blew smoke through his nose, and wheezed to the end of his pep talk.

"Look, guys, you're asking people to buy an all-American magazine. *The Saturday Evening Post!* Let them see it, feel it, even smell it. And tell them, 'You buy from me and you'll be getting a real deal. A nickel less than if you bought one at a news stand.' And . . . and more than that tell them they'll be helping you pay for college. Got it? One last thing, never take 'no' for an answer. Keep at 'em! With the third 'no' you walk away."

His heel crushed the cigarette butt on the plank floor and he sucked in the humid air. A grin cracked his red face and he added, "To light a fire under your asses, here's what I'm going to do. Two things. The first is I'm upping your commission by a nickel. So, instead of getting four bucks per subscription, you'll get the four plus another five cents. The other thing? This is real big. The two of you who sell the most subscriptions by August first, you two guys will win a trip to New York City, all expenses paid. First class hotel, a Broadway show, fancy restaurants . . . the works! Now, get off your cans and knock on those damn doors!"

TO OVER RIDE the grousing in the car, Webb switched on the radio to WBZ, a Boston AM station. Not until we had crossed into Massachusetts on US 1 did the static let up and Frankie Laine's *Mule Train* come in loud and clear. But Timmy and buck-toothed Arnie kept up their rant. Not wanting to hear another "son-of-a-bitch", Webb calmly said over his shoulder, "Mr. Furbush is an all-right man. He was only trying to light a fire under us."

"Helluva way to light a fire! He pissed me off," Timmy yelped.

"Did you see his face?" Arnie lisped. "Red as a beet. Thought he'd keel over with a heart attack."

Nat King Cole's mellow voice came from the radio, and Webb purred, "Listen to that. Nice, isn't it?" He hummed along with the lyrics of *Too Young*. The ranting stopped.

At the road sign – MANSFIELD, INCORPORATED 1775 – we turned right off US 1, passed through woodland, and approached the town's common with a stone statue of a World War I doughboy facing the business section. From what I could see as we drove by, we had come into a backwater village: a bank, diner, a couple of small shops, a Sears & Roebuck catalog store, a hardware store, a Congregational church, and the brick high school.

Like the captain of a charter fishing boat out of Pt. Judith searching for cod, Webb down shifted and drifted past one-family bungalows and weathered-shingled capes. From the radio came Rosemary Clooney's crooning *Come On-A My House*. Before the song ended, we were cruising down a street flanked with double-deckers. Webb shut off the radio and sighed, "Ah . . . here we go, boys."

He circled the neighborhood twice before stopping at a Shell gas station for a fill-up.

"We can hit this territory and finish up by three. So, Angelo and Harry, suppose you do this street, and Arnie and Timmy, you take the next one over. Okay? Get back here at noon and we'll grab lunch. You boys all set? Got your order pads and mags? I've a hunch this'll be a lucky day for you."

We scrambled out of the Studebaker, stiff-legged from the cramped forty-mile ride from Providence. Angelo and I paused by a letter drop box at the head of the street and watched Arnie and Timmy sprint around the corner.

"Does it make any difference, Angelo, which side you want to do?"

"I'll do the left side." There was a hint of fear in his voice. He crossed the street, glanced back at me, and sort of waved, dropping his order pad onto the sidewalk. The pathos on his face made me remember the sad day when Mom and Dad had left for home, leaving me almost sobbing on the parade field of Camp Yawgoog.

I was catching on to the sociology – or was it the psychology? – of the trade. For instance, you go to the back door of a double decker because the hallway gives you access to both the downstairs and upstairs tenements, and, when someone answers your knocking, you are looking into a kitchen where the lady of the house is apt to feel neighborly.

With a shaking hand I knocked on my first door of the day. On the third knock, it flew open, and I was nose to nose with a face the size of a watermelon and with a salt and pepper stubble of whiskers on its chin. A man! Only women heretofore had greeted me. I struggled for words.

"Good morning, sir. Do you by any chance get *The Saturday Evening Post*? It's the top selling magazine ----".

"Geez! I work third shift at the chocolate factory and was about to hit the sack and here comes a magazine salesman! Get lost, boy. I ain't buyin' no damn magazine. And don't bother wastin' your time goin' upstairs. My mother-in-law's a nut cake."

With the door shut in my face, I could not follow Mr. Furbush's commandment to never take "no" for an answer.

Four houses later – eight doors in all – I had made no sales. The last one really took away my final shred of hope. She was all smiles, a woman who could have been my Aunt Helen's twin sister.

We sat in her front room, and she rocked in her chair by the window, turning the pages of the April 29 issue of the *Post* that I used for a sample – Mr. Furbush's mandate. "Show this copy to your customers," he reverently said. "Look at that cover! A Norman Rockwell masterpiece! People love the guy. 'Shuffleton's Barber Shop' will really grab them, you bet!"

"Where's that piece about Yogi Berra you mentioned?" the sweet lady with a broad smile asked. "I like baseball and always listen to all the Red Sox games on the radio. Hold on, I found it."

She held the page close to her face and ran a finger from word to word. I tingled with excitement, sure of making my first sale.

"This is good, very good. Yes, I'm enjoying this. That Yogi's some character, isn't he? What a shame he's not playing for Boston."

She flipped more pages, stopping at cartoons.

"These are very funny. Did you see this Hazel one?"

When she handed the magazine back to me, I went into my spiel: "For a dime a week, ma'am, you'll get *The Saturday Evening Post* in the mail every Friday. All you have to do today is pay me a dollar, a down payment for your year's subscription. Would you please sign your name on this line?"

"Oh, no! I have no intention of buying it."

"But, ma'am, you said you liked the piece about Yogi Berra and the cartoons. And isn't this a great cover?"

"All that is true, young man. But if I took out a subscription, the magazines would only pile up and collect dust. No, just the same."

"It's only a dime a week, and you'll be saving a nickel besides."

She got out of the rocker, and I followed her into the kitchen.

"I'm a stubborn woman. When I say something, I mean it. Anyways, it's time to make myself a sandwich."

I took that to be the third "no" and retreated to the porch. Rain was pelting the sidewalk, a perfect complement to my mood. Webb was wrong thinking this would be a lucky day. My watch said it was going on to fifteen minutes before noon, time to get back to the Shell station and give him my bad news. And on the way to Providence I would tell him I quit. My mind was made up.

I looked up and down the street for Angelo, but he was not to be seen. From the house next door – a two-story with blistering blue paint and uncut grass reaching the chin of a St. Francis statue – a woman clinked a couple of bottles of milk from the box on her front porch. What the heck, I thought, there's time to try her.

It was only a few seconds dash from one porch to the other, yet time enough to get myself wet through and through. The woman I had seen fetching the milk immediately answered my knocking, looked me over, and welcomed me inside.

"What are you dong out there in the rain? Look at you, dripping and all! Come, come. Into the kitchen and sit. I'm getting a towel for you."

"No, no, ma'am. Don't bother with that. A little rain won't hurt me."

She folded her arms, cocked her head, and stared at me with an amused expression.

"I'm getting the towel."

To her back, I began my spiel: "You've heard of *The Saturday Evening Post*? For just ten cents a week, you'll get in the mail ---"

Over her shoulder she said, "Say no more. So, you're selling magazines? Into the kitchen, go!"

I sat to where she had pointed and plopped my damp order pad on the table and waited for her to stop talking and prancing about. With a towel she had pulled from a cabinet drawer, she stood behind me and rubbed my head.

"My name's Theresa Maria Moniz. You can call me 'Terry' like everybody does. Now tell me, what do they call you?"

"My name's 'Harry'. Ouch! You pulled my hair!"

"Sorry, Harry. There . . . nice and dry. You don't want to catch a cold do you? What's the magazine you're selling?"

"*The Saturday Evening Post*, ma'am."

"I told you, call me 'Terry'. Anyway, I'll buy it."

I was flabbergasted! I just made my first sale and without finishing my spiel! The clock over the refrigerator showed the time to be 12:17. I imagined Webb's going up and down the street looking for me, but so what?

"You're a nice kid, Harry, I can tell. Where do you live? Do you go to school? Don't be shy. Go on, tell me."

I was reaching for my order pad, wanting Theresa Maria Moniz to sign her name. But, brought up to respect my elders, I submitted to her inquisition. The back door opened, and into the kitchen stepped someone – a female. I knew that because of the high heels stamping on a mat. The rest of her hid behind an umbrella. When she collapsed it, she looked straight at me, wonder widening her dark eyes.

"Phyllis, you're late. Was there trouble at the store?"

"No, Mama. I waited, hoping the rain would let up."

"Go . . . go and dry off. I'm getting lunch ready."

The girl, who seemed to be my age, gave me a quick look and left the kitchen. Theresa Maria Moniz sprung into action. She rattled three plates, three water glasses, knives and forks onto the table. She opened and shut the refrigerator door, stood at the stove, and a sweet, spicy smell permeated the room. All the while she talked and talked and talked.

"Phyllis is my daughter, my one and only. On Sunday is her graduation from high school and all ready she's got a job down at the Sears catalog store on Main Street. Her marks in school were good enough for her teachers to tell her she should go to college, but she said, 'Mama, I'm going to help you. I'm getting a job'. She's a nice, nice girl. Everybody tells me how lucky I am. Hey, you like Portuguese food, Harry? My family came over from the Azores and so I do a lot of Portuguese cooking. What you're smelling is chourico frying. I go to Fall River to a market that sells it and a lot of other things from the old world. You drink milk, Harry? I tell Phyllis, 'Milk's good for the teeth.'

Did you see hers? Nice and white, aren't they?"

Phyllis returned to the kitchen and slid onto a chair across the table from me. She had changed from a damp, purplish dress into a black skirt and red sweater. Her just- combed hair matched in color the skirt, and her rouged lips matched the sweater. All in all, she was a beauty. Our eyes met.

Theresa Maria Moniz forked a couple of sausages onto each plate.

"Mrs. Moniz, this is very nice of you, but I ---".

"You forget so soon? I said to call me 'Terry'. Now, eat! And you tell me with no lying how you like the chourico. Phyllis, his name's 'Harry'. Poof! Just like that he comes to our house. I bought a magazine from him. What's the name of it again? Here, take a slice of this and make a sandwich. It's Portuguese sweet bread."

She filled the glasses with milk and sat. Phyllis kept her eyes on her plate. Her mother nudged her.

"Hey, the cat's got your tongue? Say something. Tell Harry about school . . . anything. Go on!"

"There's nothing to tell, Mama."

"Then, I'll tell. My little girl's shy, Harry. Here's the story."

WEBB'S STUDEBAKER ROUNDED the corner and braked at the Shell station where he had said he would collect Angelo and me at three o'clock. Angelo was in the front seat, looking as sad as a Basset Hound.

"Wow, I got an order!" I gushed as I squeezed between Arnie and Timmy in the back seat and gave Webb the order form with Theresa Maria Moniz's signature on the dotted line and her dollar down payment.

"Is this why I couldn't find you for lunch?"

"Sort of. You guys won't believe what happened!"

Webb turned the key and headed to West Street where what I was going to tell them had happened. He had to verify my order. He found the house with blistering blue paint and grass up to St. Francis' chin and shut off the engine. Not until I had finished telling my story did he get out of the car.

"So, her mother went on and on about how her daughter's date for the senior prom stood her up at the last minute. And there she was, stuck with a new gown, corsage, tickets – the works – but no date. No wonder her mother was so nice to me, giving me lunch and buying a subscription and all."

Timmy, the Playboy of the Western World, was all ears and asked, "When's the prom?"

"Tonight."

"You're kidding . . . tonight? What did you say?"

"I said I don't own a car, but maybe my father would drive me."

"Your father? How in hell can you make out in the back seat of your father's car? Is the dame a looker?"

"She's the prettiest girl I've ever seen, Timmy."

"Holy crap, you can't pass this up, Romeo! Here's an idea. It just so happens I picked up a cutie and I'm coming back to this burg tonight. Why don't you ride with me?"

That was that. I went with Webb to the back door to tell Terry that her one and only would be going to her senior prom after all.

THE SUMMER PASSED. Timmy and I, sometimes twice a week, drove up US 1 to Mansfield. But by August his romance with the cutie and mine with Phyllis fizzled and those jaunts stopped. Meanwhile, I was becoming a pretty good salesman, so much so that Mr. Furbush, true to his word, rewarded me with a ticket to *Guys and Dolls*. Dad had been right about thinking door-to-door selling would give his son confidence. Never, though, could he have foreseen the strange twists of circumstances that would bring it about.

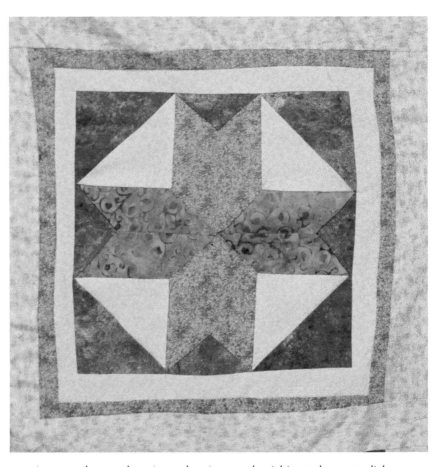

A pretty leg and an introduction to the id jarred me as did my discoveries in the rooms of Delta Upsilon.

UNIVERSITY HALL

IN MY PSYCHOLOGY 101 notebook I scribbled "Froid". Professor Hunter dropped the name in a lecture, and I thought that I should write it down in case it was important enough to remember. Because we freshmen were seated alphabetically in lower Manning Hall, Rebecca Aronson's desk, on my left, was so close that I knew she smoked cigarettes. Her presence Monday, Wednesday, and Friday at nine in the morning flummoxed me as did most everything else about college.

Until morning frost rimed the campus, Miss Aronson breezed into Manning Hall wearing pajamas. When she wore skirted ones, skin showed above her knees. Three years at an all-male academy did not prepare me for such intimate propinquity with a girl. Only once – the morning she dropped a knitting needle and I picked it up for her and she muttered "thanks" – did she speak to me. A pretty leg and an introduction to the id jarred me as did my discoveries in the rooms of Delta Upsilon.

My campus job with Buildings and Grounds had me working twenty hours a week, keeping the lounge and rooms of Delta Upsilon trash and dust free. My earnings, not much more than a stipend, paid for the text books (most were second-hand) and a monthly UTC pass (I commuted). What little money was left over I squandered to eke out a minimum of pleasure such as an ice cream sandwich in the Blue Room and eventually a cup of coffee when I took to caffeine --- another stab to blend in with the crowd.

Walking into the fraternity house each morning, an outlier through and through, discomfited me. Like the cast of *When Worlds Collide* – one of those sci-fi flicks Hollywood was dishing out in the '50's – I felt dislocated on Planet Zyra as I swished mop and rag in the rooms of Delta Upsilon. These Zyraians littered their planet with artifacts alien to me: white bucks, rep ties, Brook Brothers' 100% wool sport jackets, matchbooks collected from the likes of the Hotel Taft, the Parker House, the Village Vanguard, Sardi's. The room with a Hotchkiss pennant nailed to the wall between two windows that overlooked Wriston Quad and across the way, pinned to a closet door, a calendar with a photo of a nude red head on a swing, was nearly impossible to mop. Extension cords and wires ran from components of a Zenith stereo system to a wall outlet.

Mondays were especially tough. Weekend parties left the first-floor lounge in an utter mess. My first challenge was to adjust to the stink of stale beer. Before I could vacuum the soiled carpet, the detritus of undergraduate mayhem had to be cleared away: paper cups – beer in some of them; cocktail glasses – some smeared with lipstick; empty and near empty Beefeater bottles; crushed packs of Pall Malls and Benson & Hedges; socks, ties, mismatched shoes. But there was nothing I could do about the missing ivory of two keys of the baby grand piano or about the cigarette burns on its ledge.

The first three weeks into freshman year at Brown were hell. I simply did not fit in – socially or academically. For starters, I did not look like the guys whose messy rooms I cleaned. At home, with my bedroom door closed, I studied my reflection in a mirror: thin-faced with spots of acne here and there, irreversible features that only time could change. But the pompadour, the hair style of choice for sixteen year old boys in 1950, I could change, and I could do away with the dress white shirt and square bottomed knit tie and the loafers with nickels tucked into the tabs in the tops.

There, in the mirror, was the image of exactly who I was – a kid from a backwater village named Graniteville, naïve, inexperienced, and dressed for Sunday school. Sacrificing the coffees and ice cream bars for a month gave me the money to purchase white bucks, a blue oxford shirt with little buttons at the collar, and a rep tie. Another 25 cents and a nickel tip to Sal the barber, who had been cutting the hair of generations of undergraduates in his shop in the basement of Faunce House, got me a brush cut. Voila! I had morphed into an Ivy Leaguer, but in appearance only.

With the exception of my biology course, the other three courses demanded the writing of essays. I was woefully unprepared to compose an essay. Four years of diagramming sentences and memorizing vocabulary lists with no instruction whatsoever in paragraph construction left me ignorant of such rhetorical imperatives as cohesiveness and cogency. Whereas in high school the retention of names and dates was sufficient to get an A in American history, for Professor George the ability to synthesize data, form a thesis, and proficiently validate it was a requisite for a passing grade in his Modern European history course. I was lost.

BECAUSE THE 6:10 Centredale bus was behind schedule due to slippery roads, by the time I stepped from it in front of Charlie's Diner where I had worked the counter last summer, Forgie – the town hermit – had finished his usual supper of chili and bread and stood on the sidewalk, poking a toothpick at a back molar.

"Hey, Kid, where've ya been? Ain't seen ya for awhile."

"I had to quit. It was only a summer job anyway. I'm going to college. You don't remember I told you?"

"College, eh? I knew you was smart. You was the only one who knew what I wanted without me sayin' it night after night. Jesus H. Christ, the new guy's a moron! He keeps givin' me a menu. Anyways, how's it goin'?"

"Not bad, not bad," I lied.

"Maybe you'll come back after you're done with book learnin'? Charlie ain't like his old self no more. He sure could use ya."

I looked past Forgie and could just about make out the old Greek standing at the cash register. Warmth from the grill steamed the big window. I shivered off the urge to go inside and looked back at the graying loner who was pulling a pack of Lucky Strikes from his over-sized trench coat and deftly squeezing a match with two fingers to shield the flame from sleet and breeze.

"You know something, Forgie? If I had the nerve, I'd march right in there and put on an apron. I bet it's still hanging by the dish washer, still as dirty as ever. Honest to God I would!"

He blew a mouthful of smoke at the sidewalk, coughed, and an-gled his eyes up at me.

"Nah, Kid, you don't want to do that. I know what I'm sayin'."

"But . . . but if you only knew how I'm feeling ---."

"Damn it, listen to me! Stay with your books or else."

"Or else what, Forgie?"

"Or else you'll end up like me."

We parted, and in the autumnal darkness of November – chilled by sleety weather and stinking of formaldehyde – I slogged the mile to home, bent with the dead weight of depression. That morning in my campus mailbox I had found from the registrar's office my mid-semester grades: three D's and an F. I felt eviscerated.

Dazed by the bad news, somehow I had fumbled through the day – two lectures (hardly comprehending anything), four hours of curso-ry tidying up of Delta Upsilon's rooms, and the late afternoon Biology lab, prying into the components of the digestive system. Bisecting the remains of a fetal pig sickened me. Gone were its brain, heart, and lungs. I scalpeled a ragged incision in its belly and clumsily looked for its jejunam. I was too rapt in brooding about failing to concen-trate. Smelling formaldehyde and fingering the slimy gut of a pig were not helping.

"Having trouble, Mr. Anderson?"

Dr. Edds' TA hunched over me.

"Yes."

Thinking I was lost in the twisting tumble of pig intestines, he cut away some tissue with his scalpel.

"See? There's the jejunam beginning at the duodenojejunal flexure

where the small intestine turns toward the anterior direction.
Okay?"
"Yes," I lied.

MOM LOOKED UP from a game of solitaire and gave me a once-over. "You don't look right, Sonny. Are you coming down with a cold?"

I could never hide anything from her. At the top of the street, fifteen minutes into my walk home from the bus stop, I had sneezed and right then and there believed that the street light over me was spinning. All strength in my shoulders and legs rushed out into the darkness with that sneeze. With effort I willed myself to trudge through the slush and into the house.

"Where's Dad? His car's not in the driveway."

"Some machine broke down. He called to say he has to work overtime. But never mind that. Let's get you settled. Off with those wet clothes and I'll fix your supper. Hot beef stew sounds good?"

Too woozy to stand, I sat at the edge of my bed and kicked off my shoes and tugged at belt and buttons to undress. With one leg into my pajama bottoms, the last of my strength was spent and I fell back onto the bed, belly up, atop Professor George's text book with a slip of paper marking page 518 where Emporer Charles V of the House of Hapsburg had a set to with Martin Luther at the Diet of Worms.

FOR FIVE WEEKS I slipped in and out of awareness. After examining me, Dr. Conde summed things up in the kitchen: "It's pneumonia. His temp is 101°. But there's more going on then that. Your son is a very sick boy."

I languished in bed through my seventeenth birthday, through Thanksgiving. Not until a few days before Christmas did the penicillin, lots of egg nogs, and Mom's TLC clear my lungs. Sitting up at last and watching Mom rolling dough for a batch of Christmas cookies, I made my confession: "Mom, I'm flunking."

Instead of hearing something like, "Maybe it would be best for you to withdraw", Mom wasn't about to advise me to abandon ship.

With a pat on my hand, she murmured a string of nostrums: "I bet there are other boys, too, who haven't adjusted yet. Your teachers understand and won't fail you." Dad, on the other hand, was manly about it: "You're smarter than your mother and me put together. You've got to stick with it and finish what you've begun."

That night at my desk I wrote in my journal:

They just don't understand. College is way over my head and I'm very unhappy. Dad tells me I can't quit. He quit school and doesn't remember what grade he was in. Why does he think I'm any different?

New Year's Day fell on a Monday, and on the second of the month I returned to campus, a week before final exams began. I made the rounds, going to the offices of my professors to explain why I had been absent and to put to the test Mom's assurance that they would mercifully not fail me. But no assurance was forthcoming. "Do the best you can," each of them said.

Tension was in the air of Sayles Hall as proctors handed out blue books and the exam question. This final was a do-or-die deal. Comp 1, required of all freshmen, had to be passed or else. Heads bent and pencils moved, but the question stymied me:

"Permanence, perseverance, and persistence in spite of all obstacles, discouragement, and impossibilities: It is this, that in all things distinguishes the strong soul from the weak." Thomas Carlyle.

Directions: In five paragraphs rebut this statement.

As I scribbled, I knew I was writing drivel, poorly at that. Promptly at noon I handed my blue book to a proctor, firmly believing that Carlyle would deem me a weak soul.

Two hours later in a lab of Metcalf Hall Dr. Edds' TA plunked in front of us undergraduates the Biology 1 final exam. It had the girth of a book – 500 multiple choice questions. The first question clued me in to what I would be doing for three hours – playing a guessing game:

1. *Peristalsis (a) maintains homeostasis essential to the circulatory system; (b) begins in the esophagus upon the introduction of a boulis of food; (c) is the final phase of the mitosis process; (d) regulates electrolyte balance in the urinary system*

Without hope of doing better with the psych and history exams, I dutifully showed up for both. By Friday, my first semester of college was over. Those sixteen weeks had scarred me for life.

A TERSE STATEMENT accompanied my transcript of grades from the Registrar's office to inform me that henceforth until my grades improved I would be on probation. When the second semester began, nothing changed but the books I lugged onto the Centredale bus. In addition to the freshman comp course that I had to repeat, I had signed up for introductory courses in geology, logic, and sociology. It was a matter of blind man's bluff, for I neither knew what I was doing nor had an interest in rocks, major/minor premises, or tribal mores. This portended another semester of woe.

Even though rarely did anything of importance get stuffed into my campus mail box, I nevertheless checked it daily, usually on my way to Delta Upsilon. But an envelope bearing the Dean's return address was another story. Thinking it contained a message of doom, I postponed opening it until I was alone in the utility room in the basement of the fraternity house.

See me immediately!

In big letters was the signature of Barnaby C. Kenney. Within an hour, I was standing at his receptionist's desk in University Hall, dry mouthed and shaking. She asked for my name, and, before I could state my reason for coming, she smiled and click-clacked on high heels into his office and returned, still smiling.

"You may go in, Mr. Anderson."

The heir apparent to the university's presidency sat at his desk with his back to me. He was lighting his pipe and, when he swiveled around to me, a cloud of smoke veiled his face. From the cloud boomed the voice of a god.

"Anderson, I had a talk with your father this morning."

"My . . . my father?"

"He sat right there in that chair. He drove up from the rubber works on his break to see me."

I looked at the chair and imagined Dad's sitting there in his greasy work clothes.

"Did you ask him to come? I mean, he just didn't walk in, did he?"

"Yup, he just walked in. Obviously a man on a mission. You didn't know he would be coming to see me?"

"Honestly, no. That's the last thing I'd ever expect."

"We talked about you. Seems as though you're having a rough time of it. Is that so?"

"Yes, sir."

He puffed another cloud of smoke and tapped his fingers on his desk.

"If I correctly understand the situation, we have a solution to your problem. I'll repeat what I've told your father. You finish this semester and then take a year's leave of absence. Find a job and take a course of two at a junior college. When you come back to us, you'll be more mature and ready to handle what we throw at you. How does that sound to you?"

I nodded, afraid to speak lest I broke down. He re-lit his pipe, and again the voice of a god boomed from the cloud.

"That's settled then. Good, that's good. Now listen to me. The admissions people know their job. They would not have accepted you if they thought you lacked the brain to succeed. Therefore, you sure as hell will get your degree from Brown. In the long run, it won't make a whit of a difference if you graduate with the class of '54 or '55."

He knocked the ashes from his pipe into an ashtray and fixed his eyes on me. Eyes of an owl.

"Before you go, Anderson, there's one last thing I have to say."

He cleared his throat and sat back in his chair.

"Your father? He's a great man. Yes, indeed. A helluva great man!"

JANUARY'S THAW WAS melting yesterday's snow fall on College Hill, making my walk to the center of Providence less perilous. Behind me, Carrie Tower's bell pealed four times. Foremost in my thoughts was the morning's meeting with Dean Kenney. "I can't believe it . . . I can't believe it!" Dad crossing the campus, looking for University Hall. Where did he park? Dad standing at the receptionist's desk. What did he say to her? Dad shaking the Dean's hand. Was there a band aid on his knuckle? There usually was. What did he tell Dean Kenney? Dad, too lost for words, never used the telephone. I can't believe it!

Over laying these thoughts, the Comp 1 final exam question popped into my mind. Carlyle's definition of a hero: a "strong soul", he contended, with the traits of "permanence, perseverance, and persistence." Sure, but . . . The one thing I did grasp from Professor George's lectures – there were lots of kings, emperors, popes with these traits, though they were not heroes. Scalawags, yes, and dispensers of legerdemain.

If given the chance to try again to rebut Carlyle's definition, I would point out its glaring omission of the two paramount virtues of a hero: courage and love. For an example to buttress my contention I would cite that man over there two miles away beyond University Hall, beyond Delta Upsilon, beyond the city's panoply of politics and commerce – the shy, taciturn, grade school drop out who, as I waited for the Centredale bus, was turning a wrench in the guts of a machine to keep the US Rubber Company up and running. My father.

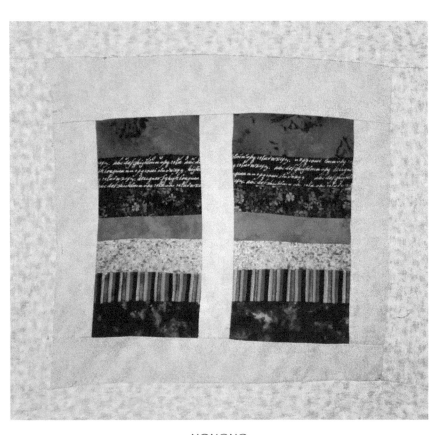

XOXOXO

BONNET SHORES

SHE MADE IT quite clear in the last letter of her freshman year at Tufts, written at her desk in Metcalf Hall, that she desperately needed a break from differential equations, statistics, calculus, and "the most boring roommate under the sun". Made even clearer was her expecting *me* to free her of the pall of mathematics and the proselytizing Sara from Rushville, Indiana.

> *I'm enclosing directions to our summer place in Bonnet Shores where I'll be staying from June 17th until the 24th. You pick the time. Can hardly wait to see you.*
> *XOXOXO*
> *Gina*
> *PS*
> *I'll be by myself. Mom and Dad are going to visit Aunt Florence in Schenectady.*

Gina and I shared similar backgrounds: children of blue collar fathers, both of us born in 1933 – she in August and me in November, both of us lived on Serrel Sweet Road – me at #38 and she at #56. But we went separate ways to get educated. Her father drove her to St. Lawrence, a parochial school in Centredale and I walked to Graniteville, a public school a half mile from Serrel Sweet Road. Her circle of friends and she played after-school games in the shadow of where the nuns were sequestered while I hop-scotched and kicked-the-can in my buddies' and their sisters' driveways.

Because Johnston had no high school in 1948, the town paid tuition to whatever secondary school I chose, and I chose LaSalle Academy to be with Richie, the kid down the street – a southpaw who was the best hitter among the gang of us who played pick-up baseball in Coyle's field. Beside that, he was my idol. In eighth grade he was the first boy to tout a pompadour, to tie a squirrel's tail to the handlebars of his bicycle, and to hold a girl's hand in public.

On the first ride aboard the 7:17 morning bus that picked us up in front of Charlie's diner in Centredale, Richie and I sat together in the first seats behind the driver, whom within a week we were calling "Pee Wee". From him I heard for the first time the word "homosexual".

"I have a cousin who graduated from LaSalle," he said over his shoulder after muttering a blasphemous "Jesus-H-Christ" when a Studebaker sedan tore out of Fruit Hill Avenue directly in front of the bus. "Terry, my cousin, would tell stories about the fags at his school. According to him, there was a lot of them, especially the Christian Brothers. One in particular, a Brother Anthony who favored red haired micks. Terry said he'd order a kid to come to his room after school and he would pants him."

Sick of listening to Pee Wee's tales, Richie and I moved to the back of the bus where the St. Xavier girls sat. "We'll show him we're not fags," Richie smirked. It took only a couple of rides to Providence for him to get the girls giggling. I envied his ease with these Catholic girls and hunched down in my seat and checked my homework.

That January, winter had its way with us. So much snow fell that Richie and I had to stand in the street to be seen by Pee Wee. Midway through the month he shivered and moaned, "Holy cow, I think I'm sick." The next day and ten days after that I stood alone at the bus stop. He had the mumps.

As I elbowed steam from the bus's window and before I opened my geometry text, someone bumped me.

"Oops, sorry. I'm clumsy in this big coat. Do you mind if I sit next to you?"

It was Gina, the girl down the road in the brown house with yellow shutters.

"Sure, go ahead. I mean . . ."

"Thanks. Golly, I thought I'd be late because my father's car wouldn't start up. You know Mr. Fairbanks who lives next door to us in the brick house on the corner? Well, he drove me to Esmond to wait for the bus with my friends just in the nick of time. How's school going? Crazy, isn't it? We're practically neighbors, but we hardly know each other. So, anyway, how is school going?"

Other than my sisters and their friends, I had not said a word to a girl since entering LaSalle, an all-boys school. I was tongue tied. On top of that, her elbow was brushing mine whenever she fidgeted. Yet I managed to gurgle, "School's pretty good."

"Do you have a favorite subject? Mine, believe it or not, is math. I'm taking geometry and love it."

"Not for me. It's my worst subject."

She spotted my geometry text and gushed, "Hey, that's the same book my class has! Where are you in it?"

I opened to page 184 and she glanced at it.

"Those ten problems are our homework."

"Um . . . They don't look hard."

"For me they are. Look at the fifth one. I'm not sure I got it right." She read it aloud:

Triangle ABC has an area of 15mm². Side AC has a length of 6 mm and side AB has a length of 8mm and angle BAC is obtuse. Find angle BAC and the length of side BC.

On the back side of what looked like some sort of prayer card she penciled numbers and just like that – plinkity, plankity, plunk – she circled the answers. Wonder- struck, I asked how she did that so fast.

"It comes easy for me, I guess."

From then on to June, Gina was my seat mate, and Richie took up with Mary Lavalle, the prettiest of the St. Xavier girls. He asked me if Gina was my girl friend, frankly noting that she wasn't exactly a looker.

"No, she's not my girl friend and so what if she isn't as pretty as Mary. She's a whiz at geometry though."

And so it went for the rest of the year and for the next two years. With Gina's help on the rides to school and occasional tutorials at her kitchen table, I passed geometry, algebra, and trig. In all that time, I dated her twice: Saturday matinees at the Community Theatre in Centredale. It never crossed my mind that she might not like *Twelve O'Clock High* or *Battleground* – shoot-'em-up, propagandistic war flicks of that postwar era that boiled my boyhood blood.

It was Gina who arranged our one and only big date. She asked me to take her to her senior prom. At first I balked.

"Mom," I whined as I talked this over with the only female in the whole world I trusted. "I don't know how to tell her I don't want to go."

"Why don't you want to go?"

"Lots of reasons. For one, I don't know how to dance. And . . . and I don't drive and I don't like Gina enough to go to a prom. Besides, I'll have to buy her a corsage, won't I?"

She made it clear that my going to the prom would please Gina very much for reasons way beyond my understanding. As for not knowing how to dance, she said she was sure that young Mrs. Davis, our new neighbor across the street, would give me lessons. To clinch things, she said that Dad would give me money for an orchid and that he would even take me downtown to Tom McCan's for a new pair of black shoes. Her persuasiveness and my wanting to always please her put me into a dilemma.

"Think it over, Sonny," she said and called to my sisters to come and help clear the table of our meat-and-potato supper dishes. I went into the other room to talk with Dad about my dilemma, hoping that he would side with me. But he was snoring in his chair as Edward R. Morrow reported over the radio that the allied Airlift Task Force that afternoon had delivered 12,940 short tons of cargo to East Berlin in 1,398 sorties.

The following morning, on the bus to Providence before Gina walked me through the mystery of solving magnitude of vectors problems, I whispered, "About the prom? Yes, I'll take you."

Gina's father, a gruff man whose hoarseness bespoke of a little used voice, dropped us off at St. Xavier, stressing that we must be prompt getting back into his car at 10:30 for a return ride to home. The nuns, who had ordered janitors to keep all the gym lights on and tamped into the heads of their students that their breasts and their escorts' carnations must not touch, paced the perimeter of the polished floor, trying to look festive as they glued their eyes upon the dancing girls.

The best thing of the night was Roger's tenor sax riffs. I sat behind him in LaSalle's band room with the reed section and knew that he was good, but not that good. His swoony improvisation of *Some Enchanted Evening* made the nuns scowl.

The front yard grass of #56 Serrel Sweet Road stayed uncut in July and August. Gina and her parents summered on Narragansett Bay in a beach cottage at Bonnet Shores. I was not that lucky. From 6:30 in the morning to 6:30 in the evening, every week day, I worked in Roger Williams Hospital's kitchen, pulling racks of steaming dishes from a dishwasher and scouring pots and pans at a double sink. My weekly take-home pay was $24.19, a tenth of which I was allowed to keep to cover bus fare and a ticket into the Community Theatre for a Saturday matinee. The rest was saved for college tuition.

The last I saw of Gina after our graduations and before she went on to Tufts and I to Brown happened in September when I was passing her house on way to the village church to do some organ practicing (the deacon had inveigled me to accompany Sunday's hymn singing after old Sybil Briggs died) and she came from her front door with Sporty, a bow legged hound, on a leash.

"Oh, hi, Harry. We're home now. What did you do all summer?"

"Work and things. What about you?"

"Nothing much to tell, really. I sat on the rocks watching the tide go in and out. Boring! But next Thursday I'll be checking into my dorm and I can hardly wait. When will you be starting Brown?"

"I'll be commuting, so I don't have to check in to a dorm. Tuesday though all freshmen have to show up for registration."

She gave the leash a tug. Sporty yelped, and she stooped to cuddle the hound. She looked up, her greenish eyes showing some sort of emotion that I couldn't make out.

"Harry, I want to ask you something. Are you scared? I mean, here we are about to start something brand new to us. A new place with people who are complete strangers. Honest, I'm scared. What are you feelng?"

Not wanting to tell her the truth lest she thought me a mama's boy, I merely shrugged. The truth was I liked things just as they were. I was going to college for one reason only: Mom and Dad expected me to. But then again it seemed that everyone else, like Richie, was going to places like Providence College.

"Gee, Gina, you shouldn't be scared, not with your brains and all. Will you come home for Christmas? Anyway, I have to go practice now. You take care. See ya, Sporty . . . be a good dog."

"Wait a minute, Harry. Do you suppose . . . well, I mean do you suppose you'll write back if I send you a letter?"

"I've never written one in my whole life! But, sure, maybe."

"No big deal. Just tell me about things like, you know, things like your courses, your new friends . . . the girls and all."

"Sure, Gina. Oh, thanks again for everything. See ya and good luck."

GINA'S LETTERS CAME once a week, chronically narrating the doings of her first semester at Tufts: acing her math courses but stuck with a lousy B average in Professor Dunlop's comp course; seeing her first football game; dismaying at the antics of the boys. I answered about every other one, glossing over my deepening misery. She should have wished *me* good luck. If I had told her the truth, I would have written that I felt as though a steam roller were running over me.

Midway in the break between semesters, along with Nick and

Charlie – two other brown-baggers – I prodigally bought a ticket at the Avon Cinema to catch the showing of a double feature that was getting a lot of buzz on campus. Three weeks later, I turned in to Professor Watts my first 500-word theme of the second semester. The assignment's topic was "A Turning Point in My Life". In five paragraphs I wrote about the irreversible impact upon my thinking that *A Streetcar Named Desire* had made.

I had come home from that afternoon at the Avon Cinema inflamed by a passion to write something that emulated the raw realism of the movie – its black-and-white capturing of the grittiness of New Orleans and the psychological wretchedness of Blanche, the ubiquitous southern heat, the steel-hard dialogue, the livid brutishness of Stanley. And the sound track – its jazz perfectly giving sound to the volatile drama unfolding. "Stella! Stella!" resonated in my head as I sat at my typewriter pecking out my first stab at writing a short story.

I loaded the story with modifiers, loving the squalor I was creating: "unshaven, muscular hoodlums lurking in rat infested city alley ways", "smirking bums loitering in shadowy doorways of seedy boarding houses", "stinking garbage rotting in dented, rusting pails." In the midst of this purple prose I plunked a bumpkin who had strayed into the ghetto, whose eyes had seen only "green rows of luscious corn and innocent faces of new-born calves". The more graphic I waxed, the stronger I felt the presence of Tennessee Williams at my elbow.

In my 500 word theme I came face-to-face with the sublimated fact that all the homey goodness that came with growing up in Graniteville - the white shirts that Mom carefully ironed, Dad's unspoken love for me, the perfect attendance pins given by my Sunday school teacher, all that organ-playing for hymn-singing, faithful Baptists - all of that goodness had been suffocating me. *A Streetcar Named Desire* punched a big hole in all that and out surged another part of me.

I stapled to my four-page short story my essay.

As usual, my returned theme had many circles, wavy lines, and marginalia in red pencil. But in large print was the grade: C-. My first passing grade at Brown! As for the short story, Professor Watts' only comment was scrawled on the top of the first page: *Sex, Mr. Anderson. There's no sex in this.*

To Gina I wrote:

> *". . . That's exactly what Professor Watts said. So, I changed the ending. Instead of my character knocking on the door of a convent for help, I have him getting saved from the hoods by a very pretty girl who let him into her house just in the nick of time. Here's an example of what I wrote. 'Her breasts pushed against her flimsy dress, and he kept staring at them and wondered what they felt like if he had the nerve to reach out and touch them'. What do you think, Gina? Is that sexy enough?"*

A month passed before she replied. Not until she added a PS to her letter did she refer to my question. Her answer was inconclusive: *Interesting, Harry. Would you let me read the whole story?* She ended with hugs and kisses. I assumed that is what XOXOXO meant.

A DRIZZLING RAIN had been dampening the roads since morning, but an hour before it would be setting the sun broke through and warmed them, creating a hovering fog. I was navigating south on Post Road into Wickford and beyond to Narragansett, a route I had down pat from many trips with my family to long afternoons of fun at Scarborough Beach. Following Gina's directions, I turned left onto Bonnet Shores Road and just ahead spotted through a break in the trees a strip of Narragansett Bay and the flashing of Beavertail light. A stranger to this bay-side community, I shifted into second and cruised past the community center, turned left onto Spring Brook Road, then right onto What Cheer Road. She said to park in the driveway of the only blue shuttered house on the street.

"Gee, that's swell of you to bring me that," she said for a welcome.

"Hi, Gina. What are you talking about?"

"Look, behind you. There's a rainbow across the bay over the light house. They say if you make a wish when you see a rainbow, it'll come true. So, close your eyes and make one."

That's how our date began. My wish was more like a quick prayer: "God, let me not be a jerk tonight." Hers she never told me. What ensued inside the blue-shuttered beach house on What Cheer Road gave me grist for the writing of my second short story. This time I larded my narrative with eroticism, entitling it "Virgins No More". I needed four days to type the first six pages, but in one night I raced through the climax:

> After we drank the second high ball and Maria put the bottle of Four Roses back in her father's liquor cabinet, we started to neck on a couch in the little parlor. The sound of a fog horn came through the open window and mixed with the music playing softly from the radio. It was very romantic. There was the smell of sea water in her hair because she was swimming all day. We kissed and kissed, and then she took my hand and put it on her breasts which felt very soft. I had never before felt a girl's breast. She sighed deeply and asked me to unbutton my shirt. Because she wasn't wearing a bra, when she took off her dress I could plainly see her breasts. My heart began to beat very fast.
>
> She wanted me to carry her into her bedroom, and I did. I carefully put her on her bed, and we kissed some more. She didn't say a word but only moaned. Then we had sex.

The following morning, I went immediately to my manuscript and saw that a flourish was needed and in long hand added, a lá Tennessee Williams, *Maria! Maria!*

Many years later, when I was in graduate school, Erich Auerbach's *Mimesis* brought to my mind "Virgins No More", a sixteen-year-old kid's callow account of a tryst. I had built its plot on verifiable details:

the whiskey, the soft music, the kissing and fondling. But the facts ended there. The rest was balderdash, a mimicry of the truth. Gina and I almost drank only one highball, we did not disrobe, I did not carry her to bed, and we did not have sex.

Here is the truth.

"Harry," she said before going to the couch, "you need to shave. Please go into the bathroom and use Dad's razor. You'll find it in the top right drawer."

"Ugh! You put too much whiskey in these drinks," she complained. She did a lot of complaining. When she ran out of things to grouse about, silence shrouded the parlor. Then she sobbed.

"I'm not happy, Harry. I'm sick and tired of math, of just about everything. There's something missing in my life, actually. Oh shit . . . kiss me!"

That was exactly what I wanted to do, why I drove 35 miles to see her. It wasn't that I had a crush on her. Simply, she was a girl who was sending me letters that ended with XOXOXO.

When my hand brushed her bosom, she commanded me to wait a minute.

"Go and shut off the lamp." Her tone was bossy.

In the dark on my return to the couch I tripped over a hassock, catching my tumble by grasping the end table and toppling a glass almost filled with too much Four Roses and a dash of Seven-up.

"Oh, shit! Now the room's going to reek of booze. How can I explain that to my father?"

Before I could find the couch, Gina had jumped to her feet. The wet carpet squished when she took a step toward me and whispered, "Let's go to my bedroom. Do you want to?"

She found my hand and ushered me in and lit a couple of candles on her dresser. In the flickering light I saw her sitting on the edge of her bed, waiting.

"What's the matter, Harry? Are you thinking I'm a slut or something?"

My eyes were fixed on a crucifix hanging over the head of the bed.

"We can't do this, Gina. We just can't."

She went to the candles and blew them out. In the darkness I muttered, "I'm sorry. I'm not Marlon Brando."

"I don't get it. What do you mean?"

"I'm all mixed up. I don't know what I mean. Anyway, I'm going home."

You've got to learn a few things before it gets dark.

ON THE BANKS OF
THE SEEKONK RIVER

WHENEVER THE OCCASION arises to express my sympathy to a be-reaving friend, I don't let a store-bought card do it for me. Instead, risking being thought pedantic, I compose in longhand a letter of condolence that usually cites a suitable literary excerpt. My reasoning is a writer, say, like Dante much more eloquently than I articulates my sincerest feelings.

To a recently widowed friend, for example, I sent this note, wishing that it would help her get through her sorrow:

> In due time, dear Dorothy, if you can hold on to Faith, your grief will abate and you will partner with Dante, whose long journey through the dark side of life has brought him face-to-face with God. At the conclusion of The Divine Comedy he describes himself to be "like a wheel in perfect motion by the Love that moves the sun and the other stars." He is at peace. And such blessed peace awaits you.

My passion for literature burst forth like a nova on the banks of the Seekonk River that sunny Sunday afternoon in 1953, a passion that has stayed red hot for these six ensuing decades. But prior to that epiphanic afternoon, I was dumb to the stuff of literature, to things like metaphor, irony, symbolism. That was no condition for a college sophomore to be in who, in six days, faced a deadline for handing in a paper to Professor Watts that would determine whether or not he passed his American Lit course.

I desperately needed a *deus ex machina*.

ARMAND THWACKED HIS notebook at my back as we left Manning Hall and crossed the campus toward Faunce House to grab a cup of coffee. He was more excited than usual after coming from a Professor Watts' lecture.

"The man's incredibly brilliant! Never in a million years would I have seen all the sex in *Moby Dick*. Ahab a eunuch, for God's sake! And . . . and all those phallic symbols? I've got to look up this Freud guy."

"You know something, Armand? I'm lost. All this about symbolism I don't get at all"

"You're missing the meaning of everything we've been reading then. What about when you did Shakespeare in high school? Your teacher must have gone into things like, say, the meaning of the ghosts in *Macbeth* and *Julius Caesar*? Right?"

"Wrong. I never had to read them."

"You're kidding! What did you read?"

"Nothing."

"Nothing?"

"Absolutely nothing."

Books, pads, cups and glasses covered every table in the Blue Room, around each sat students, some speaking seriously, some laughing, some scowling at an open text. Most smoked. Ralph – the perennial grad student – as usual held court yonder by the window, simultaneously thumbing through a stack of smudged index cards and orating to an audience of a couple of Pembroke co-eds. Armand pointed his chin at the door, and I followed him to the outside terrace and we sat in Adirondack chairs, blowing on our steaming coffee.

"So, tell me, Harry. If you read nothing for English, what did your teachers have you do?"

"Grammar. We diagramed sentences over and over, memorized

rules, and did exercises for homework."

"What about writing essays? You must have had to do that, didn't you?"

"Nope. The first time I heard of a topic sentence was in my comp 1 class. That's why I got a lousy D in the course."

"Holy shit! You poor guy."

He lit a Pall Mall and stretched his legs to the wrought iron railing. A Pembroker, hustling up the steps, spotted him and called out.

"Hey, Armand. Are you going to the Sigma Chi dance Friday night?"

"Wouldn't miss it, Francie!"

I drained the cardboard cup and hoped I didn't grimace. I had yet to like coffee. For that matter, I had yet to try a cigarette or to learn the name of a Pembroke girl.

With a wink he blew a line of smoke and smirked, "Wow, can she fill a sweater! Oh, baby, that gives me an idea for my paper. Sex, yeah! If Watts can lecture about it, I can write about it. I see it now, all the sex going on in *Huckleberry Finn*."

He took the pencil that more often than not jutted from behind his ear and scribbled something in his notebook.

"What are you talking about?"

"You heard Watts say that Freud's opened our eyes to what really makes all of us tick. It's s-e-x, sex. Yes, it's all coming together. Mark Twain's runaway boy has a problem with his sexual identity. So, there's my paper. Thank you, Francie!"

"Armand, you're nuts!"

"Hang on for a minute. Look, doesn't Huck dress like a girl? Remember that episode? That's a symbol. Get it? Anyway, what are you going to write your paper on?"

"I don't know. This symbolism stuff . . . I don't get it. Honest, I shouldn't have taken this course because I'm going to fail it for sure."

"Hell you are! Hey, I've got an idea. What're your plans for this coming Sunday?"

"Studying, I suppose. Why?"

"Well, suppose you and I get together and I'll get you started on your paper? Are you game?"

"Sure, if you are."

"Great! Get your butt here, right here on this terrace at . . . say one-thirty? I'm a good Catholic, you know, and Mass ends at noon. So, one-thirty?"

Carrie Tower's bell clanged and Armand jumped to his feet. His notebook dropped to the slate floor and his pack of Pall Malls slid from his shirt pocket when he stooped.

"I'm a real klutz, damn it! It'll be a miracle if I live to be thirty. My economics class is way the hell over at Whitehall. Gotta run! See you Sunday then. Don't stand me up."

The miracle never happened. He was twenty-nine when his Cessna's engine sputtered over Attleboro and his body was found among the wreckage not far from the high school where he had taught kids how to deal with symbolism.

HIS FOOTSTEPS BEHIND me broke my reverie. The bell in Carrie Tower announced the one o'clock hour as I stepped on to the Faunce House terrace, and in my half-hour wait for Armand I succumbed to the spell of Indian Summer. A lowering sun over the copula of University Hall warmed the silent campus. The only movement under the bare-boughed elms were two squirrels cavorting in the fallen leaves.

"Hey, I see you remembered to bring *Huck Finn* with you. Mine's in the car. Come on, we're going to the river."

I knew better than to ask what he had up his sleeve. He drove his '49 Olds 88 down Waterman Street, into Wayland Square, and through the maze of narrow East Side streets, cussing at red lights and accelerating when one turned yellow.

"Just listen to that V8! That's muscle you're hearing. Hang on, watch this."

The car lurched forward and zoomed around a van and got the speedometer shivering at 60 and screeched to a stop at an intersection.

"Next summer I'm heading West if I can get a job at Yellowstone. The roads open up out there. Then I'll let this baby go, go, go!"

He turned left, the tires squealed, and ahead loomed the Seekonk River and the university's boat house where the rowing crew stored its boats and sculls. He pulled into the parking lot and revved the engine before turning the key.

"Let's get to it, Harry. The sun's setting early, you know, and you've got to learn a few things before it gets dark. So, come on!"

He led the way to a large boulder on the edge of the river. An errant sea gull, up from Narragansett Bay, squawked from its perch on the boulder in protest and flapped off towards the Henderson Bridge, and we backed ourselves atop the boulder. Immediately he ordered me to turn to page 97 of *Huckleberry Finn*.

"I've been thinking of a topic for you, and "bingo" it came to me just like that! Bet you a coffee you can't guess when it did."

"You win. When did it?"

"This will kill you. This morning in church just after communion."

"So, what is it? The topic?"

"The river. The Mississippi River."

"Come on, Armand. You're kidding! What's it got to do with the novel?"

"My God! Everything! You're really bad off. You have to look at it not literally but as a symbol. Know what I'm saying?"

"No, I don't."

"You've finished the novel, haven't you?"

"Sure."

"Then you know the story line. Answer me this . . . when Jim and Huck are on land, what's happening to them?"

"A lot, and nothing's good. Huck's father almost kills him, for example. And Jim. He's a runaway slave."

"Right! But when they're on the raft going down the river, everything's different and for the better. You get that, don't you? Now, find the sentence on page 97, about half way down, that begins, 'So in two seconds . . .'. I'll read it:

So in two seconds we went a-sliding down the river, and it did seem so good to be free again and all by ourselves on the big river, and nobody to bother us.

With a you-got-it-now look, Armand stared at me, expecting me to shout "whoopee" or something. Instead, I shrugged and asked him what he meant by symbolism. He growled under his breath and pointed to the Seekonk River.

"There, right in front of your nose. A river! Make believe you're in a boat without oars. The boat will be moving, yes? Why? Obviously, because there's a current. Can't we say, then, when you're out there in a boat, and you have no oars, you're in the hands of natural law? Like Huck and Jim on their raft."

He took the pencil from behind his ear and doodled in his notebook.

"Here, let's say these lines are the streets we took to get here. These circles are traffic lights and stop signs. We had to stop and go and deal with traffic. In a boat, you don't have those things. In other words, what I'm saying is to get anywhere on land you have to obey rules and to watch out for other people."

He doodled some more.

"This square let's say is Manning Hall. What's going on with you when you're in there?"

"I guess I'm confused and not happy. What's that got to do with symbolism?"

He tore the page from his notebook and crumpled it and nibbled the pencil's eraser.

"Let me ask you something. Last week we had to read a couple of Emerson's essays. How are they different than *Huckleberry Finn*?"

"Different? Well, obviously Mark Twain tells a story but Emerson doesn't."

"Exactly! Yet both of them are doing the same thing, really. In other words, both of them are giving us, let's say, their *philosophy*, only in different ways. Twain wants to show us how his plays out in real life, so he makes up characters and a plot. Now get this . . . he uses symbols – like the river – to represent ideas. Comprendez?"

"Sort of."

"Not good enough. 'Sort of' won't get your paper written."

He swung his arms – once, twice – and leapt from the boulder, and, crouching, he turned his back to the breeze coming from the river and lit a cigarette.

"Are you giving up on me, Armand?"

"That I won't do. Come on, let's walk."

We slouched along the shore, not talking, and with a finger he flipped his cigarette into the water and stooped to pick up a pebble and tossed it, side-armed into the water.

"Three skips. Once, in a contest with other kids at the pond in Slater Park, I won with six skips. Anyway, you're not joking about reading nothing in high school? That stinks. I see you're wearing a class ring. Let's suppose you're so pissed off you threw it into the river. Hey, the ring didn't screw you. Why take out your anger at it? Well, why?"

"Because . . . because it represents the school."

"Yes, old buddy. Exactly! That makes the ring a symbol. You see? By throwing it into the river, you're really telling your school to go to hell."

Presto! Magically, a shroud around my brain lifted and I danced a jig, clumsily plopping a foot into the river and wetting my trousers up to the knees.

"Hold on. What's with the Mississippi in *Huck Finn*, symbolically speaking? Heh?"

"Lots of things, like freedom for one. I think I got it, Armand!"

He jotted something in his notebook, pulled from it the page, and stuffed it in my shirt pocket. His eyes gleamed like the ornament on the hood of his Olds 88, and he fisted a hand and punched my arm.

"There you have it, the title for your paper. Now it's up to you to write it."

I picked up a couple of pebbles, put one in my pocket and, with a side-armed toss, watched the other skip once.

FOR A LONG time I kept my paper in the top drawer of my desk and, from time to time, opened the drawer to glance at the circled B- Professor Watts had written on its cover page. Sometimes I rolled the little granite pebble with shiny mica flakes in the palm of my hand and remembered that Sunday afternoon on the banks of the Seekonk River when Armand got me to feel "so good to be free again". Weren't those the final words of *Huckleberry Finn*?

Today will be long, long ago.

OZARK

THE RIDE ON an olive-green, GI issue bus from the train depot in Dothan, down Ozark's Main Street, and on to Ft. Rucker was brief yet long enough for me to see that I was in the deep South. Two days earlier, when I had boarded the Florida Express in Providence's Union Train Station, the New Year's day snowfall still clung, unmelting, to tree limbs. Here, in Alabama, Spanish moss hung like negligees from old oaks.

Fresh from a two-week leave after advanced infantry training at Ft. Carson, Colorado, I was now a PFC with a machine gunner's MOS and with orders to report to the First Replacement Company, Third Army, to await re-assignment. Since my draft notice last July, the Army had shuttled me from New Jersey to Texas, from Colorado and now to Alabama. Where will I be sent next? The morning of my second day at Rucker the answer came.

Ordered to report to company headquarters at 0900 hours, I roamed the by-ways of the sprawling post, worrying needlessly that I would be late; for, when I did find the HQ building, only a clerk – a Spec 3 my age – manned the office. He squinted at my name tag stitched to my fatigue shirt and said, "Oh, you're Anderson. I got your 401 file right here. Take a seat. The sergeant's not come in yet."

Waiting is routine in the Army. I didn't mind sitting in that smallish room. Unlike bivouacking in the shadow of Cheyenne Mountain during the onset of a blizzard, the half-hour wait in a muggy room was many notches more tolerable. Besides, I was thirty-minutes closer to discharge time.

"Any calls come in, Butler?" were the first words out of the big man's mouth as he thumped into the office.

"None, Sergeant."

I jumped up and saluted.

"Who's this man, Butler?"

"PFC Anderson – the one I told you about yesterday and you said to get him in here on the double."

"Oh, yeah, yeah. Hey, Anderson, didn't they teach you in basic training you don't salute NCO's? Have him cool his ass, Butler. I've a couple of calls to make."

He gave me a once-over and went to his desk on the other side of a half petition.

I had seen a three, a four, and a five striper, but never a six striper. The gray in his buzz cut revealed that he had been in the Army a long time. Although he was out of sight behind the half petition, his voice could have passed through a brick wall.

"Ho, ho, ho, McDaniels . . . Reynolds here. I've been giving thought to that deal we talked about last night. Remember? Or were you too soused to remember, you old sonuvabitch? Well, listen up. Let's talk more about it tonight at the club. Can you get your sorry ass over there by 1700 hours? What? You heard me. And don't keep me waiting!"

I sniffed a cigar and spotted two perfect smoke rings ascend over the half petition.

"Butler! Tell what's-his-name to come here and bring his 401 with him."

9 January 1957

Darling Pauline,

I can't believe this good luck! I'm not a machine gunner any-more. My MOS was changed to clerk/typist! Because the score on the test I had to take at the induction center was so high, I've been assigned to HQ of the replacement company. My job is to

*do morning reports, cut orders, type up transcripts of court mar-
tials for the AG, and so forth. But get this! You won't believe it. I
can wear civvies, and I have my own room!! How's that for luck?*

*The CO is Captain Denton who's seldom here. It's Sergeant
Major Reynolds who's supposed to run the show, but he's not
in the office most of the time either. The other clerk (his name's
Timmy Butler from Maryland) and I really do all the work.*

*I haven't been off the base yet, but this Saturday Timmy said
he would show me around Ozark which is close enough to walk
to. I hate to rub it in but it's like spring down here. Very nice.*

*This afternoon with nothing else to do I made a count-
down chart. In 552 days I'll be out of the Army. I miss you
very, very much. Love and kisses,*

Me

ONE OF MY duties had me culling from the stack of 401 files that were
delivered daily to HQ any that recorded an IQ test score of 90 or better
and placing them on the CO's desk. Now and then when he did come
to the office and found no 401's, he asked, "Another day, Anderson,
and there's no sharp knife in the drawer? Where in hell are the brains?"

Butler and I were simpatico. We had a tacit understanding: to pre-
empt any hassles from Sergeant Reynolds, we had to make him look
good. And we did. Documents - perfectly typed, accurate, and on time
– went to his desk; files were kept in order; at all times we followed
Army protocol even to the extent of sweeping and dusting the office.
The big man with fondness for cigars and deals knew he had it made.

In return, we were given permanent passes to leave the post during down time. After three or four walks into Ozark, Dothan, and
Enterprise, we had seen all that these small towns had to offer. They
were quintessentially rural Dixie communities: a potpourri of mom
and pop stores along Main Street, an incongruous pastiche of modest newer homes and unpainted shacks and in their midst a dazzling

white plantation manor, a couple of brick municipal buildings, and more than one church – more often than not Baptist.

Enterprise, however, stood out because of a quirky statue in its business center – a monument to honor the boll weevil, the only monument in the world to honor an agricultural pest. Its fondness for cotton lured the bug to Alabama where it found this town's crop especially tasty and chomped through the cotton fields with impunity. Dismayed but not defeated, the farmers replaced cotton with peanuts and hit the jackpot. Dubbed "The Peanut Capitol of the World", in 1919 Enterprise erected this ironic icon out of gratitude to a wee, winged vermin.

CORPORAL JUNIOR HARROP was a regular visitor to the office. A gofer for the AG's lawyers, he dropped off transcripts of court martial proceedings that Timmy and I typed. He was unlike anyone else I had ever met, this skinny, loony, drawling plow boy from a backwoods settlement in nearby Georgia. I warmed to him. Eager to learn about Southern mores, I put up with his tall tales and he with my inquiries. Then, in early March, Junior, more fun-loving than ever, gave me an invitation that I immediately accepted.

"Hey, Yankee, y'all wanna go snake bustin' with me Sataday?"

Right after noontime chow, the first Saturday of March, I met up with him in the parking area behind the mail room where he was under the hood of a mustard-colored '51 Chevy Deluxe convertible, tinkering with its carburetor.

"Y'all's right on time! And look at that sun, will ya! Can't be a better day for what we're gonna do. Y'all hang in there another sec. I gotta do one more thing here and we're ready to go."

"Tell me again, Junior, exactly what we're going to do?"

"Snake bustin', old buddy."

"Which means?"

"Aw, damn it . . . I ain't gonna waste time yakin' about it. You'll see. Come on, jump in."

With its top down, the Chevy drew attention as Junior steered it through Dothan. Strollers along Main Street gawked, some waved. Horns of pick-ups beeped.

"Yee-oo!" he whooped. "I'm king of the road!"

He headed east out of Dothan onto the highway to Georgia, pressing the accelerator and switching on the radio. A Gospel choir vied with the humming of the tires and the swooshing of the wind. We entered a pine forest, passing now and then shanties with colored folk in the yards. He veered right off the highway onto a gravel road, down shifted, and coasted deeper into the forest. The air was thick with humidity and smelled musty.

"Snake country, Yankee. The big ones come out of the swamp to warm up. They stretch out in patches of sun on the side of the road. Yell out when ya see one, ya hear?"

Junior's eye was sharper than mine, and he yelled out first, pointing ahead to what I thought was a fallen pine branch.

"Will ya look at that big sonuvabitch! Hang on, old buddy, I'm gonna nail him!"

The rear tires shot pebbles into the swamp. I lurched forward. The Chevy shivered and came perilously close to the fetid water. Then, a big bump. Junior braked, and I followed him back to the patch of light where the yellow snake with black markings writhed and coiled in the throes of death.

"Jesus H. Christ! He must be all of eight feet! The biggest bull rattler I ever seen! I'm takin' him back to Rucker to show him off. Come on, help me pack him in the back seat."

I have a 35mm slide, taken in front of the barracks, of four guys clutching the snake with Junior's kneeling in the foreground, a big, buck-toothed smile on his face.

ON ANOTHER SATURDAY outing, Junior and I in the nick of time raised the convertible's top. We had been lollygagging along the streets of Ozark, filling our pockets with pecans that dropped in profusion from their trees.

"Here she comes, the rainy season. We ain't gonna see the sun much for the next couple of weeks. Ain't nothin' ya can do about it except hunker down in your bunk and look at girlie magazines. Hey, that gives me an idea! Yankee, let's you and me go to Reb's tonight. Want to? Ya can't say ya been to 'bama less y'all did some dancin' on a Sataday night at Reb's."

Junior was coming from the shower room smelling of soap and Old Spice as I entered the barracks to see what the hold up was.

"Sorry, old buddy, to keep ya waitin'. I lost track of time shootin' craps. Shit! I lost my shirt. Hey, ya got a couple of bucks to chip in for some booze?"

Booze? I had learned that Ozark and the other small towns around Ft. Rucker were dry. But I didn't ask questions and put a couple of one's on his bunk.

"Let's bug out of here, Yankee, and have us some fun."

Rain hit the convertible's top so hard that we had to yell to be heard. He turned up the volume of the radio and sang along with Elvis Presley:

Well, since my baby left me,
I found a new place to dwell
It's down at the end of lonely street
At Heartbreak Hotel

After passing Zack's Hardware, Junior took a hard left, shut off the radio, and down shifted into second gear and, as he did when we had gone snake busting - he coasted. Shanties flanked the alley ways. He stopped just beyond the only one with an outside light lit, killed the headlights, but idled the engine. What little I could see through the darkness and the rain was spooky, and I had to ask what in hell he was waiting for.

"No talkin', old buddy. Y'all will see in a minute."

Fingers tapped the driver's side window and Junior rolled it down and passed money to a black man. Whatever words were exchanged were lost in the din of the downpour. We waited. When the black man returned, he passed a paper sack to Junior.

"You hold the hootch, Yankee. Hot damn, we're in business!"

Only someone who has frequented Reb's could have found the place, for the cinder block building squatted deep in a pine forest at the end of a cul-de-sac. Junior squeezed his convertible between haphazardly parked pick-ups in the muddy lot, illuminated only by a garish red neon sign: REB'S CAFÉ. Dashing to the entrance, but not fast enough to avoid getting soaked, we went inside. Two guys in a booth across the dance floor spotted us and whistled.

"Yo, Junior! Over here!"

I could not make out what he and his pals were saying because of the cacophony in the room: their twangy way of speaking, the belly laughs coming from all quarters, and the amplified off-key singing of a Kate Smith look alike who was backed up by a quartet of local talent – a string bass, piano, drums, and an acoustic guitar. Cigarette smoke hazed dancing couples who looked like specters in the smog.

Whatever snake venom must taste like had to be similar to the bootlegged stuff that Junior had procured from the black man. One sip did it for me, but the others were draining the two bottles.

After a break, the fat lady and her band broke into a R&B number and Junior returned from a trip to the head clutching the hand of a girl who was as skinny as he was.

"Hey, Yankee, y'all ain't gonna sit on your ass all night, are ya? This here's Lou Ann and she's wantin' to dance with you. Ain't that so, honey?"

A weak grin broke her face. Blood-red lipstick and a generous dabbing of rouge hardly concealed her anemic complexion. Up I got and Lou Ann and I were dancing. Pressed together by a floor-full of whisky drinkers, we more or less took one step forward, one step back. The crowd pushed us toward what looked like a bar with a blinking Dr. Pepper sign dangling above it. Sitting on a stool too small to accommodate his obesity was a man who was leering at the ladies. Pinned to his khaki, sweat-stained shirt was a star.

"Is he the sheriff?" I shouted into Lou Ann's ear.

"Sure enough," she wheezed. Then she coughed, and I felt her rib cage rattle beneath her thin Saturday-night cotton dress.

"Are you sick or something, Lou Ann?"

"Doc Brackett says I got pneumonia."

It must have been instinct combined with luck that got us back to Fort Rucker, for Junior had tanked up with hootch and drove through the rain with his chin on the wheel, one eye closed. He leaned on me into the barracks where I left him, out like a light, on his bunk.

NEITHER TIMMY NOR Junior wanted to come with me on a visit to Montgomery. I walked alone into Ozark Easter morning to the drug store that doubled as a bus depot and boarded the 7:52 bus to Alabama's capitol city – about seventy-two miles north of Ozark.

Hoofing it only a block from Montgomery's bus terminal, I was regretting wearing my class A uniform with a tie, for summer comes early in the South. But I did fit in with the few pedestrians who were dressed in their Sunday best. Having no idea which direction to head or what to see, I followed a family of four past closed stores, hoping for a chance to ask where I might find the state capitol building. When the family obeyed the traffic signal at an intersection, even though the streets were empty of traffic, I had my chance.

"Excuse me, sir. Would you please direct me to the state house?"

"New here, are you? Well, supposin' y'all come with us, and when we get to the church we're headin' for, you keep on going for a little way until you see a sign that says – what do those signs say, dear? – I think maybe "Historic District". Just keep lookin' for those signs and you'll bump into the state house. It's a big, old building, white, with columns in the front. Y'all can't miss it."

We walked on for a couple of blocks, and all the while the man gave me a history lesson about Alabama's role in the Civil War. At the steps of the First Baptist Church of Montgomery – a building much larger than any Baptist church up North – he repeated the directions, capping them with the assurance, "Y'all can't miss it."

With the sweetest smile, his wife welcomed me to attend the worship service, adding the enticement, "Rest up out of this hot sun.

Y'all have a hike ahead of you." I watched the family climb the steps before I decided to get out of the sun.

I sat in a back pew, flabbergasted to see a full house – maybe as many as three hundred people. Sunday attendance at my church back home – Graniteville Baptist Church – averaged thirty or so and maybe as many as fifty for Easter. The choir of the First Baptist Church of Montgomery numbered at least that many. Dormant since induction into the Army, my soul exhilarated to the singing of *Christ the Lord Has Risen Today*.

With the final blessing and the organ postlude, the congregants milled in the aisles and the foyer. By the time I reached the sidewalk, I had turned down three invitations to Sunday dinner. It must be the uniform, I reckoned, that gave me away to be a stranger in a strange land.

The wife had been right in saying that the walk from the church to the state house was a hike, but I found it by following the signs the husband had said to look for. Although closed for the Sabbath, the building's portico offered up enough ghosts to make my visit worthwhile.

Embedded in the floor of the portico in the center of the six columns is a gold star that marks the spot where Jefferson Davis took the oath of office in 1861. I stood on the star, remembering the coincidence that exactly to the day, April 12, the battle of Fort Sumter was fought ninety-six years ago.

The bus back to Ozark was running late. Families who had been visiting kinfolk on the Easter holiday were returning from the big city to the hinterlands, and they filled every seat. Whatever night air came through the open windows did little to relieve passengers or blow away the odor of sweaty clothing. I gave up trying to peer over a large, dozing woman beside me to get a glimpse of the country side.

When the bus stopped, I realized that I, too, had been dozing. The driver, who resembled the sheriff I had seen at Reb's Café, stood and stretched and shouted, "Troy! Anyone getting' off here, now's the time to do it." Bodies shuffled down the aisle and out the door, replaced by others. The last to come aboard was a young black woman, clutching a soiled tote bag. She was "swollen with child." Absurdly, this Biblical way of describing a mother-to-be came to me.

She paused next to me, standing close enough for me to see a gimp bracelet, the sort of trinket kids make at summer camp. She put the tote bag between her feet and grasped the back of my seat. I heard her quietly moan. Looking at his passengers in the rear view mirror, the driver announced, "Next stop, Ozark."

The bus, back on route 231, accelerated, and the black woman nearly toppled, her belly brushing my shoulder. I looked up. Her hair was matted with perspiration. Her eyes showed an emotion like a whipped puppy. I stood and whispered, "Please, sit." She did. The woman next to her still dozed.

The bus braked, and the driver stomped toward me and raged at the black woman.

"Look a here, Nigger! Out of that there seat *now* and get yerself back there where ya belong!"

Turning to me, he snarled, "And as for you, boy, why you did that? Don't y'all know better?"

12 April 1957

Dearest Pauline,

What an Easter this has been! All by myself, I went to Montgomery to look around. I didn't plan to go to church, but I ended up going. The place was packed. I guess Southerners are religious people. As I said that, though, I thought about something that happened on the bus back to Ozark.

I got chewed out big time by the bus driver because I gave up my seat to a pregnant Negro woman. Imagine! She was in agony and I just had to do it. Nobody else would. It got really scary. These people down here really mean business when it comes to keeping Negroes in their place. Makes me think of the story Timmy tells about what happened when he hitched a ride home to Maryland with a lieutenant who was a Negro Almost all the way the lieutenant stayed in his car when they stopped to get something to eat. The other guys had to bring food to him.

Speaking of food, I miss going out for pizza. You can't find any place down here that sells it. But it's you most of all that I miss. All I want is to get this Army thing over with and come home.

Count down is 451 days. This seems to be a long, long time, but I suppose it really isn't. It'll be a dream come true when we cuddle together on a blanket at Moonstone!

Xoxoxoxox

Me

"THOSE LOUSY SONS of bitches!"

Butler and I stopped typing and looked at each other, wondering what made Sergeant Reynolds yell like that. He came from behind the half petition, shot a look of shock at us, and marched into Captain Denton's office. We shrugged and went back to work.

The voices coming through the closed door quieted, and the sergeant and captain, looking like a craps player who just rolled snake eyes, came up to us.

"You tell them, Reynolds."

"Yes, sir."

Handing Butler, first, then me a page of paper, the old war dog muttered, "These are orders come down from the AG. Read them."

Report to the commanding officer of the First Replacement Company, Ft. Lewis, Washington, at 0700 hours, 21 May 1957, to await deployment to Korea.

I went numb. Butler, who had just re-upped for another three years, simply said, "That's the Army for you." But I, grasping at straws, told Captain Denton that my date of discharge was July of 1958, thus making me ineligible to serve a tour of duty in Korea.

"Sorry, Anderson. A tour of duty over there is 365 days. Whoever cut your orders knew you would just barely make eligibility."

The inevitability of this sudden shift of fate began to set in, and I barely got a question out of me.

"Will I keep a clerk/typist MOS at least, sir?"

"No. You'll retain your primary MOS, which is?"

"Machine gunner, sir."

"I'm going to make a couple of phone calls," Reynolds snarled. "Stand your ground. This fight isn't over yet."

For the rest of the week we hardly saw Sergeant Reynolds. When he did show up, he sat at his desk smoking cigars, saying nothing to Butler and me. Nor was he on the phone with his cronies. Monday morning, as I put the finished Morning Report on his desk, he ordered me to sit down. He lit a cigar, blew a couple of perfect smoke rings, and squinted at me.

"Those bastards! They had no other way to get back at me. Like I said to the Captain, you stay in the Army as long as me and you inevitably make enemies. Butler and you make me look good, you see. So . . . those clever bastards came up with the idea to get rid of you. Without you guys, my goose is cooked."

He went to the window, and with his back to me and in a low voice said, "I have a plan, Anderson, to outwit those sons of bitches. Now listen up. Down in Ft. Meyers I have a nice place right on the Gulf. Suppose if I gave you the keys to the place and you hide your ass there for . . . say, for a couple of weeks?"

"You're telling me to go AWOL?"

"No big deal. I'll wait a couple of days before telling Butler to put it on the Morning Report. Then I'll tell the CO and some of my buddies over at the AG that the pressure of all the work around here finally got to you. Then, you come back and stick to this story."

"But I'll be court-martialed!"

"No you won't. At worse, you'll get an Article 15. Here's the point. By the time all this is said and done, you won't have enough time left in the Army to do a tour of duty in Korea. You'll stay here and everything will be hunky-dory. Well, how about it? Will you do it?"

MY FLIGHT TO Ft. Lewis included a four-hour lay-over in Denver. I checked my duffle bag in an airport locker and went into town. Spotting the gilded dome of Colorado's capitol building, I headed for it. My walk along busy 13th Avenue brought to mind the Easter morning jaunt in Montgomery. Already the memory of it was blurring. The depressive prospect of going on maneuvers in a combat zone as an infantry grunt was adumbrating everything – especially my fantasies of a happy life ahead.

At the entrance to the capitol building a posted sign alerted visitors that doors would lock at 4:30 p.m. My watch showed the time to be 3:42 p.m. The only others in the grand rotunda were two men, wearing cowboy hats, descending the stairs. Their voices and clicking boots echoed off the muraled walls. Then, I was alone.

I circled the rotunda's perimeter, studying each mural and reading the caption beneath. The seventh mural stopped me in my tracks. Like the miraculous handwriting on the wall in the Book of Daniel – "Mene, Mene, Tekel, Upharsin" – its caption portended a future event. But unlike the Old Testament prophet's foreboding interpretation (Blasphemous Belshazzar, King of Babylon, Daniel said, is doomed), this caption was salubrious, foretelling my acquiring a gift of wisdom. It read, TODAY WILL BE LONG, LONG AGO. In that moment I sensed that these words were for me.

I returned to Stapleton Airport in plenty of time to board the plane to Seattle, still unhappy but reconciled. I would let be whatever was in store for me in the coming year, braced by the assurance that all would pass.

Hungry, I sat on a stool at the bar of the airport's small bistro and ordered a ham and cheese sandwich on rye and a ten cent glass of Coors. The handwriting on the wall of the capitol's rotunda stayed in my mind, and I said to the glass, "Yes . . . already Ozark is long, long ago." I didn't give a damn if the waiter heard me.

I was wretched . . . a machine gunner on the way to war.

USS ANDERSON

THE WAITING WAS over. For seventeen wet days we had languished in the barracks of Ft. Lewis, Washington, playing chess, rolling dice, rambling to the USO to catch a movie and to fatten up on burgers and fries. At 400 hours, May 12, lights came on in the barracks and a staff sergeant, whacking his swagger stick on a foot locker, yelled: "Get your butts out of the sack! This here is moving day, do ya hear?"

Wise cracking, the tried and true way of soldiers to hide their fear, erupted:

"Hey, Sarge, we ain't walkin' to Korea, are we?"

"First chance I get, I'm gonna find out if those slant-eyed bitches are hot to trot."

"Watch out for the rice. I hear it makes your pecker stand at ease."

When wise cracking grew thin, rumors entertained the troops. In the mess hall it was bruited that North Korea had launched an offensive in violation of the truce agreement. By the time we were stuffing all our belongings into our duffle bags, the rumor had grown to apocalyptic proportions. Coming from the head, my bunk buddy, who stuttered when excited, gasped, "Holy sh-sh-sh-shit! I-I-I just heard the Ch-Ch-Chinese are crossing the 38th P-P-Parallel like a tsu-tsu-tsunami! We're heading into an all-out f-f-fuckin' war!"

Under the canvas of a deuce-and-a-half I saw nothing of Tacoma as the convoy transported us to the waterfront. The noisome mix of diesel fumes, sweat-soaked fatigues, and boot polish thickened the air and inspired a couple of wags to show off their gallows humor.

Some guys guffawed. Like me, though, most were silent, struggling to adjust to the nightmare of the moment.

Rat-a-ta-tat . . . Rat-a-ta-tat . . . Rat-a-ta-tat . . . A Navy band marched single file between the parked trucks onto the pier, their dress whites contrasting with the drab fatigues of the GI's who were lining up in company formation. The deployment of three thousand combat-ready troops to the Far East was not a covert operation. To the contrary, it was a star spangled extravaganza.

On tripods, a couple of movie cameras panned the pier. Photojournalists aimed their Canons with zoom lenses, catching every detail of the scene: a first lieutenant's kissing his wife goodbye, a row of soldiers standing at ease with duffle bags at their boots, the kids behind a chain linked fence, holding tiny American flags next to their mothers, a swabbie's hosing down the gray steel plates of the ship's prow, a sea gull perched on the muzzle of a forward gun.

A boson's whistle pierced through the band's playing Elvis Presley's *Love Me Tender*, followed by the order over the PA for troops to come aboard. The band segued into Sousa's *Stars and Stripes Forever*, and a SFC shouted, "Company A . . 'tenshun! Right face! Forward . . . march!" In single file with duffle bags on our left shoulders, we paraded up the gang plank and, as instructed, stepped on deck and saluted, requesting permission to come aboard.

I followed the man in front of me through a hatchway and down and down and down through four more hatchways to the end of the passage way into a sizeable compartment with a warren of hammocks, five deep. Shouting resonated off the bulkheads:

"The SOB's think we're sardines or what?"

"Yo, Ramos! Grab this here hammock!"

"What the hell! There ain't no fuckin' pillow!"

When the kid named Ramos swung out of the bottom most hammock and climbed onto the one over his buddy's, I laid claim to it.

The shrill boson's whistle followed by an announcement came from a speaker: "Now hear this. Anchors away at 1400 hours. All hands report on deck!"

I squeezed into a spot at the port side railing and looked down at the pier that seemed to be moving. But it was the ship that was moving. Black smoke roiled from its stacks. Behind the chain linked fence civilians waved. The band soulfully played *Now Is the Hour.* I was wretched – a machine gunner on his way to war.

FIRST FULL DAY at sea. Duties had been assigned, mess cards distributed, and cliques formed. Most noteworthy, however, an epidemic spread through the ranks: sea sickness. Its first appearance came soon after the ship had left port and was bobbing into one-foot waves of Puget Sound. All six of a knot of buddies flaunting the screaming eagle patch of the 101st Airborne Division ceased their bravado and scurried to the railing and retched.

At 0800 hours I joined the detail assigned to latrine duty, and a corporal handed me a bucket and mop.

"See those first six johns and those six urinals, Private? That's your area. It's all yours. Ain't I generous? Make it shine like a witch's tit!"

I needed all four hours of my shift to make it shine. Through the night guys must have been tumbling out of their hammocks and running to the head, for splotches of vomit smattered the deck . . . Viscous greenish yellow slime that reeked. I shut my eyes before pushing the mop into some guy's undigested supper.

Just ten months ago I had written a paper on Negative Capability for Professor Bloom's Romantic Poets seminar, not thinking that I would ever put to practice Keats' survival strategy. But as I worked the mop and emptied the bucket I tried mightily to give wings to my imagination and to conjure up pleasant visions.

Notwithstanding the stench of bile clinging to my fatigues, I could not pass up noontime mess. A swallow of hot coffee, a bite of anything sweet – that's what I needed to quell my queasiness. Another one striper punched my meal card and behind me someone asked him, "Is this the duty you've pulled?"

"Sure is."

"You're a lucky son of a bitch!"

"Hey, somebody's gotta do it, right? Look, if your card wasn't punched, you'd go through the line for seconds. And so would all the guys. Then what? Half way to Korea we'd be out of food, that's what. Think about that, man. So, this here job I'm doing is fuckin' important!"

Apparently the PFC hadn't noticed all the empty tables. Whole platoons of GI's by-passed lunch, too sick to eat.

I returned to the compartment and saw arms and legs dangling from the hammocks and heard low groaning. Still thinking of Negative Capability, I recalled the lines from *Ode to a Nightingale* that I had quoted in my paper for Professor Bloom:

The weariness, the fever, and the fret
Here, where men sit and hear each other groan

I found where I had tucked it in the toe of my dress shoe, buried deep in my duffle bag, a pocket-sized New Testament that my old Sunday school teacher had given me when, on furlough, I paid him a farewell visit. With it in hand I lurched through the hatchways and up the steps into topside.

Not yet getting my sea legs, I clung to the starboard railing, lest the yawing of the ship sent me sprawling across the slippery deck. In contrast with the dimness and miasmic air of the nether regions of the ship, the all-blue world of the Pacific and its errant wind revivified me.

Amid ship, with my back against the bulwark, I sat crossed legged and, letting chance select the page, I thumbed open the pocket testament to Chapter 27 of *Acts* and read an account of Paul's harrowing encounter with a fierce storm while he was en route to Rome aboard a ship. This chapter is not to be read at sea. Certainly not by me, not right then, when my imagination was in high gear as I put to practice Negative Capability. How terribly the 20th verse impinged upon my imagination: *When neither sun nor stars appeared for many days and the storm continued raging, we finally gave up all hope of being saved.*

Interrupted by the boson's whistle followed with the order for all hands to report immediately to their assigned quarters for a practice drill, I went below, encumbered not only with the dread of mopping up vomit next morning but also with the premonition of being shipwrecked.

DAY TWO AT sea, 0800 hours. Yesterday's scenario in the head had not changed. The same corporal greeted me.

"You look bright eyed and bushy tailed, Anderson. Your bucket and mop's over there. Look at this fuckin', stinkin' mess! What's the matter with these damn guys anyways?"

Still thinking about *Acts 27*, I wondered what the head would look like if we did get hit with a storm. The boson's whistle shrilled again. Another announcement: "Now hear this, now hear this. This is Commander Benjamin Begin, ship's chaplain. Any man who can play the piano, report to the chaplain's office on B Deck, aft, at 0830 hours."

It took a few seconds for the announcement to sink in. When it did, I leaned the mop against the bulkhead and quick-timed out of the head.

"Hey, Anderson, where in hell are you goin'?"

"Orders just came through from upstairs, didn't you hear?"

Whatever the corporal answered I'd never know because I never saw him again.

In contrast to the reeking quarters reserved for us troops, B deck resembled a corridor of a downtown office building. Its silence worried me. Had I taken a wrong route? Was I off limits? But ahead I saw a bronze sign screwed to an opened door that read CHAPEL, and in I went, relieved.

A lanky Navy officer peered at me over his reading glasses.

"PFC Anderson, Sir, reporting as ordered."

He returned my salute rather limply and told me to relax.

"I'm Chaplain Begin, Anderson. I assume you're here because

you heard my announcement. Tell me, can you play that organ?"

"I think I can, Sir."

"Let's give it a try then. How about playing the Navy hymn? It's on page 17 in that hymnal."

The electronic instrument was similar to the one I had sat at Sunday mornings since I was seventeen, leading the small congregation of Graniteville Baptist Church in the singing of their pet hymns such as *Blessed Assurance* and *Abide with Me*. I switched it on, pulled out the usual stops, and tested the two keyboards and pedals. Softly, cautiously I sight-read through the twelve bar hymn, paused, and – pressing the volume pedal – played it again, but this time with *brio*.

"Well, Anderson, it's going on 0900 hours and no one else has shown up. So, it looks like you're the one who's going to be my organist. That is, if you want to. Do you?"

"Does that mean, Sir, I get out of mopping the head?"

"Yes, it does."

"When do I start, Sir?"

"According to my watch, in about ninety minutes. Let's sit over there and I'll go over what you have to do."

THE THIRD DAY at sea. The *USS Anderson*, yet to be rained upon or tossed by high seas, carried its cargo of three thousand GI's and a complement of officers farther and farther into the largest expanse of ocean on Earth. Routines were in place, territories claimed. The Airborne guys shot craps at the end of the last row of hammocks. Another clique squatted about a bottom hammock in the second row and kept up an endless poker game. Here and there loners dangled their legs from their hammocks – one of them did crossword puzzles, another played solitaire. Most of the loners tossed and groaned.

Now and then, a Black guy, who had found room in his duffle bag for a trumpet, aimed the muted horn between his knees and made music. Some of the songs I did not recognize, but *Misty* I did and

When the Saints Come Marching In. When the kid played *Tenderly*, I hurt. That was our song, Pauline's and mine. Home on furlough, I had sold my '48 Plymouth and with the cash I bought a diamond ring and she accepted it.

I, too, had a routine down pat. From 1030 hours to 1130 hours I was the Chaplain's organist, playing a prelude, three hymns, and a postlude for his daily devotional service. After lunch, I returned to the chapel to practice and to read what Paul had to say to the bellicose Romans. Believing that I was relieved of mop and pail was an act of Providence, before each reading I said a thank-you-God.

On the fourth day at sea, more men were showing up in the chapel – a mix of officers and enlistees. Although he was quick to leave at the end of a service and said nothing to me, Chaplain Begin, I assumed, thought my playing was okay. I had clicked off the organ and looked up to see a major coming toward me, followed by a Black PFC. Awkwardly, I arose from the bench and saluted. The major returned the salute while reading my name tag.

"Anderson, I'm Major Murphy. Private Lee, here, and I have been putting our heads together and have a proposition to make. First off, though, you must have heard this man's voice belt out those hymns, right? Best damn voice I've ever heard. Anyway, to the point. He says he's been singing back home with a jazz band. By any chance, Anderson, can you play things other than hymns?"

"I played piano with a band, Sir."

"How about that! Well, here's the deal. The Navy's been going overboard – excuse the pun – to make this a five-star cruise, except for one thing. It's pretty damn boring in the officers' lounge. There's no entertainment. Some of us have wives with us, and it sure would be nice to have some music. So . . . how about you two men giving us some music? Lee would sing and you accompany him. There's a piano up there. Well, what do you say?"

Lee and I eyed each other. I guessed at what he was thinking, asking himself the same questions I was asking myself, especially the big one: Can the two of us click?

"Sir," Lee asked, "if I may make a suggestion? Before we give you an answer, I think Anderson and I should get together and talk about your idea and find out if we can come up with a repertoire. Know what I mean?"

I liked this guy. His poise and way of speaking impressed me. Beside that, he had come to chapel all four mornings. Later I would learn that Monroe Jefferson Lee had gone to Rutgers on a scholarship and got a degree in music in spite of lacking a father and coming from a project in Newark.

"Fair enough, Lee. Then how does this sound? Suppose you two go over things this afternoon in the chapel and I'll come back about 1600 hours to get your answer. Will that give you enough time?"

"There's one hitch, Sir. I have guard duty."

"No more do you have guard duty, Lee. I'll see to that."

Having twenty minutes to spare before afternoon chow and not wanting to go to the compartment, I went top side for a look at the Pacific. Borne on the breath of a stiff wind came a riff from a trumpet. I lurched with the pitching of the ship, hand over hand at the railing, in search for whoever was playing the blues. There he stood in the bow like a figurehead, blowing into the wind – the Black guy from my compartment. I crouched in the lee of a bulkhead and listened. His improvisation of a tune straight from bayou land was achingly beautiful. I had to talk with him.

THE THREE OF us – M. J. Lee, Johnny Pleasant from Baltimore, and I from a backwater Rhode Island mill town – sat in the chapel, awaiting Major Murphy. In three hours we had cobbled together enough numbers to get through a gig in the officers' lounge. Whereas their souls sprouted from the rich soil of jazz, mine had been nourished by classical music. Their heroes were Charlie Parker, Dizzy Gillespie, Louis Armstrong, Billy Eckstine. Mine were Bach, Mozart, Chopin. Johnny went right to the heart of the matter to put me in synch with them so that we could come up with a repertoire.

"You know bebop, man? Let me at that organ and I'll show you something."

He played a chord, five notes, a chord I had never come upon. The old masters never ventured into the wonderland of the blues.

"That, Anderson, is the G diminished 7th. Look . . . G, B flat, D flat, E. Got it? Then, break it up and play the notes *arpeggio*. That's the magic bullet. Hey, Monroe, let's do *Fly Me to the Moon* and we'll show this cat what I'm talking about. By the way, how in hell did you end up with a funky name like 'Monroe'?"

Our incongruous trio pleased the brass, for this gig lasted all the way to Yokohama. Harmonies were coming from the piano that surprised me. Johnny's trumpet and M.J.'s dulcet voice – music-making born in the grittiness of urban ghettoes – went into my bones and made my fingers do things they had not done before.

The major surreptitiously placed cold bottles of Coors on the piano and winked when the steward served us the evening's entrée. Like steak, for example. The other officers looked the other way.

To note the crossing of the International Date Line, we GI's were given wallet-sized souvenir cards and an announcement made it known that, although yesterday was Wednesday, today is Friday. That spawned a lot of wise cracks:

"The fuckin' Army don't know what day of the week it is!"

"What the hell? I got cheated out of a birthday!"

"Do we lose a day's pay?"

Coincidentally, with the crossing, fair weather ended. The *USS Anderson* severely pitched and yawed. Cups of coffee slid off tables, like intoxicated men on weekend passes GI's lost their footing and dropped their trays. Many stampeded to the head. An OFF LIMITS was posted on the hatch that opened to the upper deck.

Because even a short walk down a row of hammocks was a perilous journey, I expected Chaplain Begin to cancel the morning service. When I got to the chapel with difficulty, he was grasping the edge of the altar for dear life.

"Anderson, you would have made a good sailor. I've sailed

through storms before, but this out does them all! The skipper told us at breakfast that the wind is gusting up to 80 knots and is kicking up twenty foot waves. It must be hell for the troops below."

"They're not happy campers, Sir."

"If anyone shows up this morning, let's open with *Onward Christian Soldiers*. Might be good for the morale."

Nine in all showed up, including M.J. On cue from the chaplain, I introduced the hymn. We were into verse two when the ship tipped and, with my fingers still on the keys, I played a *glissando* as I slid off the bench onto the deck. Monroe, alone, finished the verse.

At dusk the storm had not abated. With each bounce of the ship, something or another smashed onto the deck and the officers whooped like rodeo bronco-busters. Johnny oiled his trumpet's valves and I practiced chord progressions. M.J. came back from gawking through a port hole.

"Incredible! I just saw a wave break over the bow."

"I kinda dig this," Johnny grinned. "Look at the brass line up at the bar! It ain't sea water they're drowning in. Hey, Anderson, give me a B flat."

He tuned up his horn and broke into a solo of *Stormy Weather*. I caught on, and we were jiving. This would be Johnny's night. He was on fire.

AFTER A DAY'S lay-over in Yokohama in order to drop off some officers and their wives, the *USS Anderson* continued its mission. Onward it sailed around the southern tip of Japan and into the Yellow Sea. The two announcements following the boson's whistle changed the mood aboard the ship.

The skipper spoke first becoming a host who was bidding a fare-thee-well to his guests: "Tomorrow at approximately 1100 hours we will tie up in Inchon, South Korea. All Army personnel will disembark. For twenty-one days you have been guests of the United States Navy. It has been our pleasure to give you safe passage. We wish you all good luck in what awaits you."

Then, with a voice we GI's were more accustomed to, the CO chilled us with the reality of the moment: "Attention, men! This is your Commanding Officer, Colonel McIvor. We have entered a combat zone. Henceforth, a helmet liner is the uniform of the day. At 1430 hours await orders to report to the paymaster at which time you will exchange all US currency for scrip. Upon disembarking, stand in unit formation to board trucks for transport to a replacement compound. That is all."

After evening mess and wearing a helmet liner, I ignored a drizzling rain and stood alone top side seeing nothing but fog. We very well could have been cruising down Narragansett Bay or strolling to the dance floor at Rocky Point's Palladium, hand in hand with Pauline, for walking to the railing was smooth and easy. The only difference was misery was holding my hand.

It had been a day without music. No hymn singing, no jazz. Already vanishing into the fog were Chaplain Begin, Monroe Jefferson Lee, Johnny Pleasant. I was again but an infantry grunt – a machine gunner with a combat life expectancy of five minutes. I went below and opened my pocket testament to second *Corinthians* and read: *So we fix our eyes not on what is seen, but on what is unseen. For what is seen is temporary, but what is unseen is eternal.* Was it luck that brought me to this page?

Although there was yet an hour to go before lights out, the compartment was hushed. No one rolled dice, no one shuffled cards. Conversations were whispered. Men moved like specters coming from the head, smelling of Old Spice. They rummaged through their duffle bags and twisted and turned in their hammocks. I lay there, fully clothed, hoping to sleep and trying to find succor in the unseen.

IN A DRENCHING rain, three thousand poncho-clad GI's wearing helmet liners huddled on deck as midshipmen hurled hawsers and secured the ship to the pier. From a transistor radio, staticky Oriental music accompanied the cacophony of shouted orders and revved up machinery.

The port of Inchon was a maelstrom of activity.

Two things struck me when I walked onto the pier and filed into formation: how wobbly my legs were and how noisome the air was. Seeing the flag of the Republic of Korea limply hanging beside the American flag and signs printed in Korean confirmed that I was standing on foreign soil. All seemed surreal.

Unlike the two weeks of languishing at Ft. Lewis and the three weeks aboard the *USS Anderson*, we were hustled onto camouflaged trucks and bounced away over gravel roads to a replacement depot where we lined up in front of Quonset huts. A lieutenant shouted into a bull horn, spelling out without mincing words what we could expect:

"Men, at all times remember this. For the duration of your tour of duty in Korea, you are in a war zone, and you must stand ready for combat. You are on high alert! Within three days orders will be cut to deploy you to battle units where you'll be issued weapons. Until then, anywhere beyond that fence is strictly off limits."

A sergeant handed him a slip of paper.

"One last thing. Anyone who can play a piano report immediately to the day room. Attention! Dismissed."

I wondered if this could be happening as I sloshed through the mud in search of the day room. No one else was with me as I entered and faced a Captain with a cross on his helmet and saluted.

"PFC Anderson, Sir, reporting as ordered."

Tapping the top of a field organ – a scaled down version of a Hammond with pump pedals, he asked if I could play it. I sat at the truncated keyboard, pumped, and played *Onward Christian Soldiers*.

"Good enough, Anderson. I'm Chaplain Creamer with the 23rd Transportation Battalion. Do you want to be my assistant?"

Two hours later, with orders cut and folded into my duffle bag, I chauffeured the chaplain in a jeep into war-ravaged Seoul and northward past rice paddies and make-shift villages – hovels pieced together with whatever salvaged stuff could be found – and parked in a motor pool five miles south of the DMZ.

Although wet to the skin and exhausted, I inspected what would be my quarters for the duration, a 12'x12' room attached to a Quonset hut that served as a chapel. I sat at a small desk across from a cot, pulled from my duffle bag a pad and pen, and began a letter to Pauline:

My darling,
At last I have a permanent address and I can write to you. A lot has been happening, some of which you won't believe. But I'm telling you the truth, so help me God.

"Shout with joy to God, all the earth!"

THE 38ᵀᴴ PARALLEL

NOW AND THEN "cat-eye" drills and fly-by harassments of MIGs alerted us to the fact that, although four years ago North and South Korea had signed an armistice, we were in a war zone, and our enemy toed the Demarcation Line at the 38th parallel just five miles north of our compound. By the time I had reported for duty with the 23rd Transportation Battalion in June, 1957, the unit's infrastructure had been secured. A barbed wire fence around its perimeter separated the Quonset huts and large motor pool from the war-scarred landscape and a small village of non-descript hovels scrabbled together with salvaged corrugated metal, plywood of various dimensions, and even cardboard.

Close by the guarded entrance to the compound, standing apart from the Quonset huts and motor pool, was a fabricated metal building with a small spire on its pitched roof. That was the battalion's chapel. An ell extended off its back side. That was the chaplain's office and my billet.

A dearth of chaplains necessitated Major Creamer to carry out his duties at five scattered compounds. Until he had determined that I was capable to be his surrogate, he showed up Tuesday, Wednesday, and Friday during my first month on duty – and, of course, every Sunday to conduct a Sabbath worship service. For all intents and purposes I became the battalion's chaplain, doing all but delivering sermons.

But there wasn't much to do. Occasional walk-ins by guys from the motor pool broke the monotony of cleaning the chapel, mimeo-graphing the weekly order of service after selecting the hymns and practicing them at the organ, and typing required reports such as a weekly inventory of issued items (e.g., furniture, space heater, type-writer, 72 hymnals). The only item that ever changed was the supply of communal wine.

There's a saying in the ranks: "Go see the chaplain". In other words, whining and griping gets a guy nowhere. Yet now and then a soldier walked into my office with a hang-dog look. My orders were clear: listen to the complaint or request; take no action; and when the visit ended, write a summary on the appropriate form and give it to Major Creamer whenever he showed up. As far as I could see, the only good coming from this was letting a man get off his chest whatever was bothering him, and the bothering ran the gamut: beefs about not getting reissued boots or waiting too long for a dentist to pull a tooth. Then there were the requests: transfer to another unit, for example, or change of date for an R and R.

Sometimes, however, I was listening to a grave confession, com-pelling me to work through the emotion and come up with some nos-trum. The skinny, carrot-top Irish kid from Dorchester, Massachusetts, was a case in point.

"I masturbated," he sobbed. "My immortal soul is damned!"

"Listen up," I said. "I went to a Catholic school and almost every day heard the kids bragging about jerking off. No big deal! All you have to do is what they did. They went to confession, did their pen-ance, and all was forgiven. Come to the chapel Saturday afternoon. There'll be a priest here doing the honors."

A sergeant's confession, however, put us in deep water.

"They say," he said, "when a female gook's slanty eyes begin to look round, then you know you've been too long in this here hell hole. There's truth in that. I know because I shacked up with one. And guess what? She's pregnant! Son of a bitch! And I'm going state side next month. Me, a daddy and I'm leaving a kid over here, never knowing if it's a boy or girl. What in hell can I do?"

THE 38TH PARALLEL ⤸

His problem was way too complicated for me to help. He had to see the chaplain. And, knowing that Sunday was the only sure time the Major would be anywhere near the 23rd Transportation Battalion, I advised the sergeant to come to the chapel then.

"Me? You're telling me to go to church? Listen, pal, all the fucking prayers in the world ain't going to pull me out of this fucking mess!"

His rush to get away toppled his chair. He gave me no chance to clear up his misunderstanding.

"Take no action," was Chaplain Creamer's explicit command. But what PFC Johnny Evans requested was different, and I took action. He was a motor pool grease monkey on the shy side. He stayed his eyes on his gunk-caked fingernails when answering a question. His first walk to the chapel came in October, a couple of weeks after getting to Korea. I looked up from reading Mann's *The Magic Mountain* when he clumped into the office and snapped a salute.

"Private First Class Evans, sir, here to ask ya a favor, sir."

"Hey, Evans, cut out the 'sir' stuff. Look, I'm a one-striper, too."

There was no hiding the fact that he was from the deep South – from Puckett, Mississippi, I soon learned.

"You ain't no chaplain? I was wantin' to see the chaplain."

"You'll have to talk with me first. Take a seat and let's hear what you have to say."

"I best stay standin'. Been puttin' a head gasket in a deuce-and-a-half all day and I'm done up to my ears in oil. Anyways, what should I call ya?"

I pointed to my name tag. He frowned and took from his fatigues pocket a smudged envelope. I waited for him to say more, curious about what favor he wanted from me. He lowered his eyes and thrust the envelope toward me.

"I got this letter from Lila today at mail call. She's my wife. She and me got married when I was on leave just before comin' over here."

"So, Evans, what's up?"

"Ah, hell, it's like this. I can't read. I can't read nothin'! So, I'm askin' if you'd read this here letter out loud to me."

103 ⤸

About every six or so days Johnny showed up, stinking of grease and gasoline. Not only was I reading aloud his wife's letters but also I was writing his replies to her. He never sat. As he dictated, he paced. By our third session he stopped turning his back to me to hide embarrassment when he ended a reply with "I love you so much and miss you an awful lot."

Soon after Christmas Johnny found me at the organ. He came earlier than usual, saying that his sergeant went on sick call and when the cat's away the mice will play.

"You're pretty good at that thing, Andy! I ain't heard an organ in a dog's age. The last time was when we buried Ma. Anyways, got another letter from Lila. This one's the second in a week. Sweet Jesus, ain't she somethin'!"

He slit open the envelope with a jack knife and handed me the letter. Her penmanship was the same as ever: puffy capitals and cursive correctness, befitting the photograph of a pretty girl that he kept in his wallet.

"Only one page, Johnny?"

He looked into the envelope and at me. "That's it. Maybe she got busy or somethin'. Go on and read it."

Dear Johnny,

Everyone here at home is getting all wound up about Christmas. Did you get my card? My sister Junie wants me to come stay with her and Junior and the kids. I'm going to do that. I don't want to be alone by myself. It's getting harder and harder being alone. Johnny, can't you tell somebody you want to quit the army?

I stopped. Before reading on, I glanced at the rest of the paragraph and folded the letter.

"Listen to me, buddy. Put a match to this and forget you ever got it. Do you hear me?"

"What's goin' on? Why ain't ya finishin' it?"

Bewilderment twisted his face. He put the letter back into the envelope and snarled, "Hell I'll burn it! If you ain't gonna read it ta me, someone else will. That's that!"

"Johnny, wait up! Let's talk . . ."

"Ah, shit!"

He bolted from the chapel.

I turned the organ off, too bothered by the pathos in pretty Lila's words, the words I could not read aloud to her man: *Johnny, if you don't come home soon, I'm not waiting. I just can't. I'm very, very lonely!*

I had been composing a doxology, putting to music the first two lines of *Psalm 66*:

Shout with joy to God, all the earth!
Sing the glory of his name; make his praise glorious!

KOREAN WINTERS ARE unforgiving. The winter of 1957 swooped into the country early, and snow clearing became an addition to my daily chore list. In fact, to get to the mess hall for a Thanksgiving turkey meal, I trudged through thigh-deep drifts. The electric space heater issued me hardly warmed my cramped quarters. The un-insulated metal walls of the chapel were no match for the bitter winds from north of the DMZ.

Two of the score or so of regulars at Sunday service – Marty Philips and Milton Shawcross (the "M&M Boys" I dubbed them) – walked with me back to the chapel after mail call on a dull, below freezing afternoon, the second day into Advent. Marty, whose voice rumbled like distant thunder, shouted over the whistling wind: "Andy, my buddy here and me . . . well, Christmas is coming on and we've been thinking. Suppose we get ourselves a choir? It'd be nice to hear some singing. How does that set with you?"

"Yeah, Andy," Milton said. "Back home in Wisconsin, he tells me, he sang with one. You sang bass, right?"

"Yup, not too good though but good enough to get my cows milking. And what about you?"

"Miss Jones said I was a tenor. She's the one who led the choir in the little Ohio church where I grew up."

There was no need to keep the pair waiting for my answer. I told them they had a great idea and, if the chaplain gave his okay, we would get a choir going. In the meantime I asked them to try rounding up some more guys who could carry a tune.

A snow squall did not deter the M&M boys and the ten others whom they had recruited from coming to the chapel the evening of the third Thursday of Advent for the first choir practice. Candles might have been brighter than the naked bulb over the organ. The generator produced only enough voltage to create a brown-out scene.

"Suppose we start off with *Joy to the World*. I'll play it through once, and then you come in. You'll find it on page 87. Are we ready?"

The twelve GI's circled the organ, squinted at the hymnals, and tested their voices to see if they could make music together. They could – not fabulously, but good enough.

Two more practices and we were ready for our debut, and on Christmas morning the choir of the 23rd Transportation Battalion, First Cavalry Division, stood smartly in their dress uniforms, shoulder to shoulder, and harmonized carols with great earnest.

Flushed with the joy of accomplishment, we sat together in the mess hall and, as Chaplain Creamer put it, "made one helluva noise unto the Lord", breaking out in song intermittently as we dug into the holiday meal. It did not go unnoticed, his ignoring army protocol to dine with us enlisted men. Characteristically an undemonstrative sort, the Major nonetheless mixed praise with swallows of roast beef, saying over and over, "Thank you, men. I'll not forget this Christmas."

TO DISPEL HOMESICKNESS the last day of 1957, Milton, Marty, and I got passes to attend a movie at the USO theatre in the Headquarters Battalion's compound, a mile's walk down the rutted gravel road past an off limits village composed of a few non-descript hovels. While we surrendered to the inanity of *Guns a Poppin*, a Three Stooges flick, a cold front crossed the DMZ. The dash back to our compound – against the biting wind driven snow – had us forgetting the antics of Moe, Curly, and Shemp.

The three MP's at the guard gate were too distracted to check our passes. A lieutenant was barking orders at them.

"Get your asses over to the motor pool on the double!"

We ran with them. Men were galloping from the barracks and forming a ring around a couple of jeeps parked on the frozen gravel of the maintenance yard. Every light in the yard had been switched on. Marty, the wide-shouldered milk farmer from Wisconsin, muscled an opening through the throng, and Milton and I were on his tail. We stopped at the edge of the circle and gawked at the guy with a pry bar who was whacking dents into the hood of a jeep.

Indifferent to the deep freeze and the snow, he was barefoot and dressed down to his skivvies. Like a rabid animal, shards of orangey light flashed in his eyes and foamy spittle leaked out of his mouth. Over and over he snarled, "God damn it, God damn it, God damn it!"

No one approached him, not even the MP's.

"Oh, no. It's Johnny Evans!" I said to no one in particular and felt my legs move.

"Andy, what in hell are you doing?" Marty yelled, pulling at my field jacket. "The poor bastard's cracked. He'll knock your head off!"

Johnny saw me coming and crouched, slamming the pry bar at the ground.

"It's me, Johnny, your buddy."

"I gotta get home. God damn it, I gotta get home!" Puffs of steam clouded his face and he shivered.

"I think, Johnny, you'll be getting home pretty soon now."

I took off my field jacket and wrapped it around his shoulders. His grip on the pry bar loosened and the MP's moved in. Two of them hauled him to his feet and the third cuffed his wrists. The last I saw of Johnny Evans was his disappearing into the cold darkness, shackled and broken. He had found someone to finish reading for him Lila's letter, I figured.

PAULINE HAD SET August 16 to be the date of our wedding. Her letters reported her progress in making preparations for the big day. For me, finances were foremost in my mind. When the eagle landed on the first of each month, I immediately made out a money order for ten dollars and mailed it to her, leaving me a scant $88.00 to make do for a month. The army fed, dressed, and sheltered me, but everything else like soap, toothpaste, razor blades, hair cuts, laundry I paid for.

"Sir," I said to Chaplain Walker, who had replaced Chaplain Creamer in January, "I'm in line for a promotion. Just about everyone else is a Spec 4. Would you put in a recommendation for me?"

I was too naïve when it came to military mores to understand why he answered that it would be better were I to see the CO and make my request personally. I did.

Captain Kosowski held a sneer on his pock-marked face as I made my request. He kept me waiting before replying. Then, with contempt in his voice, he thundered, "You want me to promote *you*? Ha, over my dead body! Promote a chaplain's assistant? Never! You're dismissed, Private."

The Captain did not return my salute. I was feeling like a pariah. On top of that, no way now could I afford a honeymoon. But fate interceded.

In February the Pentagon issued a mandate that put on notice all commissioned officers who lacked a high school diploma. Unless they earned a GED equivalency within a year, they would be demoted to their primary rank. It seemed that during the Korean war a slue of NCO's were given "battlefield commissions", and many of these men were high school drop outs. To accommodate them, the army partnered with the University of Maryland, and word came out that GED classes would start March 1. I applied for a teaching position, was accepted, and received from the university a packet containing grammar and algebra texts and all the information I needed to conduct a two-hour session per week in each of the two subjects for three months.

Fourteen officers signed up for my courses (six lieutenants, four captains, three majors, and a lieutenant colonel). The farthest corner of the mess hall, away from the clatter of kitchen noise and chattering of Koreans who were cleaning up after evening mess, was my classroom. The first hour of the first meeting was an awkward – even scary – time for me. In the first place, I was rank-conscious. After printing my name and "PFC" on the portable chalk board, I turned to face my students: fourteen sullen, combat hardened men, the light from overhead bulbs reflecting off their brass.

My voice was strained as I gave each guy a text book while explaining the A,B,C's of the course.

"Your main objective, gentlemen, is to pass the GED exam. What I have to do right now is to find out how much you know or don't know about the basic rules of grammar. So . . . I'm asking you to take this little quiz I'm passing out to you. You have twenty minutes to finish it."

The "little quiz" that the battalion clerk had mimeographed for me consisted of twenty-five questions dealing with the likes of subject/verb agreement, dangling participles, punctuation. Out came packs of Lucky Strikes, and a haze of smoke gathered over the heads of the fourteen men.

Promptly at 1930 hours I said, "Okay, time's up. Let's have these quizzes. We'll take a fifteen minute break. Stretch your legs or whatever while I grade these things."

At 1945 hours they came clomping back. With false bravado they cracked jokes, their guffaws echoing in the deserted mess hall. I stood my ground and one by one returned the graded quizzes.

"Major Slattery?"

Up shot a hand, and, as I passed the sheet to him, I congratulated him for getting the highest score: "With a 64, Major, you're at the head of the class."

The lowest score was 16. Because I knew the name of the man who had failed so abysmally, I plunked the sheet on the table in front of him and whispered, "It looks as though you have a lot to learn, Captain Kosowski."

GOOD FRIDAY, 1958, was not a good day for us troops. Right in the middle of chow time the night before, the red alert siren screeched. Trays clattered, men scrambled. The Quartermaster issued M-1's and live ammo. Engines revved in the motor pool. I signed out the chaplain's jeep, put the field organ in the back and my weapon next to it, and joined the convoy. But without the chaplain.

The vehicles headed uphill, north, toward the 38th Parallel and steered off the gravel road and bounced over rocks and tree stumps to take up battle positions. Engines stopped. With the setting sun came an eerie silence and the start of a six-hour wait. Had I been back in my billet I would be at my calendar x-ing another day and writing to Pauline, telling her that I'm officially a "short-timer". I was down to 56 days before shipping out for home.

I was snoozing when the first drops of rain hit the canvas top of the jeep. I struck a match to check my watch. Going on 2200 hours. With no room to stretch, the five hours of waiting cramped my whole body. A Korean rain storm rivals Niagara's waters. The plopping became a din.

The passenger side door of the jeep opened and I twisted to grab my rifle, but before my hand found it a guy in a sopping wet poncho was inside.

"Whoa, Andy, it's me, Milton – your tenor!"

"Milt, you scared the hell out of me!"

"Sorry about that. My truck's over there next to the ambulance. I saw you when you pulled in. This damn waiting's got to me. So I said to myself, "Damn it, I need some company." So here I am."

"Do you know what's going on?"

"Only what the grunts I drove over here were saying. Those poor bastards, hunkered down somewhere out there in this downpour!

Anyway, they were saying the Gooks shot a couple of us guys who were patrolling the DMZ. So, who knows what's going to happen?"

"You know, don't you, that in a couple of hours it'll be Good Friday?"

"So what? You think the gooks, or for that matter, our generals give a damn? Oh, that reminds me. I was going to ask you at mess if you were thinking of going to the show at the USO Saturday night. A bunch of college kids from the States are supposed to be singing. Are you interested?"

"I suppose so, Milt. That is if this thing right now doesn't turn into a big deal."

"It won't. I mean, war and Easter just don't go together."

"Yeah, right!"

He tapped my helmet liner and slammed out of the jeep, vanishing in the downpour.

"Hurry up and wait" – the Army's mantra. I was almost out of matches, as though checking the time would end this interminable waiting. The last check of my watch made me grind my teeth and shout, "It's past midnight! Holy God damn!" And I had to piss.

The rain pelted my face with such force that my cheeks stung, and my boots slurped in mud. I smelled diesel fumes and heard muffled growls of engines revving up. Coming toward me was a faint beam of a flashlight and a bodiless voice: "Alert's over! We're moving out! Remember, no headlights. Cat eyes only."

Like steaming behemoths, one by one vehicles sloughed through the mud and onto the gravel road. I had only the rain-blurred tail lights of a deuce-and-a-half in front of me to steer by all the way back to the compound.

When the walkie-talkie that sat on the desk in the chapel's office jangled at 0630 hours, I feared another all out alert. I was groggy and bumped into a chair as I groped in the pre-dawn darkness for the desk. Only three hours ago I had parked the jeep in the motor pool, turned in my M-1 and ammo clips, and hit the sack, too bushed to get out of my damp fatigues.

"Anderson . . . Chaplain Walker here. How did you do last night out in the field? I went with the artillery unit and couldn't get to you. You made out okay?"

"Yes, sir."

"Good, good. Now tell me, are we set up for Sunday? It's Easter, you know, and word's come down from HQ that General Zwicker will be coming to our chapel. We have to be on our toes. Is the choir ready to go? Have you picked out the hymns?"

"Everything's in order, sir. We're having one more practice tomorrow afternoon."

"You remember, don't you, about me including communion in the service? Do we have a couple of bottles of wine just in case there's a big turn out?"

"We do, sir."

"Anderson, you're a good man. Incidentally, maybe you don't know this. The 23rd Transportation Battalion is the only unit in the whole Division that has a choir. Makes us look good. Well, that's that. Now, if only this rain would stop."

The rain did stop – Saturday, late morning. I had to wait my turn to get at the hose to wash the muck off the chaplain's jeep. Then I sprinted to the chapel to rehearse Sunday's music. When he saw me splashing through puddles on the double, Marty – the choir's comic – brandished an axe and growled.

"What's going on, Marty? Where did you get that thing?"

"Came in mail call from home. Mom says I might need it to chop down a couple of trees for fire wood."

"Be serious. Why the axe?"

"Okay, okay. Here's the scoop. Me and Milton got the idea to make a cross and plunk it over there on the hill behind the chapel. You know, for Easter and all. What do you think?"

"Why not? First, let's get inside and practice."

I REGRETTED PROMISING Milton to join him to take in the show at the USO. In the first place, I hadn't written to Pauline since Wednesday, three days ago. Not since going to Japan on R and R had I let so much time lapse without telling her of my love for her. In the second place, the Easter excitement that had made the day special throughout my boyhood was absent. Too much with me was the noisomeness of motor pool gunk, kimchi, and fetid rice paddies, and chopping down a couple of scrub pines to fashion a cross plunged me deeper into a Golgothian mood. But I couldn't let him down.

We grabbed seats in the back of the rapidly filling Quonset hut that made do for a theatre. Standing, unsmiling, along the perimeter of a stage up front were four MP's, who jumped to the side when the lights dimmed and sixty-four bright-eyed and bushy-tailed college kids streamed single file onto it. The GI's let loose with whistles and boot banging. For the first time since coming to Korea we were seeing Americans in civvies – white shirts and blouses, black slacks and skirts. More than that – the young women! Some were blondes no less, and all had the prettiest legs that heretofore we could only fantasize about.

A middle-aged fellow with a bow tie and broad smile followed the troupe and, into a microphone, emoted, "It's a pleasure and an honor to be here with you men. We've come a long, long way to entertain you. Let's hear it for the chorus of the University of Colorado!"

Cheers, whistles, clapping. The director turned to the singers, raised both hands, and on cue the sixty-four voices burst into song. No more than four bars into *Blue Skies*, those Rocky Mountain kids not only had shushed the troops but also had them under a spell that stayed unbroken to the finale, two hours later, when they squeezed emotions with the singing of a medley from *South Pacific*, ending with *You'll Never Walk Alone*.

The audience demanded two encores. When the lights came back on and the cheering stopped, I tugged Milton's arm, not looking at him lest he saw my wet eyes.

"What are you up to, Andy? The exit's right here."

"Just follow me. I'm going for broke."

We pushed our way against the tide of bodies that surged toward the rear doors. We got to the stage as the last student was exiting, followed by the fellow with the bow tie. I shouted over the shoulder of an MP who blocked my way: "Hey, Mr. Director! I need to ask you something!" He heard me and came over, and the MP loosened his grip on my arm. I was taking a gamble, but I was putting to the test an old cliché: "Nothing ventured, nothing gained."

A COUPLE OF nattering peasants from the village, hauling a honey bucket – its two wheels creaking under the weight of latrine waste – awakened me. Had they not passed by en route to the rice paddies, I might have over slept. My watch showed that I could not get dressed and over to the mess hall in time for breakfast. But excitement replaced hunger.

Before going into the chapel to warm up the choir, I double checked myself: dress uniform clean and pressed, shoes polished, tie knotted and tucked in. The memory of pulling on my first pair of long pants and proudly walking up the street to Sunday School one Easter morning long, long ago came to mind.

The equinox sun slanted light through the window behind the organ, giving the austerity of the chapel a touch of holiness. As I ran through the day's hymns, one by one the twelve choir guys showed up.

"What's going on, Andy? Milton says you got a surprise for us."

"I'll tell you in a minute, Marty. But now hear this, all of you. You won't be singing the anthem we've been practicing."

They bombarded me with questions: "Why not? We're not good enough for a general? Is it true, a general's coming this morning?" That question I answered.

"Yeah, that's true. But he's got nothing to do with why we're not singing the anthem. Okay, I'll tell you . . ."

It was SFC Roger Dockery, our alto, who first spotted Chaplain Walker and General Zwicker entering the chapel. He shouted, "

'Ten-shun!", and we clicked our heels and saluted.

"As you were, men," the man with three big stars on his lapel barked. "You must be the choir. Scuttlebutt has it that you're pretty damn good. Carry on."

After escorting the general and his entourage to the front pew, the chaplain returned.

"Anderson, let's go over things to make sure we got everything squared away. First, why are these pews back here cordoned off?"

"Well, sir, the story goes like this."

Troops dribbled in as did a few villagers. The chaplain, looking puzzled – although I had assured him that everything was under control - walked to the altar and draped a stole upon his shoulders. Our eyes met, and he nodded – the signal to get the service under way. I looked at my watch, at the door, and at Milton. I shrugged.

"They're not coming, Andy."

I saw on his face the disappointment that I was feeling. But just as I was about to play the prelude, a most attractive young woman in a white dress came through the door, followed by another and another. Milton darted over to usher them to the pews I had cordoned off. Several minutes ticked by before the sixty-four members of the University of Colorado's chorus and their chaperones and director got seated.

All heads down front were turned, including the general's, to watch what must have looked like a miracle unfolding: this sudden burst of color and beauty.

"Holy Toledo! Have I died and gone to heaven?" one of my baritones stage whispered.

When the sound of clicking high heels, echoing in the barren chapel, stopped, Frank waved to me (last night at the USO, the director had insisted he be addressed by his first name). Too transfixed to see me gesturing the question "should I begin?", the chaplain fingered his stole and looked like a man altogether at a crossroads wondering which path he should take. I took matters into my own hands and broke the silence with the playing of Handel's *Thine Be the Glory*.

With that done, Chaplain Walker stood and intoned the Invocation, and the choir sang the response. So far so good. The Easter service had begun. Then he asked all to stand and sing *Christ the Lord Is Risen Today*. After I had played it through once, a wave of harmony crested. The alleluias shook the thin metal walls of the chapel. I had never accompanied such voices! It wasn't from nervousness that my hands trembled at the keyboard.

Included in the plans that Frank and I had laid out the night before was for the chorus' accompanist to play the organ when the time came for its singing the anthem. After delivering his sermon, Chaplain Walker introduced the ensemble and thanked them for "gracing the service with their beautiful voices". He sat and a woman who could have been anyone's aunt crossed the aisle and approached the organ.

"Will you be my page-turner, please?" she asked me.

I stood behind her and she patted in place the score – a medley of sacred music. At Frank's signal, the sixty-four kids arose. Down came his arm and voices and organ broke the hush in the chapel with *fortissimo* chords.

With the singing of *Amazing Grace*, the anthem ended followed by silence. I looked up to see what was happening. The only movement were the flickering flames of the two altar candles. A recall of a scene from an old episode of Rod Serling's *The Twilight Zone* came to me: a whole community was struck dumb by an extra terrestrial force. Later in the mess hall as my choir rehashed the Easter service, that was exactly what I said: "Those kids from Colorado summoned a spirit, I swear, that struck us dumb."

Dear Pauline,

Forgive me for not writing since last Wednesday, but a lot's been going on. I'll try to fill you in, but first I hope you had a good Easter. Was the Easter bunny good to you? He was to me.

I paused. How could I put into words the tension that had grabbed me as I sat alone in the jeep on the edge of the 38th Parallel expecting to hear shots at any minute? And I knew the futility of trying to tell her about the miracle that had happened in the chapel that morning.

I said to myself, "I'll just give her the facts. The rest is up to her to imagine." And so I wrote:

> *Four days ago we had a cat-eye alert that turned out to be a false alarm. This morning in the chapel a bunch of college kids from the States sang. Wow, were they good! So it goes. Hey, I'm down to 55 days! In less than two months I'll be on my way home. Alleluia!*

An end run around authority.

CAMP DRUM

UNBEKNOWN TO ME, I was stepping aboard a fast-spinning carousel when, 13 July 1958, I de-trained at Providence's Union Station, returning home from a tour of duty in Korea with only a canvas tote bag holding a change of underwear, some toiletries, and a Geisha doll. A souvenir bought for Pauline. Just for the hell of it, a year later I jotted down a summary of the bigger events, thinking that that might help me to finger the cause of my dizziness:

15 July	Bought new a Nash Rambler
21 July	Signed a lease for a three-room apartment at 37 Rosebank Avenue, Providence
16 August	Married Pauline Butler at Blessed Sacrament Church, Providence
10 September	First meeting of evening classes at Rhode Island College
21 September	Reported for active reserve duty with the 355th Medical Company in Warwick
17 October	Met for the first time a class of juvenile delinquents
13 April	Premature birth of Mark
20 April	Pauline's discharge from Roger Williams Hospital after recovery from toxemia
7 May	Mark's discharge from Roger Williams Hospital after recovery from pneumonia

| 26 July | Last class of summer session at Rhode Island College |
| 30 July | Reported for two-week active duty at Camp Drum |

With this list in front of me, I could see why I felt as though I were on a carousel. Or being whirled about in a tornado would be more apt.

"I don't know if I'm coming or going, Ed. God, I don't know what to do."

I had left the hospital, desperately in need of talking things over with someone and drove cross town to Ed and Pat's home. Eight months ago he, my Best Man, had straightened my bow tie in the vestibule of Blessed Sacrament Church before we walked to the altar on the happiest day of my life. Now I was in his kitchen in tears and utter confusion.

"Drink your coffee, Harry," Pat said in a way that befits a good nurse, "and go over again what's happening."

"Okay . . . As I said, when I left Pauline this morning, everything was fine. But I wasn't allowed to hold Mark. Because he was born a month prematurely, they put him in an incubator in the nursery."

I sipped at the coffee, self-conscious to see my hand trembling.

"Before going back to the hospital, I had eaten supper with Mom and Dad and stopped by Pauline's mother and father's house to give them the good news. Then I bought some flowers for her. When I got to her room, the door was shut and a sign on it read DO NOT ENTER. VISITORS NOT ALLOWED.

"I asked a nurse at the desk what the heck was going on and she gave me the bad news. 'Your wife's a sick woman,' she said. 'She's got toxemia.'

"'Why wasn't I notified?' I asked, and she said they had been trying to, but no one's answering the phone. Then she said there's nothing I could do right now and Dr. McIntyre's been with her and will come back later tonight. 'She's in good hands. So, why don't you go home and rest up.' The nurse was trying to calm me down. But I couldn't just go home. I have to talk with someone. That's why I'm here."

This episode added fright to the mix of emotions that I had been dealing with since getting off the train in Union Station ten months ago. But all was not doom and gloom. Unwittingly, the Army, although an annoyance, gave me needed comic relief.

OBLIGED TO PUT in a year of active reserve duty, with orders in hand I reported to the 355th Medical Company in Warwick promptly at 1900 hours on 21 September for my first weekly two-hour drill. About the only thing that resembled military protocol was SFC O'Malley's barking, "Fall in!" to get things underway. O'Malley was RA, going for the full twenty. We reservists stood at attention in formation and he did a smart about face and saluted the CO, a lieutenant colonel who had a GYN/OBS practice in Riverside.

"All present and accounted for, Sir."

How O'Malley knew that was his secret. No roll call was taken, and he held no clip board with the sign-in sheet. Taking his word for it, the CO sauntered front and center and casually ordered, "Okay, men, take it easy". Every Wednesday night for the year that was the only command I ever heard the doctor issue.

I stood out among the troops because only I came to the drills dressed in civvies. When we returnees from a tour of duty in Korea were being processed for discharge in Oakland, we were ordered to turn in our uniforms, boots and all, for disposal. The Army, suspecting that some Asian microbe might be stowed away in our GI issue, took no chances. The promise that our reserve units would re-issue new uniforms was made, but either this medical company had no quartermaster or its SOP was too lax to make me look like a soldier.

A uniform was hardly necessary for what duties I performed:

taking inventory of such supplies as tongue depressors and bottles of iodine; practicing CPR on a dummy; inspecting contents of kits taken into battle by medics. After SP4 Ron Mandeville, the company clerk, got banged up in a skiing mishap, throughout February and March I took his place and sat sequestered at a desk in a small office and corrected quizzes turned in by my class of juvenile delinquents.

Simultaneously, Pauline and Mark came home from hospital and orders came down for the 355th to satisfy its two weeks of active reserve requirement at Camp Drum, beginning 24 June.

"This is absurd!" I thundered to Pauline. "I'm not leaving you two to play soldier for a couple of weeks. I'll think of a way to get out of going."

Learning that a student was eligible for a deferment from active duty, I enrolled for a summer course at RIC. My CO okayed my request, but my new orders TDY'd me to a medical outfit out of Boston. I was to report for active duty 5 August at 0600 hours at its Dorchester armory for travel by convoy to Camp Drum. I parried that with an outrageous plan.

"Love, no way am I letting the Army take me away from you! What do you think about coming with me?"

"How can I do that?"

"If I can pull it off, we'll have ourselves a nice vacation in upstate New York. Would you like that?"

"I suppose so. But . . ."

"That's all I need to know. Let's see what happens."

My letter addressed to the manager of Camp Drum's guest house was succinct and couched in military jargon that I had mastered as company clerk:

To: Guest House Manager
*   Camp Drum, New York*
From: Harry L. Anderson

Subject: Request for Room Reservation

Pursuant to orders, I will report for duty with the 112ᵗʰ Medical Detachment, Boston, Massachusetts, from 5 August to 19 August.

A request follows; to wit, one room to accommodate the undersigned, his wife and son (aged four (4) months), for the duration.

Written confirmation required within two weeks.

Ten days later a hand-written confirmation, signed by a Hilda something-or-other (the signature was illegible), arrived by post. Eureka! I had nailed down the assurance of not celebrating our first anniversary separated by military interference.

WITH A COUPLE of borrowed suitcases stowed in the trunk of our compact Rambler and on the rear seat a stroller, a supply of cloth diapers, safety pins, Q-tips, baby blankets, baby formula and bottles with nipples, we drove off from Rosebank Avenue, keeping the rising sun to our backs. I had postponed notifying the CO of the 115ᵗʰ Medical Detachment until August 1ˢᵗ that I would travel to camp in my own car and report in on the morning of August 6ᵗʰ, gambling on either he would have no time to send MP's to my door to drag me off to Boston or he, too, may be a GYN/OBS doctor.

As we crossed the Connecticut River on the Massachusetts Turnpike, we passed a jeep with a sign fastened to its rear bumper that read COVOY AHEAD. I sped on, catching up on drab-olive green quarter ton trucks, a couple of ambulances, more jeeps, and several deuce-and-a-half trucks. What faces I saw of the guys bouncing in the rear of the trucks were deadpanned.

Stopping but once at a rest area in the Berkshires to change Mark's diaper and to eat tuna sandwiches, we got to the guard house of Camp Drum as the summer sun was low over the pines of northern New York. I asked the MP who checked my orders for directions to the guest house.

"Hook a right at the first intersection, Sir. It's the two-story building with a kid's swing set in the back yard. You can't miss it, Sir."

He clicked the heels of his polished boots and held a salute until I returned it. Pauline looked back at him as I drove off.

"What's with the 'sir'? Does he think you're an officer?"

"Beats me. He saw my orders with my name and rank. Maybe my civvies confused him."

As I went inside the house to announce our arrival, she stayed in the car with Mark, who was bawling for a bottle. Languor rode on a breeze that ruffled the parlor's yellowing lace curtains. A shaft of sunlight spotlighted an Angora cat curled up at the bare feet of an old woman asleep on a couch between two opened windows. A *Saturday Evening Post* went up and down on her breast with each breath. I rapped on a small desk off to the left, hoping to arouse her. That did the trick.

"Looks like Lucy and me dozed off," she yawned and sat up. "Things get quiet around here on weekends before another bunch of troopers roll in. You just got here?"

"Yes, ma'am. My name's Harry Anderson. I have a room reservation for my wife and me . . . and my baby son."

She limped to the desk and ran a finger down a page of a notebook. I wondered how she could read because her glasses were atilt.

" 'Anderson' you said? From Rhode Island?"

"Yes, ma'am."

"Forget the ma'am business. Everyone calls me 'Hilda'. I've put you in room 2D. Go up those stairs and you'll find it . . . the third room on the left. Be sure to read the house rules tacked on the door."

"Will do, Hilda." It was awkward to call a woman who appeared to be about my mother's age by her first name.

"One last thing you should know, Captain. There's two bathrooms on the second floor – one for the women and the other for you men. The four families have to share."

Room 2D was GI Spartan: a couple of metal iron beds, an armoire, and a single straight-backed chair. A Venetian blind dressed the window, and an overhead light with an unwashed dome dimly illuminated the room. A small corner shelf held a hot plate, leaving hardly enough space for baby bottles and formula. There was no amenity whatsoever, not even a carpet or sheets.

The day's long drive and the four trips from car to room 2D to empty our gear from the trunk and rear seat did us in. Too tired to figure out where we could get supper, we stayed put and attended to Mark and put into some practical order our belongings. With the two beds pushed side by side, Pauline and I entwined ankles under an olive green GI issued blanket. The mattresses were like marble slabs and their supporting springs screeched like night owls with every turn. Sleepily, we sized up the situation.

"Hey, for two bucks a day, this is what you get. Look at it this way . . . it beats being alone in a barracks. That's for sure!"

"Do you think we can handle this for two weeks?"

"After all we've been through, sure we will. I'll get a lot of questions answered tomorrow and then we'll be okay. You'll see."

She fluffed the flat pillow and sighed. Footsteps in the hallway and muffled voices from room 2C announced that the guest house was filling up. Just enough glow coming through the Venetian blind from an outside floodlight showed that her eyes had closed and her lips were parted. She wheezed a nascent snore. I shifted position, the springs creaked, and I wondered why Hilda had called me "Captain".

BOTH PAULINE AND the baby stayed curled in sleep as I tucked a buttoned-down short sleeve blue shirt into my khaki trousers and tip-toed in stocking feet, carrying my shoes, to the head. To my relief, I alone shaved at one of the three sinks. My watch said 0540 hours. My plan was to get to the mess hall, find where the 115th Medical Detachment was barracked, and introduce myself to the CO.

Luckily, the two SP4's in mess line in front of me had the Caduceus insignia pinned to the collars of their Class A uniforms. I asked if they were with the 115th out of Boston. They were. Sitting with them at table, I gave them my story and they seemed to savor it more than their shit-on-a-shingle breakfast. From them I got helpful information: Major Baldelli – a GP from East Boston – was the CO; this, being a Sunday, there would be no roll call; for the first week the unit would assist the RA's in sick bay. and the second week it would bivouac and play war games.

"Jimmy O'Donnell's the one you hafta see. He's the company clerk and I'm pretty sure you'll find him in headquarters. He's sucking up to the Major because he's getting married next year and wants a promotion. Jimmy's okay, though. He'll get you squared away."

So far so good. Frankie and Joe - those were their names – were street-wise city guys who obviously liked to see someone make an end run around authority.

"Are you ready to go?" the one named Frankie asked. "We'll show you where headquarters is."

"Wait up, will you? I'm going to try to get some coffee and whatever for my wife. She's eaten nothing since yesterday afternoon. Think I can con the KP's into it?"

"Never fear, Joey's here. Sit tight. I'll be right back."

Right back he was with a Styrofoam cup of coffee and a couple of slices of toast wrapped in a paper towel.

The old swing set in the yard of the guest house shivered and squeaked as the two medics pumped like school kids at recess.

When I returned emptied handed, they braked to a stop by digging the heels of their polished dress shoes into the dirt.

"Ain't done that since about third grade," Joe panted.

"That was a helluva lot better than playing soldier!" Frankie added.

"Pauline said to thank you guys for breakfast. You should have seen her gulp it down!"

"If I wasn't going into town later," Frankie said, "I'd get her a chicken leg for lunch."

I was sure of that. If I asked him to get me a tank from the motor pool, somehow he would. He was that sort of guy.

My new-found buddies led me to the door of company headquarters and scooted off to somewhere. Expecting to see only Jimmy O'Donnell, I sucked in a breath at the sight of a Major hunched over a PFC at a typewriter. Both gawked at me with puzzled expressions. Holding a salute, I crisply said what had been drilled into my brain during basic training three years ago: "PFC Anderson reporting as ordered, Sir."

The Major limply returned the salute, looked me over, and blurted, "What the hell's going on? Who are you?"

"I'm on TDY with your unit, Sir, for two weeks of active duty. My outfit is the 355th Medical Company out of Rhode Island."

"What's with the civvies, Private?"

"I was ordered to turn in my uniform, Sir, when I returned from Korea, and I haven't been re-issued a new one. I've been told I'd be issued one here at Drum."

The more he learned of my situation – my not coming by convoy, my residency in the guest house with a wife and child – the more perplexed he became.

"Damn it! What do we do with this man, O'Donnell?"

"I'll add him to the morning report, Sir. Simple."

"O'Donnell, you're a genius! Well, look Anderson, show up at roll call at 0700 tomorrow and we'll take it from there."

"Yes, Sir!"

By the end of the first week at Camp Drum, active duty for Pauline and me had morphed into a holiday. With a permanent pass wheedled from O'Donnell, after morning roll call each day, I drove off post with Pauline and Mark to explore Watertown and its nearby backwater villages: Carthage, Evans Mills, Black River. Blessed with a stationary high front extending from the Great Lakes to the Atlantic, we enjoyed pleasant, sunny days. A routine fell into place: As Pauline attended to the baby's needs and fixed a picnic lunch in Hilda's kitchen (Hilda allowed us to keep perishables in her refrigerator), I ran off to the mess hall for breakfast.

Frankie and Joe faithfully saw to it each morning that I would be supplied with a Styrofoam cup of coffee and toast which I carried to the guest house before I hustled to stand in company formation, dressed in slacks and a polo shirt, to shout "Here, Sir!" when Lieutenant Grady called out my name. The MP's at the guard gate, so accustomed to my Rambler, gave but a cursory glance at my pass. And always they saluted me.

Pauline became chummy with the four wives of commissioned officers and told them of my charade. None let the cat out of the bag.

"You never told me only officers and their wives could stay in the guest house," she said with alarm on one of our picnics in the shade of birch trees along the banks of the Black River.

"Honestly, Love, I didn't know that."

"What happens if Hilda finds out you're not an officer?"

"I don't know. We'll go home, I guess."

"But we can't. Aren't you on duty?"

"If I have to move into the barracks, you and Mark will have to get a motel room. But we don't have the money to do that. If worse comes to worse, the two of you will have to drive back home."

"But I'd never find my way back home! You know me and directions."

Although I felt a pang of worry, I joked, "Then I'll get Joe and Frankie to persuade Jimmie to set up a cot for you in headquarters. Look, you're a nurse and I'm with a bunch of doctors. They won't let anyone give you the boot."

We came close to eviction on Tuesday of week two. While waiting for a cheese pizza with pepperoni to come to our table (there were pizzerias galore in the foothills of the Adirondacks, and we hit most of them for our evening meals), Pauline recounted an episode that had unfolded at the guest house.

"When you went to the PX to get me stamps before coming here, Margot – you know, the one married to the Lieutenant who lisps – knocked on our door as I was getting Mark ready. She told me what happened this morning. A Major and his wife showed up and Hilda told him there wasn't a vacancy. He blew his top and ordered her to bump someone with a lower rank. According to Margot, Hilda let him have it. She told him in no uncertain terms that she bumps no one and that as far as she's concerned it's first-come-first-served. An officer is an officer, period! 'There's no pulling of rank here,' she screamed back at him."

"Whew, close call. And none of your chums let on about our conspiracy?"

"Nope! In fact, later, Margot said, they tittered like school girls, loving every second of it."

Another tense moment happened Friday morning as I left the mess hall with Pauline's coffee and toast and the guys in fatigues headed off to their details. Two Warrant Officers halted me. The taller of the two said, "I hear you've got a car. Well, here's the deal. Tomorrow, Dr. Tweedy here and I would like to see Ottawa. If you're willing to take us there, we'll pay for the gas and treat you to a nice dinner. What do you say?"

Relieved to see that that was all that was on their minds, I assented. Anyway, getting to see Ottawa appealed to me. We made plans on the spot. The next morning at 0830 hours the five of us – the Warrant Officers, Pauline, Mark, and I – were driving north toward the Thousand Islands and on into Canada.

A hard rain lashed the window of our room at dawn on Monday, the beginning of the second week at Drum. Forgetting if I had packed a raincoat, I fumbled about in the dimness for my suitcase and bumped the play yard where Mark lay asleep. He yowled, and I heard the springs of an army bed creak in the adjoining room. Pauline cradled the baby, and in my skivvies I plodded to the head, recalling that Frankie and Joe and the rest of the company were heading out into the field getting wet as hell. Just for a second I felt guilty.

As I shaved, a guy also in skivvies plunked his shaving kit on the sink beside mine. I had not seen him before. Not until he had lathered his chin did he speak.

"A helluva lousy day, isn't it! Did you hear it pouring? Woke my wife and me up. If the rain didn't do it, that kid's scream would've. Who in hell brought a baby to camp?"

I shrugged and kept scraping away at my whiskers. Our eyes met in the mirror. His graying hair made me curious about his rank. He was certainly too old to be a Lieutenant.

"What're you going to have your men do in this bitch of a weather?"

I rinsed my razor, toweled my face, and came up with an answer.

"It's a good day for character guidance."

"Great idea! Thanks."

PAULINE, WANTING TO host a farewell party on the final evening of our Camp Drum holiday, asked me to stop at a liquor store in Watertown to pick up a couple of bottles of wine and maybe some beer. She had already concocted the affair with her four women buddies who delighted at the prospect of introducing me to their husbands.

"Why are you doing this, Love? We're running out of money."

"It'll be fun. Besides, Margot and the others are chipping in. They're getting the chips and dip and whatever else."

"All well and good, but if we can't pay the tolls, we'll have to take back roads to get home."

"Stop worrying! Look at what you've gotten away with so far. We'll get home okay."

Hilda's vacuum cleaner stayed where she had last used it – between two shabby arm chairs in the parlor that held the scent of Old Spice and whatever cologne the ladies had daubed themselves with. The four couples were our age, yet they deferred to Pauline because, being a mother, she out ranked them. I, on the other hand, wearing Levi's and a Block Island tee shirt, sat awkwardly among their husbands dressed in crisply pressed khaki's with silver bars pinned to their lapels. Whenever they went to the end table to mix another high ball, their lieutenant insignias twinkled.

Saul, a Jew from New Hope, Pennsylvania, who, like the other three guys, was serving pay-back time in the active reserves for their ROTC scholarships, started off the jokes aimed at me. That clued me in that their wives had told them of my conspiracy.

"Scuttlebutt has it that a Russian spy has infiltrated Camp Drum. He's holed up somewhere until he finds a way to bust into the QAuartermaster's to rip off a uniform tghat'll fit him."

"What I heard was Hilda has given a room to her bastard son who's hard up and homeless."

Laughter stopped when, behind me, the front door opened and whoever entered brought the four Lieutenants to their feet. They saluted, and I heard a deep voice order, "At ease men. Looks like my wife and I have barged into a party. Mind if we join you?"

Saul and Marty, who had spun the tale of Hilda's bastard son, gave up their chairs to the new arrivals and sat cross-legged on the shabby carpet. Marty's plumpish wife spoke up. "Nibbles are on the end table, Colonel. May I mix highballs for you and your wife?"

I had met this fellow with graying hair, but could not recall where. He recognized me, though.

"Happy to see you again. It gives me the chance to tell you your idea worked out perfectly. Yes, character guidance was a damn good idea!"

I COULD HAVE stayed under the GI blanket for a couple more hours, but revving engines and lots of shouting outside the guest house reminded me that we had to bug out. Pauline was dressing Mark and herself. In deference to my hangover from last night's farewell party, she was waiting until the last minute to shake me awake. As though a mass of fog had rolled in from the St. Lawrence River and settled in my head, fragments of thoughts bumped into each other: What's the time? Have we done packing? I have to get Pauline her coffee.

When she spotted me coming down the stairs with a suitcase, Hilda shut off the vacuum cleaner.

"Your wife and son went to the car. She said to hurry it up. I gave her the last of the milk and things she kept in the fridge. This'll be a busy day for me, I tell you, what with a new batch of soldiers coming in later. Will I be seeing you again next summer?"

"I don't think so, Hilda. Thanks for cleaning up after last night. Thanks for everything."

"Only doing my job. Look, now, you and your missus and your beautiful little boy have a safe drive home, Captain."

I saluted her.

We passed the convoy of battle-ready vehicles lined up parallel to the parade field and, at the guard gate, an MP waved us on. Heading south on Route 11 toward Syracuse and the New York Thruway, I said to Pauline, "That wasn't so bad, was it, Love?"

"That wasn't bad at all, Captain."

Use your imagination.

SECRET VALLEY

I NEVER TOOK our seven kids to Disney World. Among other reasons, I couldn't afford to. But they explored Secret Valley, the only kids on Earth who know of it. Although I tried to cajole them into drawing a map of the place, none ever was completely drawn. When he was maybe ten, Mark, our eldest, had tried. Crudely with pencil he sketched a one dimensional house in the top left corner of a sheet of typing paper and printed beneath it OUR HOUSE. Parallel lines, representing roads, ran from the house, down half the page, curved upward and stopped at a V where Hunting House and Cranberry Ridge Roads converge. At the edge of the sheet he drew a semblance of a stone wall and an arrow pointing off into space and printed TO SECRET VALLEY.

Until last summer the place remained uncharted. That's when a surveying crew aimed their laser theodolites here and there throughout the valley and pounded into the ground wooden stakes painted yellow, and someone nailed to a tree a sign that read WILL BUILD TO SUIT.

INTO FATHERHOOD I carried a liking for the imagination, favoring it above pragmatism. "Use your imagination!" I repeated to my kids. It was my shibboleth. Almost every evening, for example, as they helped wash and dry the supper dishes, I randomly picked three nouns and gave the kids the challenge to use them in an ad lib story. Driving the backroads each Saturday morning to the town's dump with the three boys I saw to be an opportunity to prick their imaginations.

"I bet you don't know there are soldiers with cannons hiding in these woods. Who's going to be first to see them?"

The grandchild who most liked to play the "imagination game" (my coinage) was Zoë. As a boy growing up in Greystone, lacking both a brother and a playmate, I relied on my imagination to ward off loneliness. Many an afternoon, coming home from grade school, I went to the unused hen house in our back yard, climbed the wooden ladder nailed to its outside wall, and pretended that I was a hobo aboard a freight train wooshing westward through canyon land or that I was a sailor aboard a schooner whacking waves far from land. Back to Zoë.

At some point in her visits she would plea, "Let's play the imagination game, Papa." Its rules were simple: Sit together on the living room's couch, cover ourselves beneath an afghan, and pretend to be off on an adventure. I would say, "Oh, oh, we're lost in these woods." And she would say, "But look, there's a light over there!" So it went, taking turns to thicken the plot until she fabricated a clever scheme to rescue us.

ALONG WITH THE cracking of Mark's voice as it morphed from soprano to baritone came a disturbing truculence. The time had come, I reckoned, to return to Secret Valley, to reclaim his innocence that, I wished, still existed somewhere in his imagination. On our trek into the valley a year earlier with his younger brothers, although poohpoohing the fairy tale I was patching together, he ended up surrendering to the lure of the imagination game.

At that time, as I led the lads into the woods, I began the tale.

"No one has dared to walk in here since the night Black Feather and his warriors were almost captured by the settlers who a long time ago had farms where we now live. The Indians ran into these woods and hid and never again were seen, although old Mr. Baker claims he's spotted once or twice a dark skinned man crouching behind one of these trees."

"Daddy, why were the settlers after Black Feather?" Seth, who still looked for money under his pillow after someone had wiggled another baby tooth loose, was into the tale.

"My guess is the Indians were starving and were raiding the gardens around here."

In a smart-alecky way, Mark asked, "What if what's-his-name sees us coming?"

"We'll just act friendly, that's all. We'll tell him we're only looking around. Come on, keep walking."

The trace of a path gave way to a thicket of brambles. We ouched through the thorns and rested on a lichen-clad stonewall that delineated the perimeter of a long-ago paddock. Ahead was a rill yet to be staunched by summer drought. We followed its descent through a stand of tall pines and into a moraine where the water pooled before curving around a boulder and going off into the forest.

"Nobody's gonna hear us from here," Nathan whined.

"So what?" Seth was trying to be brave.

"Supposin' we need help?"

"If worse comes to worse, Nate, Dad will save us. Right, Dad? Anyways, that Indian chief must be a hundred years old. You think he can out run us?"

Mark's sarcasm echoed in the forest. I found myself whispering, "Everything's okay." There was something about the valley that made it feel church-like. Mark's shout, sounding sacrilegiously from atop the boulder, got us to our feet. "Wow, look at that!" We looked toward where he was pointing. Rising higher than the tallest pines was a wall of granite. Sunlight limned its top and, beyond, a blue sky ceiling.

"If I were Black Feather, boys, I would camp up there. Let's find a way to get to the top."

"But, Dad, what if he's there?"

"Are you a fraidy cat, Nate?" Mark mocked.

We ascended the less steep side of the cliff, the boys doing what I did, grasping saplings rooted in crevices and angling sneakers between stones.

"Any snakes here?" Seth panted.

"Doubt it," I answered. "By now the Indians would've eaten them all. Did you know snakes are a delicacy? Keep climbing! We're almost there."

On the brow of the crag we were out from the cool shade of the pines and into the warmth of a June sun. Nathan spotted a purplish Lady Slipper beneath a clump of birches and knelt next to it.

"Don't pick it, Nate. It may be all that's left of Black Feather's garden." I wanted to keep our imagination game going.

"Why'd he plant flowers?" the lad asked.

"For his girl friend, right, Dad?"

My eldest son had outgrown tales of hermit Indians. Girl friends were on his mind.

A flock of grackles cawed from the branches, their blackness contrasting sharply with the skin of the birches. With a screech they flew off when Mark poked the blade of his Boy Scout jackknife into the flesh of one of the trees and carved an "M". He was working on the letter "A" as I kept watch of his brothers who flung stones down into the valley, aiming at the pooling stream that, from the summit of the cliff, looked like a baptismal font.

"Is this an arrowhead, Dad?"

Seth, thinking he had found a relic, gasped with excitement. The pointy shard of granite was way too large to be an arrowhead, but not to disappoint him I answered, "Could be, could be. Why don't you keep it for a souvenir? Look around. Maybe you'll find something else Black Feather left behind."

"Daddy, I'm hungry," Nathan whined.

I had lost track of time. Hunger was real. Make believe, on the other hand, was a gossamer thing that vanished in the breath of reality.

Back home, I added another layer to the tale to prolong the day's excitement. "Before he died, Mr. Baker told me about his father's hearing from his father that somewhere between Snake Hill Road and Hunting House Road there's a place where Indians gathered for a ceremony You know, like you going to church on Sunday. He said they danced and chanted around a huge fire, and they even buried things like jewelry and coins. I have a hunch that the place Mr. Baker was talking about is where we just came from. By the way, the Indians called this holy place 'Potowackett', which means in English 'Secret Valley'."

Seth swallowed a bite of bologna sandwich in a gulp and blurted, "Can we go back?"

"What about you, Nathan? Do you want to go back and see if we can find the buried treasure?"

I couldn't read his expression. Was it wonder or excitement or what? But he nodded an okay.

Mark, the skeptic, slathered mustard on his second bologna sandwich and complained. "If we go back, we'll have to bring stuff like shovels. Aw, what the heck, let's do it."

My cockamamie imagination game was up and running!

BY AUGUST OF 1972, Mark, my "golden boy" (a blond, blue-eyed Adonis) had adopted the counter-cultural ways of the Woodstock Nation. He scorned barbers and hygiene, became intractable, and rejected propriety in general. He sneered whenever "imagination game" was mentioned. He was rejecting his father.

To stop or at least slow down this disintegration of bonds between father and son, I persuaded Mark and his pal, Duane, to test their survival skills by coming to Secret Valley with me for a night of wilderness camping, and to ease Seth and Nathan's disappointment after telling them that this outing was strictly for the big boys, I promised them that their turn would come before the start of school.

I set off on our expedition at mid day under a cloudless sky with the two teenage boys. Hope walked with me. I was betting on camp fire camaraderie tonight to work its magic, and for whatever the cause of Mark's puzzling behavior to be resolved. Even though we had cast aside towels, blankets, pillows, crinkly bags of snacks, pots and pans, our knapsacks weighed enough for the straps to pain our shoulders. The weight of a frozen chicken, six potatoes, small cartons of apple juice, a store made chocolate cake and various tools added up.

When thorns drew blood from Mark's leg, I almost chided, "Told you so". He stubbornly wore cut-off jeans, disregarding my warning.

"What lousy luck!" he groused. "The brook's dried up. I was going to cool off."

"Grit your teeth, boy. We'll get by."

" 'We'll get by . . . we'll get by'," he mimicked under his breath and kicked his knapsack.

"Come on, buddy," Duane cajoled. "It's not that hot."

"Says who? It must be a hundred in the shade!"

Ascending the cliff was a struggle, but I didn't admit it aloud. At the top the boys shed their shirts and took turns lifting the water jug to their mouths. With their hair matted and their naked torsos glistening with sweat, they looked like Golding's choir boys.

"Okay, we're here. Mark, suppose you pick the spot where we can build a lean-to."

He shrugged and shuffled about, finally stopping between a couple of white pines.

"How about here?"

"Perfect. Now, grab the bow saw and hatchet and cut about seven or eight saplings. Make sure they're taller than you. And after you've done that, I'll leave it up to you to build our shelter. Okay?"

I kept watch on the boys as I dug a hole for a fire pit and lined it with stones. They nicely fashioned the framework of a lean-to, lashing saplings with sisal rope to a lintel stretched between the two pine trees. For a roof, they laid pine boughs on them. With that done, they combed the ground with fingers, tossing away twigs and cones and cushioned the ground with pine needles.

"You suppose Black Feather did stuff like this?" Mark scoffed.

Duane asked who Black Feather was.

"Some dude Dad made up."

"Okay, men, let's get firewood," I ordered, covering up the hurt that came with my son's put down of imagination games.

Mosquitoes found us, and the boys doused themselves with Off and pulled on their t-shirts.

"Start a fire," I said. "The smoke will keep them away."

Duane built a little pyramid with twigs in the fire pit and, with a third match, got them lit. I juried-built a green oak rotisserie over the pit and waited for the flames to die down before I impaled the chicken onto the spit and tossed the potatoes into the embers.

"Can't beat the smell of wood smoke and roasting chicken, can you?" I shouted to the boys. They sat cross-legged in the lean-to, playing Crazy Eights with a deck of cards one of them had slyly sneaked into his knapsack.

"Whatever you think, Dad."

Splat! A raindrop hit my forehead. Then another and another. Leaden clouds uglied the sky and gusts of wind trembled the top branches of the trees.

"Gosh dang it, a storm's coming! I hope the chicken's cooked."

It wasn't. Its wings and legs held fast to the carcass. Mark jack-knived the skin and cut into the meat, and blood oozed onto the blade.

"We'll eat it anyway. Won't kill us." I was trying to sustain an esprit de corps.

Right above us lightning zig-zagged downward, followed instantly by a sizzling fusillade of thunder, and a hard rain teemed through the pine-boughed roof of the lean-to. Fright widened the boys' eyes. Again, a flash of lightning and a boom of thunder. Mark jumped to his feet, yelling, "This is crazy! Let's get out of here!"

"What do you think we should do, Mr. Anderson?" Duane wasn't rashly going to abandon ship.

"I hate to say it but he's right. Leave everything and make a run for it."

Nearing the stone wall that we had to leap over to get to Hunting

House Road, we heard shouting. Duane's father had come to our rescue. Soaking wet, we boarded his car, and I let the boys tell their war story. Now that we were safe and sound, we could have laughed, we could have turned our misadventure into a joke. Duane's father tried to. "You look like three drowned rats is all I can say."

From the back seat Mark grumbled, "Right from the start it was a lousy idea."

I NEVER RETURNED to Secret Valley. The thunder that echoed off the cliff and through the woods that August day in 1972 was but like the roaring of a mouse, an omen of more daunting storms to come. For a long time after, I was bereft of imagination, painfully learning how fragile it is when the prodigality of a wayward son and the whimsicality of Nature challenge it.

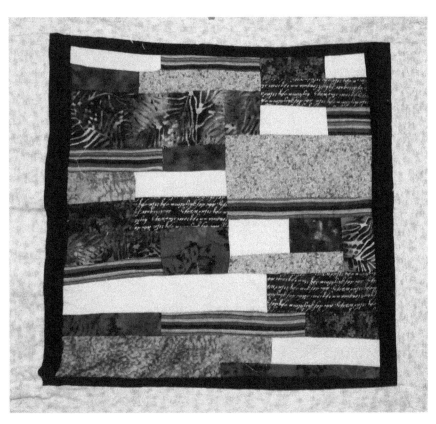

Go for it

KINGSTON

CNN CONTENDS THAT 1968 is "arguably the most important year in modern American history". Beyond argument, it was a year of chaos, highlighted by the assassinations of MLK and RFK. Morningside Heights teemed with cops' hauling protesting students from university buildings, and in the far-off jungle village of My Lei an American infantry squad massacred its civilians, and North Vietnam launched its Tet offensive, upping the daily body count and fueling the anti-war `passions that were searing America.

That year the Beatles' album, *Sgt. Pepper's Lonely Hearts Club Band*, won a Grammy. Notwithstanding the BBC's banning of it, its final cut – "A Day in the Life" (a solo sung by John Lennon) resounded in dorm rooms from Berkley to Boston:

Woke up, fell out of bed,
Dragged a comb across my head.
Found my way downstairs and drank a cup,
And looking up, I noticed I was late.

In 1968, America and I were waking up and falling out of bed.

AUGUST 16, 1968. Pauline and I sat in lawn chairs out back with a citronella candle and a half empty bottle of Andre's pink champagne between us. The three older kids, understanding that this was a special night for us, put on hold their usual bedtime antics and even forewent teasing their two younger siblings. Fourteen-month-old Nathan slept downstairs in his crib set up in our bedroom. From the speakers that I had propped in the kitchen windows came the soft sound of the George Shearing quartet – the LP I had taken with us to Bridgeton ten years ago. Our "honeymoon record" I called it.

"Happy anniversary, Love," I whispered.

"Same to you, Hon. And while we're at it, congratulations. You must feel good getting two A's."

We clinked glasses and kissed. I felt somewhat foolish to be congratulated for a good report card by a wife of ten years and, to boot, me, a father of six kids, a mortgage holder, and jobless. But, in truth, that just about summed up my status.

Exactly a year earlier I had come clean with Pauline and confessed dissatisfaction with my lot. Although ostensibly everything had been coming up roses for me since filing my Honorable Discharge certificate from the Army in a folder along with birth and marriage certificates, the path I was on would not lead to what I wanted. Albeit at age 31 the school committee had appointed me chairman of the high school's English department, three years later came the realization that the position could mire me more deeply in the miasma of public schools.

"What do you want?" she had asked.

"In a word, scholarship. I want to study literature. I want to teach at the college level."

"Then, go for it!"

"But that's impossible now. I mean, I won't do it parttime. I've been trying that, and that's not what I want. I want to be a full-time student. How in hell could I do that?"

"Where there's a will, there's a way."

"Come on, Love, enough for clichés."

"Why don't you look into it? You'll figure things out."

"*We'll* figure things out. I can't quit my job just like that without your help. Anyway, I might not get accepted into grad school."

"Why not?"

'Lots of reasons. For one, my undergraduate grades were lousy. For another, I may be too old. Anyway, I have no idea what the tuition is. Really, going to grad school is a cockamamie idea."

"The way I see it, you have to do what will make you happy. At least look into things. Okay?"

She had won the argument. Six weeks later I had a conversation with the dean of URI's graduate school, who summed up the interview nicely: "Normally, on the basis of your undergraduate transcript, your application would be rejected. However, according to your letters of recommendation and your teaching experience, you seem to have redeemed yourself. Look, I'm going to leave it entirely to Dr. Robinson, the chair of the English department, whether or not to take you on. Make an appointment to see him."

That was fine with me. With my hand on the knob of his office door, he stopped me.

"One more thing, Mr. Anderson. About the score you got on the Miller Analogy Test."

I had almost forgotten about that. The test was a killer: one hundred analogy problems to solve in one hour. When the score came in the mail, my heart sank.

"I had a bad day, sir."

"A *bad* day, you say? Perhaps you don't understand. Most people average somewhere between 9 and 14. A minimum score of 24 is required for admission into medical school. Your score of 78 is astounding, Mr. Anderson. Absolutely astounding! I've never known of anyone who scored so highly or, for that matter, who came even close."

Professor E. Arthur Robinson's office in Independence Hall befitted him: dusted, tidy, quiet. Nothing else but my folder lay atop his desk. His eyes behind glasses matched the blue of his button-down Hathaway shirt. What with his rep tie, tweed sports jacket, and perfectly trimmed iron-gray hair, the man looked a paragon of a circa 1950 university academic.

"It's going on four o'clock. We've been talking almost two hours. Thank you, Mr. Anderson, for patiently answering my questions. I think I'm ready now to make a decision."

He took from his jacket pocket a fountain pen and pulled a legal pad from a desk drawer. I turned to the window, feeling a knot tightening in my gut. Although only two days into Advent, the first flakes of winter – wet little things – splattered on the pane. The scratching of Dr. Robinson's pen was spelling out my future.

"I'm making notes here for future reference. Number one . . .

We're going to accept you into our MA program on the condition that you register for two graduate level summer courses and earn either an A or B in both. Are you amenable to that?"

"Yes, sir."

He nibbled the top of his pen and looked me squarely in the eye.

"You have a large family and you say your wife isn't working. It seems to me that finances are going to be quite tight. If you agree to be a teaching assistant, your tuition and fees will be waived and you'll be given a stipend. According to your principal's letter of recommendation, you are a very good teacher. So, I'm offering you a TA position. What do you say?"

Too amazed to speak, I simply nodded, and he scribbled another note. Recapping his pen and returning it to his pocket, he stood and went to the window.

"The snow's beginning to stick to the ground. How many miles from here to your home?"

"About forty or so."

"Do drive carefully, Mr. Anderson."

JUNE 23 – a week after the Irish had celebrated Bloomsday – I began my odyssey, sitting cross-legged in the shade of a maple tree in the rear yard of Independence Hall with a just-bought copy of James Joyce's *Ulysses* on my lap. Maybe fifteen or so others who had signed up for this seminar circled the teacher who uncannily resembled Joyce: a lanky, near-sighted man with hair that knew neither brush nor comb. Rather than taking attendance, his first words made known to us that he was an iconoclast: "Don't call me *Professor* or *Doctor* because I'm neither. Until those bastards at Columbia accept my Ph.D. dissertation, I will remain until my death *Mister Sharp.* Comprendez?"

Each two-hour class for five weeks must have physically and intellectually drained him, for he never sat and his explications of the most arcane passages in *Ulysses* replete with allusions to ancient mythologies and Biblical archetypes, linguistic nuances, Shakesperian metaphors awed us. He paced and chain smoked and exhorted us to come forth with our own analyses, and kicked the sod when he got only silence in return. By the third meeting, class size had dwindled down to eight.

In the two-hour hiatus between the morning's Joyce seminar and the afternoon's Shakespeare's Histories seminar, I forewent lunch, opting instead to hunker down in a second-floor carrel of the library. Then back to Independence Hall for an immersion into the Elizabethan Age. The histrionics of Professor Collenbach - a toothless, fifty-something, elfin man – held our attention in spite of July's humidity. Unforgettable was his recitation from memory of Hal's (now King Henry V) renunciation of Falstaff.

The more intense the work, the more keen my mind was becoming. I was acquiring fluency in the use of academic jargon common to articles published in scholarly journals. Sharp and Collenbach, whose oftentimes zany way of arriving at an interpretation of a passage was dazzling, emboldened me to follow suit. To my delight, my four ten-page papers apparently pleased those two iconoclasts, for each paper was merited an "A". The joy, the excitement of intellectual calisthenics that had for so long been elusive I had re-discovered.

The Fifth Dimension's hit song, *The Age of Aquarius*, became my anthem throughout the summer of '68 and beyond, for it aptly befitted my mood:

> *Harmony and understanding, sympathy and trust abounding*
> *No more falsehoods or derisions golden living dreams of visions*
> *Mystic crystal revelations and the mind's true liberations*
> *Aquarius, Aquarius*

I had passed probation. Let the sun shine in! Now came the wait for word from Dr. Robinson to confirm that I was a candidate for a MA.

FROM THE GARDEN where I was picking tomatoes, I spotted our '59 two-door Volvo stop at the mail box. Pauline had returned home with the four older kids from the last day of swimming lessons. At the edge of the garden fourteen-month-old Nathan and his three-year-old brother, Seth, amused each other on a blanket. With pond water dripping from her hair, Kristen ran barefooted to the garden, carrying a piece of mail.

"Mommy said to give this to you."

The damp, clasped envelope was fat. Its return address read:

English Department
University of Rhode Island
Kingston, RI 02881

In long hand above the address was written in ink: *E. Arthur Robinson.* Too excited to give thought to the picked tomatoes, I left the basket where I had set it down and hurried to the boys.

"Mommy's making lunch. Let's go wash up. Ready? One . . . two . . . three . . . Go!"

With the envelope squeezed under one arm, with the other I carried Nathan and followed Seth across the yard and into the house. Their four older siblings, still in bathing suits and flip-flops, were making mayhem in the kitchen – Mark's snapping a dish towel at the rear ends of his sisters and their screaming, "Ow, stop it!". I found Pauline at the washing machine, tossing beach towels into it.

"Look, Hon, here's what I've been waiting for."

"Yes, I know. Did you open it?"

"Not yet. I want you with me when I do."

"It's too noisy in here. The kids are all charged up. Let's go out to the picnic table, okay?"

We sat at the table, but, before I opened the envelope, she spurted,

"Look! The day lilies I planted last May have blossoms!"

I was confounded, wondering how she could be thinking of flowers as I held what would determine our fate in the next twelve months.

"Well, are you going to see what's inside that envelope?"

I did. The first sheet I pulled from it was a letter signed by Dr. Robinson, congratulating me for getting accepted into URI's graduate school. I passed it to her. After reading it, she looked up at me and said nonchalantly, "You're not surprised, are you? I'm not."

"But you know what this means? We're in for one helluva crazy year."

How right I was!

COLUMBUS DAY OF '68, a legal holiday in Rhode Island, gave me exactly what I needed close to the midway point of the first semester: a sleep-in. The only item that I had scribbled on the day's chore list the night before was "cut the grass". And that could wait until late afternoon.

The gods were beneficent. Nothing so far had upset my schedule. It was way too tight to withstand any contingency like my Volvo's breaking down or a family member's breaking a limb or any of the other hundreds of possible disasters that make cowards of pragmatists and pessimists. Because I had imposed upon myself a time limit of one year to meet all requirements for the Masters degree, I disregarded the stern advice not to register for more than two courses a semester.

An MA candidate had two options: (a) satisfactorily complete twelve courses and at the end pass a comprehensive exam; (b) satisfactorily complete ten courses and submit a dissertation. Because of my time limit and because my TA status would expire in one year and along with it the bonus of free tuition, I took on three courses a semester plus two more summer courses. And, of course, I was compiling a bibliography for my dissertation and writing it and preparing for an oral defense of its thesis.

All the while, as I probed *The Faerie Queen* and Donne's *Holy Sonnets* and the Concord Transcendentalists for meaning hidden in their metaphors, I was teaching writing – two courses at URI and two evening courses at the YMCA Institute (which was evolving into Roger Williams University) in Providence. I had to bring in money for the family.

The grass stayed uncut that Columbus Day. Demonized by a stack of unread essays, I blue-penciled those poorly written things, wondering why their authors were given high school diplomas. Shadows lengthened earlier and earlier as Indian Summer wooed us into hoping there would be no winter this year, and I slipped a rubber band around the dozen or so yet-to-be-read essays and persuaded Pauline to go for a walk,

"How are you feeling?" Her question broke the silence. "You haven't said much all day."

"To tell the truth, Love, I'm feeling as though I've bitten off more than I can chew."

"You said it wasn't going to be easy. Right?"

"Like everything else, you have to experience something before you really know it. I'm cramming so much into my head that it feels like it's about to explode. What about you? I mean, I'm not doing much of anything with you and the kids."

"But you're doing what you just have to do. Are you enjoying it? That's the real question."

We had come to the brook that flows through the Bakers' back forty and under Rocky Hill Road and on to the Scituate Reservoir. We paused and we kissed, our little ritual on these strolls.

"To answer your question, Love. Yes, in spite of the work and everything, I haven't been happy like this in a long, long time."

"That's what counts. You'll get through this."

A sliver of shame pricked my conscience.

"I'm sorry to be whining. You're the one who should be, not me. Look at what you're doing. Here you are pregnant and all the while holding the family together. Absolutely amazing!"

Again we kissed and turned toward home. That was the last time I complained.

Indian Summer was a tease, for – as the TV weatherman called it – the "Montreal Express" roared into Rhode Island the first week of November, bringing with it bitter cold and a couple of news-making snow storms.

Coping with fender-high snow drifts became yet another item on my to-do list along with deadlines for twenty-page papers. But with the coming of Christmas and the end of the semester, my mission was accomplished. With the aid of a Kingston potato farmer's tractor that towed my Volvo through a wind-blown mountain-high drift of snow I got to campus the morning of a blizzard, and with the luck of good health I soldiered through the academic challenges and my teaching assignments. And I had made headway in the writing of a dissertation. Dr. Robinson had consented to head my committee and had approved my research topic: *The Procession Motif in Hawthorne's Tales and Romances.*

Pauline, though, pulled off the greatest accomplishment. She considerately went into labor between semesters when I was home. Two days after Christmas, she delivered Rachel Leah.

DR. ROBINSON'S COTTAGE on South Street, not far from the university, befitted him. A neatly trimmed privet hedge bordered the front lawn, and flanking the brick walkway purple and white irises smiled up at us. From inside we heard a clock chime the hour. Five on the button, exactly the time he was expecting us. I thought it a great honor to be invited to dinner by the professor.

"Come in, come in! It's a pleasure to see you again, Mrs. Anderson. We had met only briefly at last year's clambake. Margery, dear, the Andersons have arrived."

From the kitchen Mrs. Robinson cheerily welcomed us. "Arthur, make our guests comfortable in the living room. There's cheese and crackers on the coffee table. You can pour the sherry. I'm almost done in here."

I had never given thought to the professor's life outside the classroom. To see him decant sherry into four wine glasses jarred me. Scratching words on the blackboard that were germane to *The Fall of the House of Usher*, or to whatever other Poe tale was under discussion, while calmly positing an exegesis – to me, that was his role, not filling stemware with sherry for a student. His wife, a merry little woman, joined us in time for a toast.

"Salud!"

And with that, the evening with the Robinsons got under way. Surely a veteran of many, many academic socials, Margery kept dinner conversation flowing, seamlessly segueing from how she has been combating the blight afflicting her azaleas this spring to the charm of Nancy Potter's just-published collection of short stories, from the "unsightly architecture" of URI's Ballentine Hall to Lady Bird Johnson's scheme to beautify America's interstate highways.

Darkness had come to the windows as the professor poured coffee and his wife placed a bowl of vanilla ice cream with butterscotch glaze at each seat. He snapped on the Tiffany chandelier and softly recited, "Was never evening yet but seemed beautifuller than its day."

"Arthur, it's the rising sun that's most beautiful!"

"But, dear, Browning's a poet and poets, you must know, prefer the melancholy that comes with sundown."

"Fiddlesticks! Tulips fold their petals at sundown. I think they have more sense than poets."

She stood and collected the bowls and spoons, and Pauline trailed her to the kitchen, insisting to lend a hand in cleaning up.

"Your ham casserole, Mrs. Robinson, was delicious!"

"I've been making it since getting the recipe from a woman colleague of Arthur's at Ohio State way back when."

The kitchen door shut, and Professor Robinson and I felt the silence in the room. A grandfather clock in the far corner chimed the half hour. Seven-thirty. He finished his coffee, dabbed his mouth with a linen napkin, and cleared his throat.

"I've invited you this evening because I want to make a proposal. First, however, I must tell you that your performance is making quite an impression in the department. With that said, you're probably not aware that finally, after many, many meetings over the span of three years, the powers that be at the university have approved the English department's plans to launch a doctoral program, beginning in the fall of 1969, that is the first semester of the next academic year."

He went to the clock and wound it. I waited, wondering what he was thinking. He turned, adjusted his glasses and cleared his throat again and said, "Initially, only seven candidates for the Ph.D. will be chosen. Harry, I – or I should say 'we' – want you to be one of them."

I could not respond. He returned to the table, folded his hands, and took in the wonder, the confusion that must have come to my eyes. In his avuncular way he went on.

"I know that this comes as a great surprise. I also understand that, given your circumstances, you have a lot of thinking to do. If you accept, your TA status will be extended for another year. All in all, you'll have five years to complete requirements, including, of course, the writing of a book-length dissertation. Let's leave it at this for now. Wait until the end of this semester to give me your answer."

We were home before ten and thanked my mother and father for babysitting. Pauline immediately went to bed, but I hunched at the kitchen table strewn with note cards and books, alternately re-reading highlighted passages of *The Scarlet Letter* seminal to the procession motif and re-playing Dr. Robinson's stunning words, "Harry, I want you to be one of them".

It was with profound relief that I shut off the kitchen light at two o'clock. I had drafted the first paragraph of my Hawthorne dissertation and had an answer ready to give to the professor.

AGAINST THE BACKDROP of utter chaos, I came to the successful conclusion of my year-long quest for a Masters degree. As I was acing the last two courses and getting through the oral defense of my thesis, the events of the summer of 1969 were forming a plot- line too implausible for Beckett or Ionesco or for any other Absurdist playwright. Almost every day from my car radio I learned of another plot twist: a massacre in My Lai; a cult slaughter of seven west coast glitterati led by a man, ranting that he was God; a human being's kicking up moon dust; a could-have-been President's abandoning his extra-marital girl friend to drown; a drug-fueled orgy of 400,000 kids in the muck of a cow farm.

An apocalyptic mood permeated the campus. There were deaths galore making news: Nam body counts; rock and folk musicians dropping from drug OD's; assassinations; lynchings and bombings; and the spread of HIV. Not impervious to this mood, in a why-the-hell-not state of mind I stayed on at URI for another year with a schedule similar to the previous one. This time, though, I was aiming for a Ph.D.

Along with November came my usual bout with melancholy. Wednesdays were particularly tough because they began with an eight o'clock writing class that I taught and ended twelve hours later with a three-hour seminar. I would not see my family on Wednesdays. In an Ishmael-like state of mind, who "whenever I find myself growing grim about the mouth, whenever it is a damp, drizzly November in my soul . . . then, I account it high time to get to the sea", I left campus and strolled the East Matunuck beach, hoping that the salt air would refresh my wits before the start of the seven o'clock Fielding seminar at the home of Dr. Selnick.

The surf was high but obscured by the absence of light: no moon, no stars, no lamps of any sort. Only the steady voice of breaking waves told me that I was at ocean side.

Fifteen months of unbroken study had sated me, and the turmoil of the times had me floundering like a castaway in a rudderless skiff. Into the breath of an on-shore wind I read the roll of my closest companions whose agonies had become terribly real to me: *Dimmsdale, Mersault, Swann, Falstaff, Hester, Ahab, Parson Adams.*

Parson Adams . . . My seaside interlude ended. I had but twenty minutes to get to Dr. Selnick's house in Kingston where he and his eight graduate students would try to discern what in hell Fielding intended when he created that burlesque parson. Troubled protagonists we adroitly examined, but a kindly, happy-go-lucky rube of a clergyman perplexed us.

Giving thought to what I might contribute to the upcoming discussion shifted focus from my November melancholy to the immediate problem of trying to make sense of another piece of literature. I huffed over the sand dunes toward my car, ready to press on, ready for three hours with *Joseph Andrews* and then a long drive home to look in on my sleeping kids and to kiss Pauline goodnight.

MAY 4, 1970, the first balmy day of spring, a day too nice to keep my 11:00 a.m. freshman comp class cloistered indoors in an engineering lab. The penultimate meeting of the class for the semester, therefore, took place on the lawn of Bliss Hall on the northern edge of the campus. The lesson for the day was to explicate William Butler Yeats' poem, *The Second Coming*.

I asked Michelle, whose wardrobe seemed to consist only of tie-dyed shirts and frayed farmer's overalls, to start things off.

"Okay, Mr. A, you want me to say what the man – what's his name? Yeats? – is writing about? Well, like he's telling it like it is. I mean, bango! It's all over for you and me. For everyone! Isn't that what the man's saying?"

"Whoa, Michele! What lines would support your interpretation?"

"How about lines four, five, and six? I'll read them:

Mere anarchy is loosed upon the world,
The blood-dimmed tide is loosed, and everywhere
The ceremony of innocence is doomed.

Okay? Like, just what I said. Bang, we've had it! We're doomed."

"Well, yes, sort of. But it would be nice if you gave us your thoughts about why Yeats thinks we're doomed. Look at his diction, for example. What's the connotation of 'anarchy' or . . . or of 'ceremony' and 'innocence'?"

"Okay. 'Innocence' makes me think of kids. Like, aren't they supposed to be innocent? I mean, like they're naïve?"

"You're on to something, Michele. Say more."

At that moment – only a stone's throw away from where the class circled on the grass – eight or nine students packed at the flag pole, gesturing with clenched fists and chanting, "Down with the pigs . . . Down with the pigs!" From every corner of the campus more students came running. Michele jumped up and shouted, "I gotta find out what in hell's going on. I'll be back." The rest of us watched her race barefooted to the throng. She returned in a couple of minutes and gasped the news.

"Oh my God! Somewhere in Ohio the National Guard just shot and killed a bunch of college kids!"

The class stared at me, and I told them to go. I lingered in the shade of Bliss Hall long enough to see the kids' hauling down the American flag.

The university canceled all classes for the rest of the day, allowing me to get home at mid afternoon. That, for me, was a lucky break, for I had an Herculean task to do. Notwithstanding careful planning to space out assignments, the inevitable happened. Bunching up at the same time were three deadlines: the writing of two twenty-page papers and the reading of Melville's 500-page *Pierre*. I had no time to give thought to the Kent State fiasco.

Billy Pilgrim: Vonnegut's Existential Anti-hero I entitled the first paper. Having thought it through on my drive home and being up on existentialism, I had the paper blocked out and reached the twentieth page in time to help Pauline get the kids to bed. As she nursed Rachel downstairs, upstairs I knelt at bedside with the older ones to say nightly prayers. And then back to my typewriter I dashed to start the writing of the second paper, a discourse on Spenser's Blatant Beast.

A bit after midnight I had finished it, and, with no time to edit, I inserted them into plastic folders. On to the reading of *Pierre*. Come dawn, I had the book read. Unshaved and woozy, I was back to Independence Hall by 8:30 a.m. But the drive to campus had been nightmarish. Coming from the car's radio were the anthems of the Sixties, songs like *Everybody's Talkin'* and *The Sound of Silence*, and all the while, resonating in my head, were the screams of scores of angry kids and Michele's succinct summary of *The Second Coming*: "Bang, we've had it! We're doomed!"

MORBIDITY CLOYED THE campus mood the summer of 1970. But I soldiered on, registering for three seminars to finish course requirements for the Ph.D. and receiving approval from my committee of my dissertation topic. One more year to research and to write it would bring to fruition my quixotic stab at living the life of a scholar. But poof went that dream when Dr. Robinson reminded me that the tenure of a TA was limited to two years, leaving me with no other choice but to find a high school teaching job.

As Yeats predicted, "Things fall apart; the centre cannot hold." My over-worked Volvo was first to go, a blown head gasket sending it to the junk yard. Hastily, we bought a huge Dodge station wagon and, a week after the last meeting of a Tennyson seminar – my final course ever at URI – the nine of us squeezed into it along with newly purchased camping gear and drove off to Bar Harbor for the family's first vacation in three years.

By the light of a Coleman lantern I sat at a picnic table in Acadia's campground not far from Thunder Hole and wrote a letter to Dr. Robinson. Before writing the final paragraph, I paused to appreciate the spectacle of a first-quarter moon rising over Frenchman Bay.

Achingly, I penned the paragraph:

So, time simply ran out for me to write the dissertation. That may be a disappointment for you as it is for me and I am sorry. You surely know that I have done my utmost to reach the goal. However, I have learned from you a lesson that exceeds in value any degree: the core of good teaching is giving a student self respect. I hold in my heart profound gratitude.

In the tent, surrounded by my sleeping family and breathing in the sweet scent of spruce and sea, I fell asleep to the sound of silence.

When you're ready, Mr. Anderson, you may proceed.

PHILADELPHIA

DRIVING THE STREETS of a city that I had not visited – especially a city the size of Philadelphia – terrified me. With sweaty hands I exited the New Jersey Turnpike onto Route 30, crossed over the Delaware River via the Benjamin Franklin Bridge, and entered the center of the City of Brotherly Love. I had studied the AAA map and had fixed in my mind the street layout. What I had to do was find Walnut Street and follow it, straight as an arrow, to the university.

The AAA tour book informed me that Philadelphia is the first planned city in North America and that Ben Franklin ingeniously platted it to replicate a grid. Nice! But the neatly drawn blue lines on the map do not inform you of one way streets and detours. Serendipitously I found Walnut Street but strayed when a construction barrier forced me to turn right.

Every attempt I made to get back onto Walnut failed. Making matters worse, the last of the disappearing sun was fading. I squeezed the steering wheel and cursed, "Damn it, damn it! Why did I come here? This is so stupid!"

Pauline, who had been sitting mutely since crossing the Delaware, broke her silence. "Up ahead there's a police car. Why don't you stop and get directions?"

A cop was doing business with a bunch of teenagers. I walked up to his partner who stood by the door of the cruiser. A garish purplish light of a neon sign above the entrance to a nearby storefront church discolored his lips. The letter "U" in CHURCH OF THE LIVING GOD was unlit.

"Officer, I'm lost. Please direct me to Walnut Street."

"Holy crap, mister! You better get the hell outta here and pronto!"

"I want to, but how?"

"Where exactly are you going?"

"To the University of Pennsylvania."

He looked dazed, started to say something, stopped, and ordered me to stay put. He went to the cop who was shooing the kids away, and the two of them returned to the cruiser. One of them said to me, "You're a lucky guy we were here. Get back into your car, lock the doors, and follow us."

I WAS DRESSED and perking coffee by 6:30 the next morning. The suite assigned us – our "home" until August 5 – was on the 22nd floor of Harnwell House, a high rise dorm on Penn's campus. From the window of the sitting room/kitchenette, I watched 747's land and take off. The airport seemed to be about five miles away. In the adjacent room Pauline stayed abed, sleeping off the effects of yesterday's doings.

Banking on the coffee to help unscramble my wits, I drained two cups before jotting down a list of what had to be done ASAP. First, of course, was to find the library, meet my fellow seminarians, and size up Professor Lustig, who would be leading the seminar. Then, I had to get to the security office to secure a photo ID and a parking sticker. Everything else, like shopping for groceries, Pauline and I would do later.

Had I not acquiesced to Mary Beth's insistence, I would be home , happily fussing in the garden. From the day she came to my office at school to give me the brochure that announced the coming summer's National Endowment for the Humanities seminars for teachers she badgered me to apply. To spend half a summer with teachers did not appeal to me. Furthermore, I thought myself too old to sit around in a classroom and try to look smart. I told her to give the brochure to someone else. But the woman persisted and persisted, arguing that the experience would be wonderful.

More to quiet her than for any other reason, I finally read the brochure and mailed off an application. Certain of having no chance of acceptance, I nevertheless chose the Dante seminar to be held in Florence, Italy. Pauline, on the other hand, felt so sure of my getting accepted that, for a Christmas gift, she gave me an Italian/English dictionary. I was chosen an alternate and never used that dictionary.

Meanwhile, at Penn Dr. Irma Lustig was beating the bushes to find three more people to sign up for her seminar. If she could not attract sixteen teachers, her seminar would be a no-go. Somehow she was given the names of the turned-down Dante applicants and was making telephone calls. Now another woman was nagging me.

"No, Mary Beth. No . . . absolutely no! I can't think of anything more dull than reading Boswell's *Life of Samuel Johnson*!"

"Look at it this way, Harry. Philly's a great city, and you'll get a stipend as well as free lodging. Go for it!" Pauline got into the act. How could I win?

And there I was, strolling along Locust Walk on a fine June morning en route to Penn's library. I came upon a bronze statue of Ben Franklin, his legs crossed, lolling on a bench. Many hands had rubbed his head that shone in the sun. I partook in the custom, talking while rubbing: "Hey, Ben boy, come with me. You're good for a lot of laughs."

There was no need to inquire where to go, for immediately upon entering the Van Pelt Library I spotted a hand-printed sign: DR. LUSTIG'S NEH SEMINAR, ROOM 202. At the room's door waited a diminutive woman whose coal-black eyes behind dark rimmed glasses took measure of me. I guessed her age to be perhaps sixty-eight or even seventy. With a voice resonating with authority she welcomed me.

"Good morning . . . I'm Irma Lustig. And your name?"

"I'm Harry Anderson."

"Ah, yes . . . from Rhode Island. My late husband and I enjoyed occasional visits to Newport. Whatever, I'm very, very happy about your enrolling in this seminar. Well, come in, come in. We're about to start."

I did not question her sincerity, yet it did little to raise my spirit, and neither did room 202's austerity: bare beige walls, no windows, fluorescent overhead lighting, and an oak conference table. I sat in one of the two vacant chairs, Dr. Lustig in the other, directly across the table from me. Her first order of business had us sixteen strangers taking turns to introduce ourselves.

Other than noting that seven men and nine women made up the group, that the common denominator among us was that all were teachers, and that our homes were scattered all over the map of America, from Nevada, Nebraska, California to Maryland, New Jersey, Pennsylvania, I had nary an inkling as to the uniqueness of anyone.

Three hours later I walked back to Harnwell House, clasping an unabridged edition of Boswell's *Life of Johnson* and quailing at the intimidating prospect of having to read all of its 1,042 pages. More than that, Dr. Lustig expected each of us to deliver a one-hour oral dissertation on a topic we chose from a list of topics she had prepared. At least, I thought, she did not ask for a twenty-page, footnoted paper.

However moribund the topic of death, I chose it, calculating that my turn to speak would come at or near to the end of the seminar, thus giving me five weeks to read Boswell's tome.

EXTRACURRICULAR ACTIVITIES BRIGHTENED our Philadelphia sojourn. Because the seminars met Monday, Wednesday, and Friday, we had four days to ourselves, giving us plenty of time to explore the city, its environs, and each other. An extended dry spell with daily temperatures in the 90° range encouraged several field trips: Cape May, Hopewell, Longwood Gardens, Bryn Mawr, Lancaster. Of the out-of-staters, only I had a car. Consequently, someone – usually Fran Reinehr – rode with us.

Pauline and I had reconnoitered the neighborhood adjacent to Penn's campus in search for a grocer, a bank, and a church and found all three within walking distance. When overhearing Fran's asking for directions to the nearest Catholic church, I told her that she should come with us Sunday morning. She did. Not only was that the first of six Sabbath walks to St. Agatha but also the start of a close friendship.

Fran Reinehr, born in Fargo, North Dakota, and in 1988 was teaching grade 4 in Lincoln, Nebraska – a single mother of a grown son and daughter – was a prairie woman to the core. Sweet but tough, self reliant yet vulnerable. She published a creative non-fiction book about a not-so-crazy hermit woman of the plains named "Crazy Mary" and composed wistful poetry. Marlboro's had lowered her voice an octave, and Budweiser's were fueling her *joie de vivre*. A mystery ride to a warehouse on the bank of the Schuylkill River cemented our friendship.

To her profound dismay, Fran found herself in a big, mid-Atlantic city that outlaws what Rhode Islanders call "package stores". To pur-chase a six-pack, one had to go to a tavern and pay an exorbitant price. For a week she groused about that until finally a fellow semi-narian named Mike, who was a Philadelphian, gave me the solution.

"We'll come for you this afternoon, Fran, about two o'clock. But where we're going I'm not telling you."

"Give me a hint at least."

"This side of Paradise."

The drive from campus to the address Mike had given me was quick and easy. In the parking lot of a big box building, she stuttered a question: "What in hell is this?"

"Let's go in and find out."

The building was cavernous, its floor-to-ceiling shelves packed with cases of beer. As broad and dazzling as the Nebraskan prairie at sunrise, a smile spread across Fran's face, and she hugged me and hugged me with the strength of a buffalo.

THE THREE OF us – Pauline, Irma, and I – chewed through six inch Hoagies at a sidewalk café on Chestnut Street. The professor had sched-uled one-on-one lunches with us seminarians, and July 3rd was my turn.

Her aim was to get acquainted with each of us. But, as Pauline would note that evening, "The woman is lonely. We learned more about her than she did about us."

Before the first bite into the sandwich she set the tone of our *tête á tête* by insisting that we call her "Irma".

" 'Doctor Lustig' is much too formal. I was born on the other side of the tracks, you see, and there I remain . . . essentially. With that said, let's hear about you."

I nodded to Pauline, who seemed quite comfortable with this learned woman. Off she waffled about our seven kids, our gardens, her job at Providence College's Student Health Center. I chomped the Hoagie, savoring its salami and prosciutto and olive oil drenched roll, waiting my chance to ask Irma her meaning of "born on the other side of the tracks".

"Ah, Pauline, you're a nurse! Most recently I've watched nurses in action. Before my husband died, he was cared for by these lovely women. They are truly special people."

Well after I had finished eating the Hoagie, Irma talked on and on about her husband's illness, finally ending the dirge with "I continue to grieve."

Silence. She picked the onions from her sandwich and placed them on the paper plate. "I detest onions!"

"Irma, if I may, why did you say you were born on the other side of the tracks?"

Out came her story: The daughter of a blue collar father who frowned upon girls' going to college but gave in to her persistence and allowed her to enroll at Temple, dropping out to do war work in a factory and returning to write a paper on Samuel Johnson that so impressed her teacher that he persuaded his counterpart at Penn to get her into its graduate school with a scholarship where her Ph.D. dissertation – *Boswell's Portrait of Himself in "The Life of Samuel Johnson"* – caught the attention of Frederick Pottle of Yale, the world's preeminent Boswellian scholar, and together she and Pottle authored books and articles about Johnson and him.

"Pottle also has died, leaving me to carry on the work. I'm trying, indeed. But it's become very difficult now, especially with grief weighing me down."

Hours later, in our room in Harnwell House, as we reviewed our two hours with Irma and after Pauline had summed up by saying that we had been with a lonely woman, I stood at the window watching landing lights of jets descend over the distant airport and feeling melancholia set in.

"I think I've got it, Love."

Pauline, on her way to bed, stopped.

"Got what?"

"Irma's problem. She's never gotten rid of the stigma of being born on the other side of the tracks. To boot, she's old and alone and hasn't found a disciple. I may be wrong, but I think she's on to something in this Boswell/Johnson thing but can't put her finger on it. Damn it! It's too complex for me to figure out. This I'm sure of, though. Irma needs those guys, and she needs her seminar maybe even more."

"You lose me. Are you coming to bed?"

I hit the light switch and thought of doppelgängers.

EACH DAY WAS proving Mary Beth's prediction to be right. Our Philadelphia stay was becoming unforgettable. With her mind set on making it so, Irma threw an Independence Day party in her tenth floor apartment. All sixteen of us plus the four wives walked together from campus, down Walnut Street, across the Schuylkill River bridge, through Philly's center, to the Society Hill Historic District where Hopkinson House haughtily awaited us. Our spirits were high, our camaraderie lending credence to the meaning of "Philadelphia": the city of brotherly love.

We were shocked at first when Irma greeted us at her door. Whereas at the conference table in the Van Pelt Library she assumed an austere appearance – no make-up and wearing colorless skirts and sweaters - that evening lip stick glistened, rouge reddened her cheeks, and a blood-red dress with sequins screamed "Party Time!".

She made sure that we were not wanting refreshments. Bowls of nibbles were on end tables, bottles of wine chilled in ice buckets on a kitchen counter, mounds of tiny sandwiches and an array of pastries on bone china platters spread across a cherry wood table.

Three hours into merry-making, over the clinking of glasses and clanking of plates and clashing of voices a BA-BOOM shut everyone up. Hidden by the men who circled her, Irma shouted, "It's starting! Come see." We raced with her onto the balcony that overlooked Penn's Landing. In the gloaming, pyrotechnics sputtered and burst above the Delaware River, their flashes of vivid purple, white, red light silhouetting a million shrieking spectators squeezed along the river's banks. Off to the left, the white spire of Independence Hall gallantly loomed.

"Unforgettable!" I shouted to Pauline.

WITHOUT GUSTO, I plodded on with the reading of *The Life of Johnson*. Try as she did to infuse her seminar with excitement, Irma was not lighting fires under us. My colleagues dutifully, dispassionately tackled their chosen topics – more or less paraphrasing Boswell rather than coming up with inspired exegeses. Discussions following each oral dissertation were dull and pedantic. Exactly one week before my appointed time to fill an hour with comments on the topic of death, I had trudged through 800 pages of *The Life*, leaving 200 more to get read, and had yet to see why it could be germane to Boswell's biography of a corpulent, disheveled, 18th century bag of wind.

"To hell with it," I said to Pauline. "Let's pack a picnic and take in tonight's concert at the Mann Center."

Arriving before the Philadelphia Orchestra tuned up, we had our choice of spots to spread a blanket. When our tuna sandwiches and tossed salad were eaten and the bottle of Riesling nearly empty, twilight had come and the musicians were tuning up. A westerly breeze coming straight from Amish country hardly brought relief from a heavy humidity.

"How about that, Love! Claudio Abbado's the guest conductor. Did we luck out!"

The center piece of the concert was Richard Strauss's *Death and Transfiguration*. I read the notes in the program that explained the tone poem's four movements:

I. Largo (a sick man near death)
II. Allegro motto agitato (struggle between life and death with no respite)
III. Meno mosso (dying man reviews his life)
IV. Moderato (sought-after transfiguration)

An idea exploded in my brain. Transfixed, I moved with each nuance of the music that was depicting an artist's almost unbearable wrestling match with his mortality - painfully, pathetically, heroically seeking reconciliation, redemption, transfiguration.

"Yes, I got it!"

"Shh," Pauline hushed.

What stirred me to excitement was thinking that Strauss could have composed the sound track to a bioflick of Samuel Johnson. He had done in twenty-six minutes of music-making what took Boswell 1,000 pages of prose to do.

SEQUESTERED ALL DAY Tuesday in a carrel on the third floor of Penn's library, now empty of students, I finished reading *The Life* and began culling from it the passages I had underlined that pertained to death, noting page numbers on a clipboard. The next evening I returned to the same carrel. The more I read Boswell the more ideas I scribbled down, and the heavier my clipboard was becoming.

Thursday, the eve of my scheduled turn to deliver the goods, was a fretful day for me. Fran and Pauline, correctly thinking it best were I left alone with my angst, ambled away to shop for souvenirs. I re-read my notes, spreading the pages across the kitchenette table, onto the chairs, and upon the divan. Try as I did to sequence them into a coherent order, I wasn't succeeding. Three hours into this frustration, I fled from the apartment that had become stuffy. No breeze came through the open windows to stir the air.

In the small yard of Harnwell House, beneath the canopy of a few larch trees, I paced, I pondered, but I could not come up with a linchpin – a key idea that would unify all those allusions to death interspersed throughout *The Life*. Yet, ironically, I was gaining an intimacy with Old Sam. The crux of my problem lay with an imponderable mix of facts: Johnson's extraordinary intellect, his mercurial personality, and the ineffability of death itself.

Oddly, however, I knew what was troubling the man. Indeed, what has been troubling me and everyone else for that matter. Even Shakespeare. Hamlet's lament - "The dread of something after death" (isn't that how the line goes?) - sums up the cause. Johnson's life-long fear of death and the elusiveness of a reason for our mortality profoundly nettled him.

Thus went my thoughts, stopping at the recalling of last Saturday's concert. Strauss nailed it down, I concluded. It took music, not words, to do it.

When Pauline got back to Harnwell House with her purchases and asked how I had made out, I answered with a shrug.

"I'll be a happy camper, Love, by this time tomorrow."

I CAME TO room 202 of the Van Pelt Library for the final meeting of Irma's seminar with fear and trembling. The glory of a perfect mid-summer morning did nothing to ease my dread of certain humiliation ahead. Chairs scraped, voices hummed. Fran touched my shoulder as she bent onto a chair. The last to enter was Irma, who glanced around the table and, with forced cheer, wished us a good morning.

"Well, fellow scholars, we've come to the finale of our five-week study of *The Life of Samuel Johnson*. After we hear Mr. Anderson's comments on the theme of death in Boswell's masterpiece, we'll have a summing up. So, when you're ready, Mr. Anderson, you may proceed."

" 'Death had always been to Johnson an object of terrour', Boswell tells us." That's how I began. Had I the gumption to be a smart ass, *that's all I needed to say* I would have said. Old Sam, after all, had been snappish and down right debasing all his life, albeit in most clever ways. And he got away with it. The next line from Boswell, however, irrevocably led me into an oration that was tantamount to a Sunday morning sermon:

My readers are now, at last, to behold SMAUEL JOHNSON preparing himself for that doom, from which the most exalted powers afford no exemption to man.

I had planned to cite that line toward the conclusion of my talk, but the jitters caused this slip up, committing me to comment on how Johnson may have prepared himself for imminent death as well as Boswell's meaning of "most exalted powers". Throw in his sudden shift in tone - almost foreboding - I had on my hands a sermon-in-the-making.

What followed spontaneously sprung from a mother-lode of experiences: the teaching of Greek tragedies and their theme of apotheosis; my familiarity with Existentialism and the Kierkegaard "leap unto faith" notion; my upbringing in the Christian faith; the lasting memory of witnessing my mother's death, when she lapsed into a beatific bliss. Most of all, at that moment, I was oddly feeling a kinship with Johnson. All of this coalesced and merged with Strauss's *Death and Transfiguration* that continued to resonate in my mind.

Approaching the end of my allotted time, I paraphrased Boswell's account of his friend's final hours, emphasizing that Johnson had emerged from the privacy of his room purged of fear. Because neither had anyone witnessed the man's behavior behind closed doors nor had he told anyone what transforming thoughts ran through his mind, "we can only speculate" I said. But present to witness Johnson's death was the Honorable John Byng who, in a letter given to Boswell by its receiver – a Mr. Malone – reports: "No man could appear more collected, more devout, or less terrified at the thoughts of the approaching minute."

I paused, badly needing a sip of water to wet my tongue and throat that were becoming dangerously close to shutting down. The hour was just about up, and I had to add a conclusion. It went something like this:

"Mind you, Johnson lived in a time dubbed 'The Age of Reason', and he was a staunch advocate of reason. Almost from the start of his biography Boswell reports that reason over and over again clouded Johnson's thinking in matters concerning the soul and those 'most exalted powers'. Yet, on page 1,377, we hear Old Sam praying:

Almighty and most merciful Father . . . Have mercy upon me, and pardon the multitude of my offences . . . Support me, by thy Holy Spirit, in the days of weakness, and at the hour of death; and receive me, at my death, to ever lasting happiness, for the sake of Jesus Christ. Amen.

Boswell avers that this prayer was 'uttered fervently'.

"Were it not for the theme of death in *The Life of Samuel Johnson,* we would have but a chronicle of an extraordinary 18th century man, surfeited with accounts of gossipy London tea parties and clever rejoinders. But, to use a musical metaphor here, by sustaining as a counterpoint throughout his masterpiece the death theme and sounding it *pianissimo* at the end, Boswell has given us an epic, and to Samuel Johnson, its hero, immortality."

I doubt if I could have said more. My tongue was just about stuck to the roof of my mouth and I was trembling. I averted eye contact with anyone around the table and awaited Irma to ask a question or to make a comment as was her practice to do so following an oral presentation. But there was only silence in the room. I nervously neatened my pages of notes and returned them to my clipboard, still waiting for Irma to say something.

Finally, I looked across the table at her. She had taken off her glasses and was knuckling her eyes. "What in hell?" I thought.

Embarrassment shot through me. Then, as in slow motion, her hands came together. Clap . . . clap . . . clap. The eminent Dr. Lustig was applauding! And then my colleagues joined in!

EN ROUTE BACK to Harnwell House to collect Pauline and onward to pick up Fran and drive to Fairmount Park for our last field trip – a picnic - I sat beside Ben Franklin, whose bronzed face would forever hold its impish smile.

"Hey, Ben. I have to ask you something. You were a contemporary of Samuel Johnson, right? Did you ever get to meet him?"

OUR BELONGINGS TUCKED into the car and our room key returned to the office of Harnwell House, we drove off campus onto Walnut Street into Center City and up the ramp onto Route 30. We were going home. This time I knew the way.

"That was a lot of fun, wasn't it?" Pauline yawned, needing another cup of coffee.

"Yeah, a lot of fun. I can hardly wait to tell Mary Beth all about it . . . That is if I can remember."

Wah-kohn-ton-kak! The dirt devils come to give you peace.

FORT ROBINSON

ON HANDS AND knees I unzippered the door of our dome tent and looked about, swearing that I had heard footsteps. If there were a stalker on the prowl, I would see him, for he had no where to hide – no bush or tree or gully. Moreover, a full moon's light illumned every detail of the prairie. Way off in the vast emptiness the wail of coyotes broke the silence. Not wanting to rouse Pauline, who softly snored in her sleeping bag, I did not call out, "Who's there?"

It would be a week before the Nebraska Game and Park Commission's people, the overseers of Fort Robinson and its adjacent campground, officially opened for the summer; therefore, we may have been quite alone in this 22,000 acre state park. Had I called out, "Who's there?", no one would have answered.

Yesterday we had broken camp at sunup in a prairie hamlet named Raymond just outside of Lincoln, where we had been staying for five days while visiting Fran Reinehr, who, upon learning of our plan to see Mt. Rushmore and the Badlands, suggested that we pitch tent at the state park since it was close to South Dakota. To get there from Raymond required a nine-hour drive through the Sandhills, a landscape of undulating dunes protected from erosion by a covering of mixed grasses that stretches to the horizon, unbroken by buildings or highways. "What the ocean is to you," a guest at Fran's 65th birthday party said to me, "the Sandhills are to us Nebraskans."

Between naps on the long drive Pauline read the brochures that Fran had passed on to us. From time to time she read aloud to acquaint me with the area.

"Listen to this, Hon. *The Nebraska Sandhills, which compose approximately 19,300 square miles of sand dunes stretching across Nebraska, contain 12.75 million acres of range land. With dunes that are as high as 400 feet, as long as 20 miles, and slopes as steep as 25%, the Sandhills are the largest sand dune region in the world.*

"Wow, that's impressive! Now, get this: *Highway 2 has been called one of the ten most scenic drives in the country. It's one of those places that everyone should see at least once.* Did you know that?"

"No. In fact, I know next to nothing about Nebraska. Did I tell you about bumping into Randy Smith at the library the day before we left to go on this trip? When I said where we would be heading, he laughed. 'Who in hell wants to go to Nebraska? There's nothing there!' That's exactly what he said. But here you are reading this amazing stuff. How about that!"

We drove into the campground of Fort Robinson after dark. Because it was deserted, we had our pick of where to set up camp. The car's headlights enabled us to see what we were doing as we emptied the car of our gear and staked the tent to the ground. After we had eaten the rest of a picnic that Fran had packed for us, we stayed at the table and read with the aid of a propane lantern.

"Here's something interesting, Hon. I'm reading about Chief Crazy Horse. There's so much history about this place! It says here that Crazy Horse was chief of the Oglala Lakotas. Did I say that right? Anyway, and I'm quoting, *He surrendered in May 1877 and, as he resisted imprisonment at Fort Robinson, a guard fatally stabbed him in the back with a bayonet.* Did you know that?"

"No. I told you, I know next to nothing about the history of where we are. So, this Indian guy was killed here. Read on. Tell me more."

"Well, he was only 37 when he was killed. And . . . and, let's see, he defeated Custer in the battle of Little Horn. Oh, there's a bunch of things about him. What else would you like to know?"

"What else is there to know? How savage was he? How many white men did he scalp? I'm sorry. I've seen too many Westerns, I guess."

"What I'm reading makes me think Crazy Horse was anything but a savage. Like, for example, when his wife died and then his three-year-old daughter he fell into deep mourning. Once he went off alone into the Black Hills and had a vision. It sounds like he was something like a mystic."

At that I turned away from the crossword puzzle I was working on. Curiosity was setting in, and I asked if the brochure gave any information about his vision.

"Yes, it does. Here's what crazy Horse's cousin named Black Elk said about it and I quote:

Crazy Horse dreamed and went into the world where there is nothing but the spirits of all things. That is the real world that is behind this one, and everything we see here is something like a shadow from that world."

"Sounds like the Chief was a weirdo, doesn't it? Is there more?"

"Just this, and then it ends. Again I quote:

Crazy Horse was known to have a personality characterized by aloofness, shyness, and aloneness. He was a queer man and would go about the village without noticing people or saying anything. All the Lakotas liked to dance and sing, but he never joined a dance, and nobody ever heard him sing. But everybody liked him, and they would do anything he wanted."

I STOOD BY the tent, barefoot, and winced. The coarse prairie grass bit into my skin. The full moon was lowering in the western sky, and behind me light of new day, our first morning at Fort Robinson, limned the Red Cloud Buttes across the way. Maybe, I thought, it wasn't footsteps that aroused me in the middle of the night. Maybe, in my sleep, I had entered Crazy Hose's "real world". I shivered, although the May morning was mild and no breeze blew across the high plains.

INTERSTATE 90 IS the usual route taken by visitors to the Badlands. But we crossed into South Dakota from the south, necessitating a drive through the Pine Ridge Reservation, home to an estimated 25,000 Sioux. I did not realize, however, that we were in Indian territory (my road map omitted that information).

We had had a meager breakfast at the campground – Saltines and peanut butter and over ripe bananas – intending to stop at a diner for bacon and eggs and coffee. But an hour or so into the drive we were getting deeper and deeper into a vast emptiness. It was only the two of us. Dusty dunes, sun-parched grass, and an infinite cloudless sky.

"Hey, Love, look! Up ahead I see a house! Civilization at last."

Ten or so houses hugged the west side of the two-lane road like a child's play village in a sand box. As we drove past them, we saw that they wee actually hovels. Their clapboards, long without paint, had taken on a mournful gray patina. Blistering sand storms and blinding blizzards had done their job. Cardboard squares replaced missing window panes. Cars without wheels rusted in yards. Young men, smoking cigarettes, loitered on a porch that tilted precariously. One of them pissed through the railing. A half-naked, barefoot lad shyly waved at us.

Just beyond the last hovel on the opposite side of the road a crudely hand-painted plywood sign nailed to a cottonwood tree read WOUNDED KNEE. I hit the brake. Two teens – a boy and a girl – sat at an aluminum kitchcn table to the side of the sign.

"You're not stopping, are you?"

"Why not? Let's see what those kids are selling."

Pauline did not have to tell me why there was fright in her voice. I steered off the road onto prairie grass and stopped parallel to the table. She stayed put with the windows rolled up and kept watch as I approached the table. The two kids stood and rearranged the items for sale.

"My name's 'Harry', and yours?"

"Mine's 'Joshua Strong Wind,'" said the boy.

"Mine's 'Anna Belle Singing Bird,'" said the girl.

That introduction began a conversation that bested any lecture given by the most learned Native American scholar. Eager to talk about Wounded Knee, Singing Bird and Strong Wind took turns recounting tales of Sioux lore passed on to them by their elders, I presumed. They talked of the Ghost Dance and Wovoka, of Chief Sitting Bull and Crazy Horse, of the massacre of 1890 when the 7th Cavalry shot to death 350 Sioux men, women, and children.

A woman who had seen the coming and going of many moons and who was standing some distance from the table, peering at the nothingness of the prairie, sidled up behind the kids and gave me a once-over. She was unmistakably a Lakota: her skin, as eroded as the stone of the Red Cloud Buttes and as dark as their color, stretched tautly over her high cheek bones, and her eyes, as black as crow feathers, hinted at having seen a lot of suffering. A breeze from the west ruffled her ankle-length yellow dress, yet could not undo her graying hair that she knotted into a tight bun.

"Have my grandchildren not shown you these?" She pointed to the items on the table. "All are authentic Lakota, made by the women and children of Wounded Knee. Young people are all talk, forgetting what must be done to carry on. Singing Bird, though, made this basket."

"I'll get my wife. She does the shopping in this family."

Before going to the car, I looked around to make sure those big guys had stayed put.

I stood next to the old woman and watched Pauline hold up to the sun a beaded necklace. She was not conscious of how incongruous she looked: brand new Levi jeans, a University of Nebraska t-shirt that Fran had given her, skin as white as the cumulus clouds gathering on the horizon, and strands of ash-blond hair lifting in the breeze.

"Your woman is beautiful."

"I was thinking that of you. What is your name?"

"I am 'Black Shawl', a very proud name to my people. That was the name of Crazy Horse's wife."

What luck, I thought. This woman is willing to talk. I had much to learn about Wounded Knee. After going over the stories of the Sioux wars, she went on to tell of the ensuing fate of her tribe.

"When the United States government confined us to the Pine Ridge Reservation, it did more than that to us. It took away our way of life and our spirit. What you see is useless land. Crops cannot grow on it. Cows and sheep cannot graze on it.

"The reservation is very big. It goes from here all the way to Sioux City, but only a year ago a small hospital was built. It's the only medical place a Sioux can go. Many of us die young. With no jobs here, people are very poor. Men mostly go into Nebraska to spend most of the money the government gives them to buy beer.

"When I was very young, the government brought doctors from Germany after the war to sterilize girls because the Sioux population was growing. My mother sent me to live with her sister off the reservation until the doctors went away."

Pauline called to me. "What do you think of this, Hon? Singing Bird made it herself."

The girl was helping her with the clasp of a beaded necklace.

"Very nice, very nice. The blue beads match your eyes."

"What's Strong Wind wrapping?"

The boy held up a leather strap with "Wounded Knee" burned into it. "A bookmark. After school I make them."

"I bought one for each of our grandkids. A perfect souvenir, don't you think?"

Black Shawl came to the table. "I do my share, too. This I made. It's a dream catcher. See these threads inside the hoop? Lakota children believe bad dreams get caught in them and only good ones enter their minds. When I'm making a dream catcher, I think someday all my people will be free of bad thoughts."

Pauline gushed, "I'm buying one of those!"

The sun was at its zenith, and there was no way to escape its blaze on the open prairie, but Black Shawl and her grandkids had no intention to close up shop. But we had to move on.

"Okay, Love, let's skedaddle."

Pauline hugged her purchases to her breast and smiled a farewell. I nodded to Black Shawl and left unsaid my shame for having lived so long in ignorance of the tragedies of the Great Plains. We took three steps toward our car, but Singing Bird's shriek stopped us.

"Haho, Unci! Yumni! Omakiya-yo!"

Everyone gaped at where the girl was pointing. A brown-gray funnel of sand, about ten or so feet tall, whirled up and down the grassy dunes, coming at us with great speed. A smaller funnel joined it, and the pair do-si-dosed, veering off to the north and vanishing.

"Wah-kohn-ton-kah, Singing Bird," whispered the old woman

"What was that all about?" I asked her.

"When trouble comes, we speak our language. Singing Bird was frightened by the Dirt Devil. But when I saw two and how they danced together, I told her they are good spirits. You and your woman are good people and I think the Dirt Devils came to give you peace."

In the rear-view mirror I saw through the dust stirred up by our tires Strong Wind and Singing Bird fussing with the unsold items on the table and Black Shawl counting dollar bills. A dream catcher dangled from the mirror.

All the way to the Badlands, we had the narrow road to ourselves. The feeling of experiencing something preternatural intensified as we mingled with a few other off-season visitors who had come to view this 244,000 acre National Park.

"My God, this is unreal!" I had to gasp.

We had entered a land of disintegration. What once had been a range of buttes, eons of tempests had mutilated them, eating away grass and scrub pines and whatever else had clothed them. Their remains – monolithic stubs of stone – grimaced like teeth in a skull.

Yet to get to Mount Rushmore as we had planned to do, after three hours of rambling in the utter silence of this ruined landscape we circled back to our car.

"That was like a walk through the valley of death, Love. Ain't we having fun?"

OTHER THAN A few security lights in the eaves of the old cavalry barracks and headquarters building now rental lodging for summer's tourists, Fort Robinson was in darkness. I aimed a flashlight here and there in search for firewood. None. In the Sandhills a cowboy will not find as much as a handful of twigs for a camp fire. I did find, however, a stone marker surrounded by fist-sized rocks embedded in mortar. Focusing the beam on the marker, I read the chiseled inscription:

ON THIS SPOT
CRAZY HORSE
OGALALA CHIEF
WAS KILLED
SEPT. 5, 1877

I had no need of a flashlight on my walk back to the campground, for the full moon had popped up out of the prairie. Its half-light transformed the scene into a surrealistic setting. My mood was funereal. All day I had been steeped in the lingo of a hangman: *massacre, bad this* and *bad that*, the hills were *black* and even the old wounded Knee Sioux woman had *black* in her name.

A chill rode on a breeze that fluttered a brochure that Pauline held close to the Coleman lantern. She had pulled on a sweater over her University of Nebraska t-shirt.

"Sorry, Love, there was no firewood to be found."

"That's odd. Remember the old John Wayne movies? He and is pals always made coffee over a campfire out there in the prairie.'

"Aw, the movies never did get things right. It's all make believe. Anyway, what are you reading?"

"Something I picked up at the Crazy Horse museum or whatever they call the place. You know, where his statue is being made. It says here that when finished it'll be the largest one in the world. Get this. It'll measure 563 feet from top to bottom. Incredible!"

"Funny you should mention that. Just now I stood on the very spot where Crazy Horse was killed. You know something? Honest to God this guy is beginning to haunt me!"

Her elbow was on another brochure, one that she had collected at Mount Rushmore. On its cover was a photograph of the four Presidents: Washington, Jefferson, Lincoln and Teddy Roosevelt.

"I just thought of something ironic, Love. Just down the road from Mount Rushmore is where Crazy Horse's statue is being built."

"So?"

"Think about it for a minute. Two monuments in close proximity to each other. Historically, though, the men they memorialize were enemies."

A coyote's cry, coming from the shadows of the Red Cloud buttes, stopped me.

"Ooo . . . that's eerie, isn't it? Well, anyway, go on. You're talking about the statues, the monuments . . . whatever. I still don't get what you mean about irony."

"Ah, forget it. I think too much, and besides, I'm too tired to think straight. Let's douse the lantern and get some sleep, okay? I want to pack up early tomorrow and get away from here. My plan is to be in Minnesota before dark."

I FELT FOOLISH sitting in the car at one-thirty in the morning, shivering even though sweat had dampened my t-shirt. A stiff breeze was assaulting Fort Robinson with impunity. It wasn't the flapping of the tent that had awakened me. Rather, it was a damn awful, loony dream. I was running through dunes, struggling to keep up with a stick figure of a man. A dirt devil pursued us. I tripped and tumbled into a gully, and the stick figure stopped and came to me and covered my body with his. His eyes were dilated, frenzied. A swash of yellow and white paint zigzagged down his cheeks. Then the dirt devil morphed into the figure of a man wearing the blue uniform of a cavalryman who resembled Teddy Roosevelt. He smirked as he aimed a long gun at us.

To drown out the lugubrious wailing of coyotes, I pulled in a Sioux City country western station on the car radio. Tammy Wynette was midway in the singing of her signature song:

Stand by your man,
And show the world you love him
Keep giving all the love you can
Stand by your man.

Pauline crawled from the tent, stood, and looked about. She heard the radio and came to the car.

"Are you all right?"

"I had a bad dream and needed some fresh air, that's all."

"Well, come on back. It's chilly out here. Why don't you bring that with you?"

She pointed to the dream catcher dangling from the rear view mirror.

"I will. It may work."

By the shore of Gitchee Gumee/By the shining Big-Sea-Water.

ONTONAGON

WE HAD AGREED to meet half-way, Paul and I and our wives. I had left it up to him to choose where, expecting it to be in the vicinity of Buffalo because that seemed to be about midway between Harmony, Rhode Island, and Lincoln, Nebraska. Moreover, we could zip right along on interstate highways. But his letter revealed that his reckoning and mine were at odds:

April 8, 2009

Dear Harry,

    I've made reservations at Peterson's cabins for the 5th and 6th of August. The price is the most reasonable I could find in the area. I'm enclosing a brochure of the place that includes directions to Ontonagon, which is in Michigan's Upper Peninsular.

    Fran and I are eager to see Pauline and you after too long a time. Wishing you a safe drive.

Ontonagon? To say the least, I was shocked. Not only had I never heard of it but also its pronunciation baffled me. What I did know, however, was that I did not want to drive to Ontonagon.

Several days passed before I wrote back to Paul, wanting to mull this over. On the one hand, a 1500 mile drive to a remote outpost in the wilderness of the UP did not set well with me. On the other hand, I did not want to offend Paul. But I longed to see Fran, whose health has been failing since our visiting her in Lincoln three years ago.

While sitting on this dilemma, I learned that our fifteen-year-old grandson, Matthew, was almost flunking algebra and had acquired a dislike for math. I telephoned his home. Rachel, his mother, answered. I rattled on about meeting friends in Ontonagon in August and caught her by surprise when I asked for her permission to let Matthew come with us, that is if he cottoned to spending eleven days with old people.

"He's having trouble with math, I hear. Well, I have an idea that might help him."

"You lose me, Dad. How can a trip to – what's the name of where you're going?"

"'Ontonagon'. I think that's how it's pronounced."

"Anyway, how can a trip to there help him with math?"

"He'll be my navigator, you see, and will have to calculate time and distance. And I'll have him keep account of every cent we spend. What do you think?"

"I'm for anything that'll work. Sure, it's okay with me if he goes with Mom and you. But first you'll have to see if he wants to go."

He did. By my watch, the time we backed out of Matthew's driveway Friday morning, August 4th, was eight o'clock.

"Here we go, kid!" I shouted. "Note the time. In nineteen hours driving time we'll be in Ontonagon."

ROAD CONSTRUCTION HALTED us at center span of the Mackinac Bridge, affording Matthew a chance to gawk at two of the HOMES: to the right was Lake Huron and to the left Lake Michigan.

"This is really cool, Grandpa. Wow!"

"Okay, okay . . . It's really cool, but you're not off duty yet. When we're off this bridge, we have to head left. Am I right, Matthew? Check the map and tell me what route we have to take to get to Manistique.

On the double because we're moving!"

A woman in a white hard hat and yellow vest waved us past a work crew, and we were off the bridge and over the threshold into the UP. Ahead, spanning the highway, was a large green traffic sign, its white letters reading SAULT STE. MARIE↑ and MANISTIQUE←.

"Go left, Grandpa. Manistick is that way. Take route 2."

"'Manis-*teek*, Matthew."

"Whatever, but that's the way to go."

"You read the sign?"

"No . . . I found it on the map before I even saw the sign."

Pauline nudged me and smiled. She knew of my plan to boost his confidence in solving math problems. Thus far into the trip he had been alert and had been keeping meticulous records as I had instructed. At the outset, before backing my Saturn out of his driveway, I asked him to examine the contents of the black computer carrying case that I had handed him.

"You are my navigator, Matthew and accountant. In this case are the tools of the trade: maps, ledger, pens, a calculator. Let's call it your 'office', okay? Henceforth your job is to record in the ledger every cent we spend and to keep track on the maps exactly where we are at all times. Comprendez?"

So far so good.

Route 2 hugged the northern shore of Lake Michigan, close enough to catch sight of vacationers splashing in its water.

"How about that, Matthew? The lake looks like the ocean, doesn't it? But can you tell me what's different about it?"

"No big waves."

"Sure, but what else? The smell. It doesn't have the salty smell like Sand Hill Cove back home."

To pique his imagination I recounted the legend of Paul Bunyon and his pet blue ox, Babe.

"The story goes that Paul Bunyon's foot prints had sunk into the land during spring thaw and that's what created the Great Lakes."

When no response came from the back seat, I asked Matthew if he were taking a nap.

"I'm awake, Grandpa. I'm figuring how far we are from Ontonagon"

"Good show, kid! So tell me, how far is it?"

"Wait a minute . . . ah, about 270 miles."

"Really? That far? Okay, now tell me this. We're doing fifty-miles-per-hour. At that speed, what time should we be in Ontonagon?"

"I would say . . . close to six o'clock."

"Is that Central Time?"

"Oops, I forgot the time difference. So, make that five o'clock."

Again Pauline nudged me. My plan seemed to be working.

"Whoa, see that sign ahead? ENTERING THE HIAWATHA NATIONAL FOREST. How about that! Matthew, did you read Longfellow's poem, *Song of Hiawatha*?"

"Never heard of it."

"Honest? Too bad. In seventh grade my English teacher had the class memorize the first twenty or so lines of it. I think I still remember them. Want to hear?

> *By the shore of Gitchee Gumee,*
> *By the shining Big-Sea-Water,*
> *At the doorway of his wigwam,*
> *In the pleasant Summer morning,*
> *Hiawatha stood and waited . . .*

Da dah and so forth. Gee, Love, I surprise myself!"

As ever, on our drives Pauline was my silent partner. When she did speak, it was usually to ask to stop.

"We've been on the road since having breakfast at the motel in Bay City, and it's going on noon. I bet you're hungry, Matthew. I am. Have you seen all the signs advertising pasties? They seem to be popular here. Let's try one for lunch, okay?"

ALTHOUGH THE WALL clock in the office of Peterson's Cottages showed the time to be 5:32, the sun blazed above the pines and birches. We would learn that in these parts summer's sunsets came late. Checking in turned out to be more than signing a form and getting a key. The proprietor – Luke Peterson – did all but ask me what shoe size I wore.

"Remember," he repeated, "folks here come to get away from noise. So, no fussin' about after ten. Here's the key to 'Gitchee Gumee' – that's the third cabin down. Park your car on the side so's you're not blockin' the lane."

"I have a question, Mr. Peterson. Have our friends, the Olsons, checked in yet?"

"Olsons, Olsons . . . you must mean the professor from Nebraska. He's kinda short with glasses and is a quiet talker? You can't hardly make out what he's sayin'. Yeah, they're here. Came in about two ours ago. Their cabin's 'Sunset', the one next to yours."

Before getting into the car, I bent at the window and flashed the cabin's key.

"Everything's copasetic, Love. Paul and Fran are already here. So, let's unpack the car and get supper going. Oh, Matthew, your timing was off by a half hour. It's half past five."

"I didn't know we'd be stopping for pasties, Grandpa."

"Your point's taken, Kid. Now, our cabin's the third one down this lane. Mr. Peterson told me there are eight of them and each has a name. Guess the name of ours. Here's a hint. It comes from the Longfellow poem I recited for you. Well?"

"Hiawatha?"

"Nope, but a good guess, Matthew."

Pauline yawned. "We give up. Tell us, and let's get to the cabin."

"'Gitchee Gumee'! Can you believe the coincidence?"

PAUL, MATTHEW, AND I patched together the sparse provisions we had on hand for our late supper as Fran and Pauline chatted on the small deck of the Olson's cottage, named "Sunset". When Paul called the women in for supper and spotted a procession of people carrying lawn chairs, he asked where they were going.

.   "A woman told me they're going to the lake to watch the sun set," Fran answered. "Maybe we should skip eating."

"No, no, dear. Everything's all ready. We'll hurry."

"Oh, Paul, you're a barrel of monkies."

Dinner conversation was puzzlingly constrained, attributable, I guessed, to Paul's fatigue and to Fran's out-of-character reticence. When she did speak, out came strange non sequiturs. I did pick up on, however, that retirement from teaching literature at the University of Nebraska did not suit him nor did hers from teaching grade 4 in Lincoln's schools.

Matthew broke the awkwardness when he sprang to his feet and said, "Grandpa, you're going to miss the sunset! I'll clean up and you go."

"You're a good lad, Matthew. But cleaning can wait. You must come with us."

"Paul's right," Pauline said

We all stood and Fran asked, "Where are we going?"

"To the lake, dear, to watch the sun set. It must be quite a show."

"Don't forget the tickets, Paul."

The five of us strolled to the end of the lane, up an embankment, and on to the shore of Lake Superior. At the edge of the calm water the people we had seen passing by the Olsons' cabin sat in their aluminum chairs taking in a dazzling sunset. At that time of evening, the sun belonged to Ontario, leaving its remnants to the sky over the Keweenaw Peninsula.

"Wow!" Matthew blurted.

Obviously awed, Paul stage-whispered, "God Almighty, what a miracle of colors!"

At that moment I regretted thinking him daffy for choosing Ontonagon for our rendezvous.

On a bench atop a knoll Pauline and Fran sat side by side and Paul examined a piece of petrified driftwood, and Matthew and I stuffed our pockets with multi-colored pebbles. Like gems, hundreds and hundreds of them gleamed at water's edge. I moseyed over to Paul and asked, "Is Fran okay?"

"Ah, you caught on to something, have you?"

"Well, it's pretty obvious she's not her old self. In the first place, never in the twenty years I've known her has she sat at table without a bottle of Bud. On top of that, twice she fumbled with my name. And . . . and her eyes! I don't know how to put it. They see, but they don't see. Am I making sense?"

Evading my question, he pointed down the shoreline toward the western horizon to where the serrated profile of the Porcupine Mountains, made purple by mist and luminous sky, loomed.

"Those are the so-called 'Porkies'. Fran and I plan to take a drive to them tomorrow Want to join us?"

He gave a last look at the driftwood before tossing it into the lake, and, over his shoulder, he coughed up one word: "Alzheimer's". Then he faced me. "Fran's undergoing tests at an Alzheimer's clinic in Omaha."

Luke Peterson kept true to his word about no noise allowed after ten. Pauline and Matthew had hit the sack, and I rocked alone on a wooden glider on the unlit deck of 'Gitchee Gumee', spooked by the incongruity of utter silence, although I was in the midst of the brawn of a vast forest and the world's largest inland sea. Notwithstanding being at this latitude, I was working up a sweat by swatting an invasion of mosquitoes. A light came on in Sunset Cottage and I wondered if maybe Fran had called out to Paul, frightened perhaps by not remembering where she was. I strained to hear voices, but the silence seemed to deepen.

Fran had laughed the laugh that distinguishes someone who for too long had had little to laugh at when, two decades ago, I first met her at Penn where both of us were enrolled in Irma Lustig's Samuel Johnson NEH summer seminar. It was her robust manner and her jolliness that attracted me. But there was a flip side to this persona which came forth at a South Street bistro on the evening of Bastille Day.

After dining on crab cakes, Pauline, Fran, and I got into the festive mood of the college crowd and ran up a hefty bar tab. The Budweisers rendered Fran confessional, and she stammered non-stop the story of her life, beginning with an account of her girlhood – the hard early years of a North Dakota daughter of a German sod-buster who sheltered his family in a sod house and eventually broke from seeing too many crop-killing droughts, sand storms, and brutal blizzards. Then, made foolish and desperate by poverty, she married the first guy who kissed her and followed him to Texas where he abandoned her and their two kids. Alone, she fought the odds, raising her son and daughter and, incredibly, getting a teaching certificate.

Life finally became rosier for her when, hearing of an opening in a humanitarian project headed by a University of Nebraska professor named Dr. Paul Olson, she applied, was accepted, and she and her kids moved to Nebraska. But the sun went behind the clouds again for her: a highway accident killed her beloved brother and cancer did in her son.

The sting and anger that came with learning of Fran's death sentence was numbing me, there on the deck of 'Gitchee Gumee'. Before I had asked aloud to Paul what was booming in my head – "Why did you have me come more than a thousand miles to tell me this?" - he had answered my unspoken question: "Fran insisted on making this trip even though I tried to talk her out of it. She said she must see you and Pauline before . . . you know what I mean."

I knew.

RATHER THAN RIDING with the Olsons to the Porcupine Mountains, we opted instead to drive in the opposite direction to tour an abandoned copper mine. Breakfast in Sunset Cottage, graciously prepared by Paul, had gone well. Apparently the midnight clicking-on of a light did not spoil a good night's sleep, for Fran seemed to be clear-witted. She questioned Matthew about school, scolded me for drinking too much coffee, and helped Pauline to clean up. I smiled when she chided Paul for burning the toast, miscounting the number of place settings, and not finding the dust pan and broom.

"Paul, you're a real absent minded professor!"

En route to the copper mind I asked Matthew what he and the professor had talked about after breakfast.

"The 'professor'?"

"Yup, he's a professor."

"Well, Grandpa, it was like I was back in school. He went on and on telling me things like what's the population of Ontonagon."

"And what is it? I know nothing about the town."

"Gee, now I have to take a test? That's not fair. Like, I didn't take notes or anything."

"I'm not testing you, kid. I'm asking only because I'd like to know. So, tell me. How many people live in Ontonagon?"

"Something like a little more than a thousand, I think he said. What I do remember though is a lot of them came from Finland and they're called 'Yoopers'. Don't ask me why. Gee, the professor sure knows a lot!'

From then on, the two of us, when referring to Paul, used the so-briquet "Professor".

The way to Adventure Mining Company along narrow back roads was well marked. For two hours, with headlamps attached to white hard hats, we explored the stopes of the mine A woman of college age, working her summer job, led the tour, rattling off historical facts and statistics and giving Matthew a lot of fodder to feed the Professor. Seamlessly, she presented her scripted talk as we tourists ducked through adits and sidled along narrow, subterranean passage ways.

"In the 19th century at the height of the copper-mining boom numerous villages sprang up throughout the Keweenaw Peninsula to house the influx of people who came here, especially from Cornwall in England and from Finland. Their mining experience was invaluable. In less than a century, after millions of tons of copper ore had been excavated, the mines were abandoned. This particular one has been retained by the Adventure Mining Company. The State of Michigan has designated it an official Heritage Site and oversees guided tours such as this one. Are there any questions?"

Two days later – a Sunday – after Mass at Holy Family Church and a quick picnic lunch on benches overlooking the lake, I asked Fran, who would not miss going to a Sunday Mass, if she were steady enough on her feet to climb the stairs of Ontonagon's lighthouse. Paul, not a churchman, had opted to stay put and get some reading done.

"I'm not an invalid, Harry. Of course I can climb stairs. Let's go!"

Had she known that the measurement from the ground floor to the lantern room of the Ontonagon light was 39' (or three stories), Fran may not have been so cocky. Moreover, the stairs were steep and narrow. Add to the mix August's warmth, she was in trouble at the 14th step.

"Let me rest a minute," she puffed. "You others go. I'll be okay."

"Pauline, Matthew and you go. I'll stay with her and we'll wait for you outside."

Up they went, following two other tourists and the garrulous guide, Mr. Onni Niemi, and Fran and I sat on a step. She unlaced and re-laced her sneakers, chortling like a school girl to cover up her embarrassment.

"I don't know, Harry. Something's going on with me, and I don't know what it is. Imagine if I were to take my last breath here and now in a lighthouse of all places! Me, a prairie girl!"

She laughed again.

"Remember Virginia Woolf's novel, *To the Lighthouse*? Why in hell do I think of that? Oh, Harry, I'm going crazy!"

"No you're not, Fran. Come on, let's get outside. Ready? Down we go."

She wagged her head and stood. "Uh, uh . . . You forget, I have my mother's Irish blood. I'm climbing these damn steps all the way to the top!"

When we reached the lantern room, the docent was telling his six listeners about the role Ontonagon's port and its beacon had played during the acme of the copper industry. Upon seeing Fran and me, he paused.

"Goody, you made it! I'm about to explain how the ore got from underground to the bulk carriers anchored just over there. I'm warning you, though. It's a grim story."

"Before you begin, sir, may I sit there?" Fran panted.

"You mean on this platform? Of course you may. This is where the light was placed before it was moved to the Historical Society's museum over on River Street after use of the lighthouse was discontinued in 1964. Okay? So let's get to the story.

"Copper miners worked ten-hour shifts for $3.00 a week, drilling and blasting through solid rock to get at the red stuff embedded in it. Then the ore, of course, had to be gotten out of the mine. That was a trammer's job. Once a rock car had been loaded with red ledge, he used brute strength to push the car uphill out of the passageways and onto open ground. And next the ledge went, at first, onto horse-drawn carts and eventually onto trucks and transported to a freighter.

"The life of a miner was fraught with danger. On average, each week one man lost his life by falling down a shaft or by being crushed under a slab of rock. Some even died by suffocating in the noxious dust. Beside this danger, these miners went to work in the dark and went back home in the dark. Imagine! I haven't mentioned the winters in the Upper Peninsula. For half a year this whole region is buried under up to 22 feet of snow!"

Dramatically, Onni went silent and with his fingers combed his full head of grey hair and sighed.

"Now, look out there at the lake. Isn't that picture perfect? Don't be fooled, though. Lake Superior's waters are treacherous. Over the years an estimated 6,000 ships and 25,000 lives have sunk to the bottom. Not all that long ago, in November of 1975, a ferocious storm packing winds of up to 90 miles an hour whipped across the lake and walloped the *Edmund Fitzgerald*. Waves exceeding 35 feet swamped her, the largest Great Lakes freighter ever built. She went down with her 29 member crew just shy of Whitefish Bay. Do you know of the

Canadian singer, Gordon Lightfoot? His ballad, *The Wreck of the Edmund Fitzgerald*, has made this catastrophe famous."

Not until we had returned to our car did anyone speak.

"Ghastly!" Fran murmured. "Don't you think so, David?"

That night en route to the lake for a last look at the sunset Matthew asked me, "Grandpa, why did Fran call me 'David' when we came from the lighthouse?"

"I don't really know. Maybe because she was tired or maybe because she was thinking of someone with that name."

TUCKED BETWEEN OUR visits to the mine and to the lighthouse was the fish supper at a roadhouse at the end of Ontonagon's main street. On our walkabout through the center of the village with Fran and Paul, we had been seeing signs tacked to telephone poles and taped on shop windows: FISH FRY FRIDAY 5:00 TO 7:30 AT PORKIE'S PUB (or SYK'S CAFÉ or ROXEY'S).

"What do you say, Harry?" Paul asked. "Shall we give this fish fry a try tonight?"

"Sure, if Fran is up to it."

"I'm up to it. What about you, Matthew? Every kid likes hamburgers."

Arbitrarily we picked Syk's Café and had to wait until after six o'clock for a table. Middle-aged men and women and some much older far outnumbered the few younger customers. Most of the men held their overalls up with suspenders crisscrossed over flannel shirts, August's warmth notwithstanding. And the women . . . they were not out to impress anyone with new store-bought dresses.

"Are these Yoopers, Grandpa?"

"Could be. Ask the Professor, Matthew."

Paul, glancing about the room with checkerboard curtains at the windows – management's only stab at pleasantry – hushed his answer: "I deduce that they very well may be because – have you noticed – how oddly quiet it is? Finns, as you may or may not know, are not garrulous."

I did notice the quietness, quite odd since every table was full. No TV's, no canned music, no laughter or conversation. Just the clinking of knives and forks and *ssst's* of cans of Pepsi being opened. The Yoopers had come to eat the harvest of their great lake, not to party.

PAUL, MATTHEW, AND I strolled to the lake for a final farewell, but the horizon and the Porkies had vanished in the thickness of an early morning fog. Off in the distance the dolorous voice of a fog horn from the lighthouse and the soft splashing of wavelets coming ashore broke the silence. Matthew, looking like a specter, ran to the edge of the lake and collected more of the colorful pebbles. He was wearing the sweat shirt he had purchased yesterday at the gift shop of the historical society. ONTONAGON was embossed across its front. I waited for Paul to say something. When he did, his voice was frail and seemed out of place in this vast, eerie emptiness.

"It's like this in the Sand Hills before a storm. Extraterrestrial, don't you think?"

"There's nothing in Rhode Island that comes close to this. Look, I'm shivering, yet there's no wind and the air is warm. Why?"

"Exactly! Makes me want to give credibility to the Existentialists."

"Come on, Paul. You can't give in to their notion of Absurdity and Nothingness."

"Lately, I've been on the verge of doing it. It's very difficult for me to watch Fran slip into the void. Well, anyway, let's collect the women folk and head for home."

"Hey, Matthew, we have to go!"

Standing on the moss between "Gitchee Gumee" and "Sunset Cottage", Pauline and Fran looked lost in the fog.

"Are we all set to shove off, Love? Matthew, check to see if your office is in the car and be sure to note the time and the mileage. Oh, one last thing. Would you please return this key to Mr. Peterson?

Thanks. Well, Paul, it looks like it's time for parting." I shook his hand and thanked him for everything, especially for choosing Peterson's Cabins for our reunion.

I waited for Pauline and Fran to break their tearful embrace before giving Fran a farewell hug. Her eyes held a mix of confusion and sadness.

"Fran, my dear, dear friend. Honestly, you're more beautiful than you were back in Philly when we first met. Remember that summer so long, long ago?"

She frowned and lied, "Yes, I do. Well now, are you going somewhere?'

"We're off for home, and so are you. Your beloved prairie awaits you."

"I suppose it has to. Are you keeping someone waiting, too?"

"I don't think so."

"I'm sorry about that, . . ."

She had forgotten my name.

"WHAT ARE YOU doing back there, Matthew?"

"Oh, just some office work, Grandpa. I've figured out we'll be at the motel in Bay City about 5:45 p.m., that's if we don't stop for pasties."

"Too bad it was so foggy when we crossed the bridge. You didn't get to see Lakes Huron and Michigan."

"That's okay. No way can they beat Lake Superior."

"Anyway, kid, I have to say you're doing a fantastic job as my navigator!"

"It's been fun, Grandpa."

"Not like school, right?"

"Right! Except the Professor made me feel like I was in school."

"That's just his way, kid. He can't help it. But I bet you've learned a lot. In fact, more than a whole shelf of books could ever do."

"I don't get what you mean."

"Matthew, you have a good mind and more than that you're sensitive and observant. Years from now, if you remember this journey and go back over everything about it, I'm pretty sure you'll get my meaning. For now, concentrate on what exit off I 75 we have to take to get to Bay City. Comprendez?"

What in hell are you doing here?

D.C.

"HARRY, WOULD YOU take a look at this, please?"

Without a "good morning" or "how are things going?", with two hands she held up a clasped envelope, her eyes showing excitement. Usually Kathy Finnegan, Mansfield High School's assistant principal, at least smiled before getting down to business. I gave the envelope a quick glance and read the return address:

U.S. DEPARTMENT OF EDUCATION
400 MARYLAND AVENUE
WASHINGTON, D.C. 20202

"May I have a minute, Kathy, to catch my breath? I'm coming from the first meeting of the new school year with my AP kids and already I'm pooped."

She followed me into my office, and we sat. I rubbed my eyes, put on my reading glasses, and took the envelope from her.

"This looks official. Are the Feds up to their tricks again?"

"You'll see when you read what's inside."

She lit a Newport and waited. When I looked up, she asked what I thought.

"If you're asking my opinion about nominating our school for a blue ribbon award, I say it's a good idea. But the deadline for submission of application is September 21st. Today's the 8th, which leaves about two weeks to do the paper work. Did you study the instructions?

They want to know everything – description of the town, the curriculum, extra-curricula activities, the school's philosophy, budget breakdown. *Everything*. This can't get done by deadline!"

She crushed her cigarette and paced the small office.

"It'll take some doing, I know. But I think we can do it. It all depends on you, though"

"Me? What are you talking about?"

"I'm pretty sure the faculty will buy into this. My idea is to break teachers down into groups of three and assign each group a specific area according to the list given us in the instructions. They'll have one week to find the information asked for, and then all the data will be passed on to you."

"Why to me? I'm not following you, Kathy."

She lit another Newport and blew the smoke out the open window. With her back to me she said, "Because you're going to write the nomination document."

I was too dumbstruck to respond. She faced me.

"There's nobody else who can do it. Here's my plan. At the end of the day – next Tuesday – I'll make sure you'll have gotten all the information you'll need. Then, we'll get a sub for you and you stay home the rest of the week to do the writing. What do you think, Harry? Will you do it?"

I SAT AT my desk, cleared of everything except a typewriter and a stack of folders, each about two inches thick with pages of data. I had re-read again the U.S. Department of Education's booklet of instructions and understood quite well what I had to do: distill all that information down into a twenty-seven page narrative that is complete, clear, coherent, and cogent. Cogent? How does one make the giving of statistics cogent?

I rolled a blank sheet into the typewriter, leaned back with arms folded, and sat like that until Pauline bade me "good night" with orders not to stay up late. Frustrated and angry at myself for letting

Kathy persuade me to agree to her plan, I attacked the keyboard: %*##!^&&&&&.

Lights out.

Wednesday, the first day of my hiatus from school, I was back at the typewriter before the birds had awakened. Sleep dissipated the fuzz that had clogged thought, and by the light of a new day I proof-read the first paragraph, liking its tone and hoping it would resonate throughout the document:

Three years ago the 12,150 residents of Mansfield, Massachusetts, had to accept the fact that builders of industrial parks, malls, condo-miniums, and trophy houses had big plans for their sleepy, little town. With two Interstate highways running through it, a municipal airport, an Amtrak train station, and acres of open land. Mansfield inevitably would be in the cross hairs of developers. Indeed, they have arrived, and earth movers are quickly altering its complexion.

By sundown I had reached page 9. At that pace, I would finish my writing before deadline. When I returned the stack of file folders and handed Kathy the twenty-seven page nominating document Monday morning, she beamed her glee.

"I knew we could do it! Now we wait. Sometime before Christmas we'll hear from Washington about whether or not we're in the run-ning for the blue ribbon. Thanks, Harry. Now get to your class. The kids have been missing you."

THREE DAYS BEFORE the school closed for the holidays, Ed Russo, the principal, called for a department head meeting. Instead of passing out an agenda to the eight of us, he said that Kathy had an announcement to make. She took a letter from its envelope and read the opening sentences:

Congratulations! Reviewing your nomination proposal, the National School of Distinction selection committee has deemed Mansfield High School eligible for a Blue Ribbon award.

Not one to exhibit emotion, Mr. Russo, waiting for the hand-shaking to stop, reminded us that all was not yet said and done, that another hurdle lay ahead: in April three deputy commissioners would fly up from Washington for a three-day inspection of the school to validate the nomination document. Kathy, on the other hand, could not conceal her joy.

"Come on, Ed, smile! You know you've got a great school. Everything will come up roses."

Her optimism proved to be justified. Five weeks after the Feds had come, snooped, and gone home, an official letter, signed by Lamont Alexander – head of the U.S. Department of Education – reached Mr. Russo's desk. The principal interrupted classes to broadcast over the PA an announcement:

"Word has been received from Washington, D.C., that Mansfield High School has been declared a National School of Distinction. In September, in a ceremony at the White House, President Bush will present the prestigious award to representatives of our school."

PAULINE AND I walked onto the tarmac of Logan Airport on the morning of Saturday, September 24th, and boarded the sixteen-passenger, turbo prop Delta business express plane that would fly us to National Airport in Washington, D.C. Learning that I had been chosen to represent the faculty at the awards ceremony, a colleague had obtained for me two buddy passes from her son-in-law, who is a Delta pilot. They were valid, though, only on weekends. Because, therefore, the four-day schedule of planned events leading up to the White House ceremony began Monday morning, for two days Pauline and I would be on our own.

To find a place to stay for two nights, I searched the AAA Tour Guide for affordable lodging, almost gagging to see the high cost of a hotel room in the D.C. area. Eventually I came upon a Day's Inn listing, advertising the lowest rate by far. An added boon – the motel abutted the National Arboretum. I telephoned for a reservation.

As the plane descended for landing, I nudged Pauline.

"Look at that view, Love!"

There they were – the Washington monument, the capitol build-ing, the Lincoln memorial – gleaming in the sunlight of a perfect September day.

The taxi ride from National to Days Inn, close by the intersection of Bladensburg Road and New York Avenue, NE, not only was quick but also uninteresting – a stretch of urban drab. At the entrance to the motel's office, the driver shifted into park, popped open the trunk, and idled the engine.

"Sorry, folks," he rasped. "You hafta get your bags yourself. I ain't getting out."

I gave Pauline a that's-how-it-goes-here look, and we stepped from the cab. When I passed a twenty through the partially lowered window and said, "Keep the change", the guy asked, "You're sure you got the right address, Buddy?" I nodded and he rolled up the window, and, as soon as I pulled our luggage from the trunk and slammed shut the hood, the cab's wheels squealed. It was back onto New York Avenue, heading south, before we got to the door of the office.

Inside, I filled out a sign-in card. The desk clerk, a good look-ing young black man examined it, looked us over, and handed me a room key.

"To make sure everything stays okay, I'm giving you a room on the second floor. One more thing. Come here."

I went to the big window and looked to where he was pointing.

"See the McDonald's across the avenue? Well, listen up. Don't go anywhere near there after dark!"

We found room 201. Although the smell of bathroom cleaner cloyed its mugginess, the room was shipshape.

"Help me open the window," Pauline asked. "It's stuck or something."

It wasn't stuck. Metal stops screwed to the frame made sure that it stayed closed permanently.

"Oh, oh. Why are there those bars? I don't want to make you ner-vous or anything, but I've been noticing a lot of red flags."

"What do you mean, Hon?"

"You know, warning signs. The taxi driver, for instance, who wouldn't get out of the cab and his asking if I got the wrong address. And the desk clerk warning us to stay away from the McDonald's. Now, this locked window and those bars."

"So?"

"So, something's not right. But if we hunker down here, we'll be fine. Right next door is a Chinese restaurant. It's only for one day, and first thing Monday morning we'll call for a taxi and meet up with Kathy and Mr. Russo."

BEFORE SETTING FORTH in search of a haberdashery, I clicked the remote until getting the weather channel. I did not want to get caught on the streets of D.C. by a sudden cloud burst. With a slight southern accent, the cute announcer assured her viewers that this, the last Sunday of September, would be warm and dry.

"Are you ready, Love? Don't take your pocketbook with you, just in case."

"We really shouldn't be doing this."

"I know, I know. Look, maybe you should stay put."

"No way am I staying here by myself."

"Well, if you say so. But I have to do this! I can't spend a week here without underwear – what with meeting the President and all. And there won't be time to go shopping when we meet up with the others. It's now or never, so let's go!"

"I can't believe I put your things back in the dresser. That was very, very dumb."

"We went through all this last night. So forget it. Are you ready?"

With the sun to our backs, we crossed New York Avenue and strayed into a shaded neighborhood, its small bungalows and tiny front lawns flanking the street. My plan – to ask someone for directions to a shopping center – overlooked the unlikelihood of meeting no one. Twenty minutes into our walk and we did not see a man, woman, or child. Nor had any kind of vehicle come along. Nothing but an eerie silence.

"This is weird, Love. Here we are in the capitol of America and the street's deserted. Maybe I was right in thinking the bad guys would still be in bed, sleeping off last night's partying."

From an overpass that spanned the mainline Boston-to-Washington railroad tracks, we saw the great dome of the national capitol.

"What bizarre irony," I had to say.

I saw movement ahead. A door opened and a smartly dressed young black woman with a Bible in hand stepped into the morning's humidity. She spotted us and froze.

"Good morning," Pauline smiled.

"What in hell are you doing here?" She could not conceal her astonishment.

"We're looking for a store that sells ties. Can you please give us directions?"

"Ties? You're looking for a place that sells ties? Man, you're crazy! Don't you know where you are? Yeah, I can give you directions. But it's down a way on Rhode Island Avenue and no buses run on Sundays. You have to walk. Sweet Jesus, you *are* crazy!"

As we parted in the direction she was pointing, she shouted to our backs, "May God walk with you!"

The city was waking up, at least along Rhode Island Avenue. In quick time we found a haberdashery and came face-to-face with a security guard – a bullish black man in a blue uniform who eyed us suspiciously. I felt his eyes burning into my back as we mingled with other customers – all black. With great relief, I spotted a rack of men's underwear, took six tee shirts and six jockey briefs, and turned to tell Pauline, "Bingo! Now let's get out of here – on the double." But she wasn't behind me.

Before panic set in, I saw her conspicuous blonde hair in the next aisle. She was rummaging through a display of sweat shirts. "What in blazes are you doing?"

She held up a black sweat shirt with WASHINGTON, D.C. emblazoned in white and asked if I liked it. "A souvenir," she said.

"Yeah, yeah . . . but come on! Hubba-hubba!"

My watch showed that the noon hour was nearing, and I figured that the bad guys were getting up and ready for another day of prowling. On the way out I consulted with the hulky security guard, hoping he could tell me a more direct route back to the motel.

"Nope. You hafta go the way you come."

"Can I get a taxi?"

His eyes widened.

"Are you kidding? No taxi comes anywhere near this neighborhood. Mister, you gotta hoof it! I wish you luck."

Not until we came upon a sprawling housing project did I realize that we, mistakenly, had turned off Rhode Island Avenue onto a wrong street.

"We didn't come this way. Shouldn't we better turn back?"

"Too late, Love. We'll lose precious time. I'm pretty sure this street will take us to New York Avenue."

"I don't believe this! Look, the project goes on and on. Where does it end?"

The detritus of poverty was everywhere: discarded mattresses, shards of smashed beer bottles, foul smelling pampers. Often we had to step onto the street to get around trash that piled on the sidewalk. From somewhere within those graffiti-covered brick walls came a rap recording, so loud as to resound in the ominous alley between buildings. I got a whiff of cigarette smoke and scanned the door stoops and windows, searching for a peek at the smoker, and finally meeting the eyes of a shirtless, twenty-something male with a big Afro. Even in the gloom of the alleyway, the look of astonishment on his face was visible. He dropped his cigarette and sagged onto an about-to-collapse lawn chair.

Pauline squeezed my arm and staged-whispered, "Let's walk faster."

"Did you see the look on that kid's face? I bet he's thinking he's still high on dope."

"I don't care about what he's thinking. I'm scared."

We walked on, a bit faster. Ahead, the sidewalk was cleared of people and I heard no footsteps following us. We passed the last of the project's sprawl, rounded a corner, and saw the golden arches of a McDonald's.

"That must be the place the clerk warned me about. So, our motel is just across from it. We're almost home, Love!"

Resting a bit in our motel room before a visit to the National Arboretum, I read the bulky Sunday edition of *The Washington Post*. A full, four-page spread with the headline THE MURDER CAPITOL OF NORTH AMERICA riveted my attention. Worthy of a Pulitzer, it reported the chilling reality of daily life in the very neighborhood that we had naively entered in search for underwear.

Pauline came from the bathroom wearing her new sweat shirt.

"Do you like this, Hon?"

"Ha! In a way, it goes along with what I'm reading. Listen to this. Where we were this morning – are you listening? – an estimated 60,000 ex-cons live. Can you believe – *60,000*! Muggers, drug addicts, what have you! But there's more. Every day lots of people are dropping dead from drug overdose. And . . . and so far this year there have been 479 homicides!"

She turned to the full length mirror screwed to the bathroom door, tugged the cuffs of the sweatshirt, and asked, "When are you going to try on what you bought to see if they fit?"

MONDAY MORNING WE drove off in a cab to rendezvous with Ed and Kathy. I wondered what the driver was thinking as she headed from the ghetto to Georgetown. The lithe young black woman with corn curls had shown no reaction when I told her our destination: the Fairmont Hotel, 24th Street, NW. Curiosity got the best of me when I saw on the ledge of the cab's dashboard a book.

"That book, *The Sociological Imagination*? You're reading it?"

She put it on the passenger seat and answered, "Are you surprised or what?"

"I'm a reader – mostly novels. Seeing a book like that in a taxi of all places . . . well, yes, I'm surprised – and curious."

She half turned and laughed, a laugh tinged with bitterness.

"What you really mean is what's a black gal like me doing with a book like this? Right?"

Traffic picked up on Pennsylvania Avenue. Her skill at weaving through it impressed me. At a red light, she looked at me in the rear-view mirror and said, "For your information, mister, I'm writing a Ph.D. dissertation. Now I bet you're *really* surprised."

Too much was going on on the streets to continue the conversation. At the curbing in front of the Fairmont Hotel, she stopped and hustled to the trunk and had our bags on the sidewalk before we were out of the cab.

"You owe me fourteen bucks, mister."

I gave her a twenty. She shifted her eyes to the crowd dodging each other while hauling their luggage on little wheels from cabs to the hotel.

"The thing about driving a hack, you get to see first hand all kinds of people. Good stuff if you're into sociology. It's none of my business, mister, but I have to ask . . . did you actually spend the night over there on New York Avenue? On second thought, forget I asked you that. From the look of things, you're gonna sleep better tonight. You are lucky. That's more than my cross-town brothers can say."

THE US DEPARTMENT of Education had booked rooms in the Fairmont Hotel for us delegates from the 250 secondary schools that were declared National Schools of Distinction. We out-of-towners brought into the high ceiling, plush carpeted lobby a carnival atmosphere. Behind me in the check-in line, a couple of school superintendents groused about having to queue up. Coming from a room off the lobby and carrying Styrofoam cups of coffee, four middle-aged men babbled like boys on the first day at summer camp. Off to the side beside a rack holding tourist brochures, a suit-and-tie fellow flounced a street map and seemed to be arguing with his companion, a woman who resembled Eleanor Roosevelt.

Pauline's role at the moment was to keep watch for Ed and Kathy. When my turn was next to sign the register, I caught her attention and mouthed, "Are they here?". She gave another look-see at the crowd and shook her head.

"Sir . . . Sir?" The desk clerk forced a smile. "Do you have a room reservation?"

I said I did and filled in the registration form. As he handed me the room's card key after examining the form, he looked up at me and asked, "You are Harry Anderson, from Mansfield High School?"

"That's right."

"I have a note here that says someone wants to meet you. Would you please wait a moment, sir?"

With puzzlement, I watched him scurry away. The man behind me muttered, "What in hell's going on? I've been in this line a good twenty minutes. Wouldn't you think a four star Washington hotel would be more efficient?"

When the clerk returned, with him were three primly dressed women with ID tags looped around their necks. The eldest of the three, the one wearing cat-eyed reading glasses, did the introductions.

"I'm Louise Spindlethrift, under secretary of the Federal DOE, and these are my assistants, Margo and Melanie. Let me shake your hand, Mr. Anderson. There, at last! Ever since reading your nomination document, we've been anxious to meet you. Honest to God, what you wrote is the best by far of the hundreds that came in from all over the country! We just had to tell you that in person. Congratulations!"

The one named Margot blurted, "Tell him what Dr. Schneider said."

"Of course. Dr. Schneider was one of the team that visited your school last spring. Remember? Well, anyway, he had sat in on one of your classes, and apparently you blew him away! He still talks about you. In fact, just the other day he told me about pleading with you after class to reconsider retiring. Is it true what he says that he was crying? Dr. Schneider is not the sort of man to do that."

I knew that I was looking like a fool, standing there speechless and all, and was relieved when Louise Spindlethrift and her assistants dashed off to continue their governmental business.

Glancing about for Pauline, I found her amongst a clutch of new arrivals gesturing to Kathy and Ed and their mates. From all appearances, the week's extravaganza was up and running.

A NASTY SQUALL delayed our return flight to Logan. We bided the wait in a café off the main concourse of National and, snacking on crab cakes, we reviewed our week in Washington.

"I'll never forget the look on Mr. Russo's face when he saw our room. What was the cost per night? Wasn't it something like $359? And we were charged half that. Still, that's a lot of money."

"That wasn't a room, Love. It was a *suite*. Imagine, a telephone in the bathroom! Lucky us, though, that Mansfield picked up the tab."

Pauline flipped the pages of her journal in which she recorded a summary of each day's events.

"We did a lot in five days! Seeing the monuments and the Smithsonian, but the funniest was ending up in a gay restaurant Tuesday night. It was Kathy who caught on when she noticed she and I were the only women in the place. Anyway, what stands out the most for you? I bet I know. Having lunch with President and Barbara Bush and seeing Mr. Russo going up on stage to get the award. Am I right?"

I stirred sugar into my coffee and stared through the rain splattered window and flinched when a flash of lightning zig-zagged over the Potomac. I thought of the cabbie with corn curls who drove us from the ghetto to Georgetown and imagined her in her cab reading *The Sociological Imagination* while waiting to pick up a fare. I thought of the stunned black woman on her way to church, the one who wished that God walked with us and imagined her behind locked doors praying for a safe night. And I thought of the shirtless young man in the alleyway of a sinister project and imagined him, wet to the bone, sloshing down 24th Street, NE, hoping the price of a joint hadn't gone up.

"Hon, you didn't answer me. I asked what you'll be remembering mostly about this trip."

"Do you want the truth?"

"Yes, of course."

"Last Sunday . . . our walk on the wild side."

I want to believe in Camelot.

ST. GENNYS

ONCE UPON A time, for six enchanting days, I roamed the lanes of Camelot. Bobby Masterman, that is, swore to it, and I wanted to believe him. For nowhere else had I felt such ineffable peace, such joy that passeth understanding, such complete harmony with time and place. Here is my story.

Other than snatching a few winks aboard a British Airways overnight flight to Heathrow from Logan, Pauline and I had not slept since leaving home more than twenty-four hours ago. Although quite woozy, we properly had made our way through customs, found the Victoria Coach Station, jostled through the throng of holiday makers, and queued up to purchase tickets to Exeter.

Daylight was fading when we plopped into seats on the coach from Exeter to Bude. Darkness had obscured the paddocks and moors of England's West Country we passed through well before we stepped from the coach onto the deserted street of this town on the coast of the Irish Sea. Our destination still had not been reached. According to directions mailed to me by Mrs. Penhallow, proprietor of the Churchtown self-catering cottages, we had eleven more miles to travel.

Within minutes after I made a phone call from a phone booth, a taxi collected us. Not sure of the pronunciation of "Gennys", I ordered the driver to take us to "St. Jennys". He said he had no idea where that was. Flustered, I tried again, saying, "Churchtown, where there are self-catering cottages."

He looked puzzled. Pauline, her face bloodless from fatigue, poked me and sighed, "Spell the name for him."

"G-e-n-n-y-s. Got it?"

"Bloody right I got it. If you said it right in the first place, we'd be 'alf way there."

"You pronounce it for me."

Sounding the *genn* to rhyme with *again* and the *ys* to rhyme with *hiss*, he pronounced "St. Gennys".

"You're a Yank, aren't you? 'Ave you 'eard of that Irish stout, Guinness? The place you want almost sounds like it. Remember that. Now, get in. I'll 'ave you there in two shakes of a lamb's tail."

He idled the engine, and Pauline and he watched me knock on the door of cottage #2 on Churchtown Lane.

"I'm Harry Anderson, and over there in the taxi is my wife, Pauline," I said to the woman who came to the door. "We've found the right place, I hope? A self-catering cottage owned by Mrs. Penhallow?"

"We've been expecting you," she answered, glancing beyond me. "Mind you, you shouldn't have taken a taxi. It's too costly. Had you telephoned, Bobby and I would've collected you. Well, be that as it may, what matters is you and your wife have arrived, and I imagine you're both done in. I'll get the key and show you what Mrs. Penhallow has booked for you. Oh, my name's Joyce, Joyce Masterman. Bobby, my husband, and I are caretakers of her four cottages. But first things first. You follow me and we'll chat later."

I went back to the taxi and said, "Eureka, we made it!"

The driver yawned and shuffled to the rear of the taxi and took from its boot our knapsacks and two tote bags.

"Pay me ten pounds, Mate, and I'll be off."

He stashed the two five-pound notes I gave him in a shirt pocket and said before driving away, "You Yanks got lucky. We haven't seen those stars since a fortnight ago. Rain, rain, rain everyday. Looks, though, it's gone now. Jolly good, 'taint it?"

I introduced Pauline to Mrs. Masterman, who had come from her cottage with a torch, aiming its beam on the damp cobblestones.

"Come along now, and step carefully. The way's terribly uneven."

Deep darkness obscured whatever stood to our left or right. Without the parabolic beam to follow, Pauline and I surely would have strayed. When the woman's key clicked open the door and she switched on an overhead light, we blinked and then gasped. We had entered an overwhelmingly charming room. Rough hewn beams above, walls of flat, smooth brownish red stones, and a slate floor. Only a table and four stools in an alcove beyond a sink, cooker, and fridge furnished the room.

"'Tis the kitchen. Upstairs are the loo, the lounge, and a bed-room. Before this was made over to accommodate holiday makers, the headmaster stabled his horse here. At one time, you see, there was a parish school on this property. But come see. Mrs. Penhallow has brought in a few provisions to welcome you."

Lined up on a narrow counter were small boxes of tea bags and sugar cubes, a couple of scones wrapped in plastic, a tiny jar of quince jelly, a tin of lemon biscuits, and a bottle of cream sherry.

In deference to the late hour, Joyce Masterman whispered, "I'll be gone now to let you two snuggle in for a good sleep. If you are in need of anything, you know which door to knock on. Nighty-night, loves."

For the first time in many hours, Pauline and I were alone. Standing in the silence of this 16th century room evoked a feeling of déjà vu.

"Oh boy! This is like expecting Silas Marner or . . . or Tom Jones to walk through that door at any moment! Isn't this incredibly great? Are we really here?"

"We're really here, and I'm really tired. Let's go upstairs, okay?"

When I opened my eyes to the morning sun, through the window from the bed I saw the Norman steeple of St. Gennys Church a mere hundred yards away. Pulling on my trousers, I dashed to the other window and viewed verdant paddocks rimmed by hedgerows and grazing sheep here and there. Beyond, on the horizon, Dizard Point – a rugged headland – pointed its brow toward the Irish Sea.

I let the temptation to wake Pauline pass and hurried down to the kitchen, pausing to inspect the lounge and loo. Unlike the kitchen, the lounge had plastered walls and a carpeted floor. Quite cozy. With what Mrs. Penhallow had provided, I scrabbled together a breakfast. Overhead, I heard Pauline's puttering and then the shower's running. As the tea kettle began to rattle on the cooker, Mrs. Masterman tapped at the door.

Apologizing for her early visit, she thought I ought to know that milk delivery was soon and perhaps I might wish to place an order, saying, "Since you have no auto and the nearest purveyor is four miles away, I should give you this." The order form she handed me listed everything we would want: eggs, milk, butter, meats, vegetables, bakery goods.

"Mr. Thorngate will leave what you've circled this morning. Mind you, he'll come around again Tuesday. You can put your payment in the box outside by the door."

I had not noticed the previous evening how badly Mrs. Masterman limped. My eyes followed her as she hobbled up the cobbled path, and I regretted her painful start of a new day, feeling duty-bound to tell me about the milkman. Already I was warming to this woman who seemed to be at least ten years my senior.

Fully awake and fortified with scones, jelly, and tea, Pauline and I walked out into a dazzle of blue sky and Cornish lore. We rambled up the lane past the church and past the other cottages – sturdy, quaint structures made of brownish red flat stones indigenous to the West Country. To get over the hedgerow that separated the lane from the paddocks beyond, we climbed a stile and stopped. Ahead, the land rose steeply and between us and the horizon wildflowers grew, untouched by sheep, forming a palette of many colors.

We walked on, side-stepping foxgloves and butterworsts, Queen Anne's lace and bluebells. So steep was the incline that whatever lay below could not be seen. Knowing that we were heading west toward the Irish Sea, I feared that we might come to the rim of a precipice and tumble over. We changed direction to walk parallel with the horizon and came to where the paddock sloped downward, to where the vista below stunned us to a halt.

For a long time we reclined in the tussocks of cotton grass and gaped at Crackington Haven, an inlet of the sea, flanked by crags and paddocks and so far below us that we could not hear the breaking surf of an in-coming tide. The only sound came from a shiftless breeze and a plaintive baaing of a lamb looking for its mother.

"Close your eyes, Love. Good. Now, imagine yourself back home and driving in thick traffic, say like in Warwick past the malls. Smell the diesel? Okay? Ready? Now, open your eyes and look."

"Oh, my God!"

THE SUN COULD not warm the nave of St. Gennys church. Erected about 1215 A.D., its stone walls and vaunted, timbered ceiling retained centuries of the cold of wintry weather coming down from the North Sea over the mouth of the Bristol Channel and into Cornwall all the way to Lands End. We shivered in the pew, awaiting the start of the Sabbath service.

Too few worshipers to have a permanent rector, the parish faithful made do with itinerant retired priests. The one who conducted that day's service fit the paradigmatic figure of an Anglican prelate seen in the novels of Dickens and Thackeray. His diction befitted that of an Oxford don, and his homily – perhaps repeatedly delivered from parish to parish – was too arcane to be understood by the sun-burned shepherds and their wives of north Cornwall.

In the vestibule, as the final measures of the postlude echoed in the emptying church, Mrs. Masterman gave us a cheery good morning and introduced us to her husband, who could have been a stand-in for Alec Guinness.

"Never mind the 'Mister Masterman', dear." Turning to us he added, "Unless you call me 'Bobby', I won't have the slightest idea to whom you're speaking."

"As for that," she smiled, "you have my permission to address me as 'Joyce'. We spotted you two strolling by yesterday. Is our little corner of the world to your liking?"

"No words can describe its beauty!" Pauline answered.

"And your accommodations?"

"What Joyce means," Bobby interrupted, "does your water closet flush and the telly . . . does it flutter like it often does?"

"Bobby hasn't always been so cheeky. He gets worse with each passing day."

We stepped into the lane and he asked if we liked tea.

"Bobby's inquiring because we would very much enjoy your coming to our cottage this afternoon for tea."

Although I knew the answer, nevertheless I asked the time we would be expected.

"Would four o'clock be fine?"

Pauline and I tarried in the churchyard, absorbing its antiquity. Most of the grave markings had been obliterated by storms and lichen. Celtic crosses graced the buried bones of the ancient folks who had sailed the sea to Christianize this land of moors and myths. We tarried until three and then ambled to our rooms to prepare for a tea party.

Joyce welcomed us at the door of #2 Churchtown Lane and led us to the lounge where Bobby sat with an atlas opened on his lap.

"Come," he said, "and show me where your home is."

I bent to a map of North America and pointed to Rhode Island. His insistence to tell him the history of the state got me to talk about the Wampanoags and King Philip's War. I paused in my accounting of Roger Williams when Joyce limped into the lounge, carrying a tray laden with a tea service. Pauline scolded her for not asking for help.

"Help? Of course not, Love. You are our guests and this is the proper way to go about business at hand, bad knee or not. Now, you sit down. I'm going for the cake."

"I'm a devotee of history," Bobby said, paying no heed to the 'business at hand'. "That's the principal reason why I came to Cornwall after my redundancy in Leeds. You see, since boyhood I've had a keen interest in King Arthur. You may or may not know that Camelot is hereabouts. It's bothersome to me that most think Arthur and his roundtable of knights is folderol, mere fanciful tales made up by old story-tellers. Tut, I say! They may call me daft, but I swear Camelot is real!"

Joyce poured the tea and sliced a white layer cake with lemon icing, reprimanding Bobby. "Enough of your fairy tales. Our guests may not give a tinker's damn for Arthur and his knights."

I contradicted her. "To the contrary, Joyce. I've read Malory's *Morte d'Arthur* and I want to believe in Camelot."

Stirring a sugar cube in his cup of tea, Bobby grinned. "Well, well, well. 'Tis good fortune that's brought you here! Before this week's out, I'll show you the very spot where Camelot once proudly shined. What do you say about that, Dear?"

"You have a bit of icing on your cheek, Bobby. Do be less excited and like a gentleman take your tea."

"Yes, indeed, we'll go to Camelot! Tomorrow? Shall we go tomorrow?"

I WAS HAPPY not to be driving the narrow roads of Cornwall, especially after learning from Joyce that the hedgerows flanking them are stonewalls disguised by burdock, knapweed, and spear thistle. The Mastermans lost a son whose car veered into a hedge. Joyce was a careful driver. A jack rabbit could have out-run the vintage, two-door Opel. Her bad knee notwithstanding, she worked the clutch pedal with agility.

When the distinctive Norman tower of a church loomed ahead, Bobby announced that he would take us on a look around of St. Juliot.

"We'll avoid the rest of Bocastle," he said. "It's become too twee. Brings in holiday-makers, though. But the church you must see."

The Opel was the only car in the car park of the ancient church, built about the same time as St. Gennys. Their architecture inside and out was similar: brownish red flat stones, vaulted ceiling, narrow, stained glass windows – their interior dark and cool. Bobby rubbed the rim of the baptismal font, its stone bowl made ovoid by centuries of use.

"When Thomas Hardy courted his wife-to-be, Emma, they worshipped here. In fact, at that time he was an architect and had much to do with the reconstruction of this badly deteriorating building. Over there, if you look, is a window dedicated in Hardy's memory."

As we strolled back to the car park, Bobby kept up his commentary, a tone of reverence resonating in his voice: "St. Juliot is nicknamed 'The Cathedral of the Moors', or at least in earlier times that's what the Celts had called it. Quite a bit of history here."

At the Opel, where Joyce was waiting for us, he sang out, "Drive on, Dear, to Camelot!"

To us she said, "He means Tintagel, of course."

"Ah, bosh! Like all those other skeptics, Joyce thinks Camelot's a silly fairy tale. One only has to read Jeffrey Ashe's book to believe. Have you read it, Harry? No? Well, you must."

Our visit to Tintagel circumvented its quay and castle ruins atop a headland overseeing the ocean.

"If this weren't August, I'd have Joyce let us have a peek. Unfortunately, we'd have too much twee to put up with. Look at all those tourists poking about! Were Arthur to see this, his mind would be pudding. We'll make do with a stop at St. Enodoc. 'Tis said to be the oldest Celtic church in Cornwall."

However charming, these old churches did nothing to pique my imagination enough to envision King Arthur. Disappointment rode with me to Reddivallen Farm, where the Mastermans took us for lunch. We sat at a backyard table adjacent to a 17th century converted farm house beneath a canopy of trees and ate a plowman's meal of pasties, biscuits with clotted cream, and tea. Enhancing this bucolic scene were sleeping sheep under a wain to escape the blazing sun.

On the return drive to Churchtown, we came upon a stretch of treeless, flat, empty countryside. A swath of asphalt paralleled the narrow road. Sheep chomped at the grass sprouting from cracks in its surface. Joyce, off-handedly, told us that we were passing by an abandoned air field from which American war planes had taken off on bombing raids over Germany.

She said nothing else. Bobby and Pauline dozed. I said nothing either, keeping to myself my thoughts: bombers and Camelot? Incongruous! A landing strip and ancient churches? Blasphemous! Burdock, knapweed, and spear thistle could camouflage the peril of a hedgerow, but nothing had yet masked this artifact of war.

That evening in the lounge of our booked stable, as Pauline watched a BBC show on the telly, I began to read *The Quest for Arthur's Britain*, the Jeffrey Ashe book that Bobby gave me to keep.

"YOU AMERICANS HAVE brought us good weather," Bobby said. "Haven't they, Dear? Usually, every other day we have to use our bumbershoots."

"Hush, Bobby. I haven't driven this road in ages. I must concentrate. You keep alert as well and tell me where we must turn off."

He tugged at his wrinkled, tweed cap and shook a finger at the windbreak, shouting, "Keep going, keep going!"

The plan for the day was to picnic on Bodmin Moor, a ten-by-ten-mile of desolation noted for dozens of migrating birds, its granite tors, and its legends of murders, ghosts, and a preying black beast. Pauline and I fretted about Joyce's dubious ability to hobble even a short distance through heather and furze, but in deference to the famed "stiff upper lip" stoicism of the Brits, we kept our worry to ourselves.

She had the grit to get from the Opel and ascend a hillock where Bobby had spread a quilt.

"Good show, Love! You would've been given a seat of honor at Arthur's round table."

"Stop your palaver, Bobby, and help me get down on that quilt."

Pauline had patched together a passable bill of fare made up of this and that, left-overs from Mr. Thornberry's last delivery: ham slices on wheat rolls, cheese, peaches, chocolate biscuits, and bottles of apple juice. We ate like trenchermen in the midst of a vast wilderness beneath the bluest of skies.

"Pauline," Joyce sighed, "I believe I'm truly happy."

Bobby pulled his cap lower onto his brow and jumped up, excited by a thought.

"Let's you and I, old chap, go for a ramble and have a look for the Beast of Bodmin Moor!"

The ramble turned out to be an hour's hike that might have been longer had not Bobby reached for another sprig of yellow-flowered gorse and slipping on the verge of a mire. A foot slid ankle-deep into a turbid pool.

"I say! Shall I tell Joyce to blame the Beast?"

Our return to the women could have brought the house down in a vaudeville theatre: Bobby's clutching a bunch of gorse in one hand and a muddied shoe in the other, cursing each time he stubbed a toe on one of the hundreds of granite stones that littered the way, all the while panting a lecture peppered with esoteric allusions to Riothamus, Geoffrey of Monmouth, Utherpendragon, Camlann – inserting now and then deprecations aimed at disbelievers of King Arthur.

The women had cleared the quilt of plates and nappies and worriedly scanned the moor for our return. Joyce's first words to Bobby: "Act your age and put your shoe back on!" He handed her the bouquet of wildflowers, kissed her cheek, and dramatically bowed.

"For you, me lady. To gather them I nearly drowned in a mire. This young Yank saved my life."

With quilt and picnic hamper tucked into the Opel's boot, we squeezed into the car. "Remember, Dear," Bobbie said. "We're to show our guests Dozmary Pool."

On the eastern perimeter of Bodmin Moor, unhidden by hedge or trees, Dozmary Pool's languid water added a dollop of blue to an otherwise dismal landscape. Were it not imbued with Arthurian lore, a traveler more likely than not would pass by without hardly noticing it. Joyce, to give Bobby time to explain the pond's fame, slowed the car to a crawl.

"The king, knowing he was mortally wounded in the battle of

Camlann, ordered his knights to carry him here – the very spot where the Lady of the Lake had presented him with Excalibur. I can almost hear Arthur's dying words."

Like an actor on stage he emoted, "Sir Bedivere, heave my gallant sword into the depths of Dozmary Pool! It must be returned to the Lady of the Lake!"

"Have you finished, Bobby?" she asked and accelerated.

TO SPARE JOYCE from a painful walk downhill from Churchtown to Crackington Haven, Bobby took to the gravel lane in the Opel, the final evening of our Cornish sojourn. Extraordinarily, the succession of fair days continued as did the high temperatures. No one in the gathering of villagers who had come to the shore for a sausage sizzle and a brass band performance carried a sweater for warmth at twilight.

Barefoot children squealed as they romped in the froth of breaking waves, and the hum of adult conversations sounded in counterpoint. The aroma of sizzling bangers over hot coals mixed deliciously with the briny ocean air. The romping and the chatting stopped when the twelve musicians tuned their instruments.

The Mastermans had come to quell Sophie's insistence that they must hear her play the tenor horn (she was their twelve-year-old granddaughter). In the tradition of England's brass bands, the instrumentation consisted of flugel, tenor, and baritone horns, a trombone, euphonium, tuba, and percussion.

Over the music and the clatter of pebbles roiled by the outgoing tide, I shouted into Pauline's ear, "Haven't we given ourselves a perfect anniversary gift? This is absolutely magical!"

I took her hand, and, seeing this, Bobby turned to Joyce and caressed her arm. She gave a wee start and returned her eyes to Sophie, whose cheeks puffed up as she soloed the opening bars of *Over the Rainbow*.

Accepting my invitation to close out the evening with a farewell dink at the nearby Coombe Barton pub – its front porch just a few feet beyond the high water mark – the Mastermans hugged their grand-daughter and the four of us went inside. We took a table at the window that faced the inlet. Pauline ordered a shandy, Joyce a glass of tomato juice. When I ordered a pint of Whitbread ale and Bobby said, "Make it two", Joyce scowled.

"I know your thoughts, Love," he said. "But isn't this a special occasion?"

"If it's so special, Bobby, then remove your cap."

The discomfort that Joyce had taken with her into the pub little by little eased as we reviewed events of the last few days. "Tell me, please, what stands out mostly?"

Joyce's question flummoxed me, but Pauline came forth immediately with her answer. "Our tea party last Sunday when we first talked and, as I keep saying to Harry, we're so lucky to meet you!"

Everyone looked at me, waiting for my answer. Had I had another pint, perhaps I could have sorted out a single moment that I would recount over and over to friends back home. I looked past Bobby, whose back was to the window. A huge reddish sun, smack between the two promontories that hugged Crackington Haven, hovered bare-ly above the line where sky and sea met. I motioned my head toward the window, and Bobby looked. We all looked.

In no rush to make its exit, the sun gallantly, imperceptibly van-ished. To have spoken would have been sacrilegious. I placed my hands on Joyce's and Bobby's and finally whispered, "I see Arthur at Doxmary Pool." Then I said again, "I can answer your question now, Joyce. This very moment I'll cherish. It culminates everything."

The driver stowed our knapsacks and tote bags into the belly of the coach, keeping its motor idling. No other passengers were travel-ing to Exeter this early. On the drive to Bude, only Bobby was up to talking. The topic of his morning lecture concerned the birds indig-enous to Bodmin Moor. Having done with explaining of the nesting, eating, and mating habits of buzzards and wheatears, at the open door of the coach he moved on to the tiny meadow pipets. Pauline and Joyce stood apart, softly chatting.

"It's time we get cracking," the driver called out.

Pauline hugged Joyce, then Bobby. Through tears, she muttered how she hates farewells. With arms around Joyce, I thanked her, feeling at a loss to come up with better words to express my emotion. The morning light glistened her moist eyes. I squeezed Bobby's hand and followed Pauline aboard the coach.

From its window, as the driver pulled away from the curbing where a week ago I had used a telephone to order a taxi for a ride to a place whose name I could not pronounce, we saw the last of the Mastermans. Joyce was limping toward the old Opel and Bobby was tugging his tweed cap lower onto his brow.

When I could speak, I merely said, "There is a Camelot, isn't there, Hon?"

I restore outhouses.

WATERPLACE

WITHIN SIGHT OF the Evans Road schoolhouse – an 1850 (circa) one-room building that the Glocester Heritage Society had had moved to a field in the rear of town hall and had restored – an out-house moldered in Mrs. Ryan's backyard. Acquiescing to her son's insistence that she knock it down, she had another idea and showed up at a monthly meeting of the GHS to inquire if maybe the Society would like to partner it with the schoolhouse.

"My thinking is, what's a one-room schoolhouse without an out-house?" she said. "It's yours if you want it."

I thought she made an excellent point, and so did Tom Samson. The two of us volunteered to look into the matter.

Mrs. Ryan introduced Tom and me to the privy on the morning after Memorial Day. To get to it the three of us had to stomp through a thicket of chokeweed and wild grape vines and zig-zag around junk such as bicycle frames, a rusted push lawn mower, a corroded wash tub, and a headless plastic Santa Claus.

"Obviously, Harry," Tom chortled, "this thing's not been used in a long, long while. But that's good for us, right?"

We stepped aside to let Mrs. Ryan open the door. When it didn't budge, Tom grabbed the rusted latch and tugged the door open, and a long-handled scythe toppled out, bopping him on the head. A squadron of wasps circled their home base in the eave over the door.

"That's enough for me, boys!" Mrs. Ryan shouted. "You do what you have to. I'm getting out of here."

"Boys?" Two old geezers with nothing better to do on a sunny May morning than to gawk at the insides of a decrepit two-holer. We could have been at a wake, for we were viewing a mausoleum of deceased farm tools: the scythe for one and an assortment of shovels and rakes, a hoe and a post digger. A length of garden hose coiled from a nail, and a dented watering can squatted on the lid of one of the holes.

"What do you think, Harry?"

"Well, at least we can say we took a look."

"Did you notice how this baby wobbled when I opened the door? Look, the floor boards are rotted out and those studs look like carpenter ants have got to them. One thing's for sure. If we try to move this, it'll collapse."

"Then let's tell Mrs. Ryan she can keep her outhouse. Thanks anyway."

"Let's first think about it, okay?"

He walked around the building that had outlived its use, tapping its weather-worn clapboards, standing tip-toed to inspect the roof, and kicking its sill. He closed the door and grinned.

"I like a challenge. I think maybe we can save this thing. Want to give it a try?"

I had to think about it. As he again circled the privy, I tossed the scythe onto the bicycle frames and eyed the wasps that were returning to their nest.

Maybe we're nuts, but okay. When do we start?"

"How about tomorrow? Bring some tools, like a hammer and crow bar. Okay?"

WITH JUNE CAME wind gusts out of the Carolinas. Cheerily, the hostess of WCRB's *Classics in the Morning* program gave the day's weather forecast: lots of sunshine with a high of 72°. She was introducing *Rhapsody in Blue* as I pulled into Mrs. Ryan's driveway and parked behind Tom's

Camry. My watch said 9:21, nine minutes before the agreed upon start-ing time. I was wrong to think I would beat the old warrior to the punch.

"About time you showed up," he snickered. "I figured you either forgot or, worse still, you chickened out. Put your hammer and pry bar back. I thought we'd clear the area before doing open heart sur-gery on the shit house."

He heaved an old muffler with a tail pipe still attached onto a growing pile of junk at the top of the driveway and pulled from a pocket in his jeans a pair of work gloves and tossed them to me.

"Catch! I bet you didn't think to bring along gloves."

"Wise guy, eh? Well, I got something I bet you didn't think to bring."

I went to my car, put my tools into the trunk, and returned with an aerosol can of hornet spray and aimed it at the nest.

"Good for you, killer! I did forget."

"Bull's eye!"

"Now, put those gloves on and help me. Quitting time's high noon and, by damn, we're getting this helluva mess cleaned up by then. Let's roll!"

The remains of a sump pump was the last sizeable piece of junk to be thrown into the pile. Mrs. Ryan stepped from the screened-in porch to look things over. I asked if her son had a pickup truck and, if so, maybe he would take the junk to a recycling place and get some money for it. As we talked it over, an engine roared to life.

"I say, look what your friend is up to," she shouted over the noise. "He's a go-getter alright."

Tom had brought a weed whacker and was cutting a swath through the thicket. He idled it and yelled, "Harry, find a rake and get rid of the cans and glass and stuff that was hidden under these weeds."

We worked past noon, determined to finish the job. It had taken almost five hours to give us easy access to the privy. We leaned, sweat-ing, against our cars and, before driving off, looked back to where we had cleared. Now exposed, the outhouse was a sad remnant of yesteryear: precariously tilted, lichen clinging to the curling cedar shingles on its roof, missing clapboards, and mounds of saw dust about its rotting sill.

"How about that, Tom? Who could have thought that a couple of old duffers could have done that?"

"Don't get too smug, old boy. Just look at that poor thing ready to fall down. Maybe we've bitten off more than we can chew."

"We won't know until we try. See you tomorrow – same time, same place?"

"You got it! And don't be late."

Mrs. Ryan limped from her porch, waved to us, and gawked at the outhouse. As I backed out of the driveway, I kept my eyes on her. Like the old privy, she too slightly tilted, and I wondered what memories she might be recalling.

THROUGHOUT JUNE AND most of July, Tom and I put in three-hour days, Monday to Friday, restoring Mrs. Ryan's outhouse. Only twice rain kept us home. The project immediately became a brain teaser. Discovering that the lower third of all four walls were so badly rotted that they had to be excised and replaced, we had to use ingenuity to figure out how to stabilize the structure before sawing off its legs. By nailing 2x4's to the tops of each corner stud and slanting them downward and nailing their ends into stakes hammered into the ground, we had the building braced. And thus the cacophony of reconstruction began:

Hold the tape at the end of that two-by. Where the hell's my pencil? You'll need the level. Out of the way . . . I'm going to saw this off. Keep an eye on the wall. Damn, we should've run a couple of 2x6's first! Okay, that's a snug fit. Perfect, I'll toe a 12 penny nail into the piece. That should do the trick. Crap! We need more 2x4's! Wish we had a table saw . . . Too much trouble lugging the thing back and forth. Ready to rip up these boards? I get 63 and 1/16 inches. See what you get. Better safe than sorry. Suppose we put a diagonal two-by between those studs? We're moving right along . . . got two walls done in three weeks . . . should be almost done before winter. Oh, oh . . . we goofed! Didn't give the damn door enough clearance! Would you believe I forgot the plane? How in hell can we do the roof without a plane?

Shortly after noon of the last Thursday of July Tom and I squatted in the shade of a maple tree that must have witnessed the comings and goings of users of the privy, for its circumference was at least four feet. We had nailed the last shingle onto the roof, opened and closed the privy's door a half dozen times, and used the level to double check the plumb of the walls. We felt pretty good about the outcome of our work.

"With some caulking here and there and a couple of coats of paint, she'll be a beauty!"

"The prettiest gal in town, Tom."

Mrs. Ryan, her apron dusted with flour, limped to us, carrying a pitcher and two glasses.

"Saw you boys sitting out here and thought a drink of cold lemonade might hit the spot, what with this humidity and all."

I told her that the job was done and asked what she thought of it.

"Looks okay from here. But you haven't done what I asked you to do."

"And what may that be, Mrs. Ryan?" Tom looked befuddled.

"I asked you to get that thing out of my yard. Remember? How are you going to do that?"

Tom downed the lemonade in a gulp, stood and brushed sawdust from his pants, and looked at me.

"Harry's the one with the answers. I only came along for the ride."

"Who are you kidding, Tom? You've been clerk of the works from the get-go. You tell her how we're going to move the outhouse."

He shrugged, saying he had to hurry to pack up his tools and get to school in time to take his daughter to the dentist.

"Wait up a minute. Didn't she graduate a long time ago? And besides, the kids are on vacation."

A woman who knows the wiles and ways of men, she smiled and looked me in the eye.

"You haven't thought of how that outhouse is getting from here to yonder, have you? Well, I've got an idea. See that whatcha call it over there . . . a trailer? Belongs to the Glocester Light Infantry. They use it to cart their cannon whenever there's a reenactment they have to go to. Why don't you telephone Peter Rao? He's the head guy, a nice fellow. I bet he'll let you use it."

NOT ONLY DID Peter Rao lend us the Glocester Light Infantry's flat bed trailer but also he volunteered his muscle to help get the outhouse out of Mrs. Ryan's back yard. Another telephone call brightened the picture. My neighbor, Dick Howath, whose pick up truck had a hitch, said, "Sure, I'll tow the whole shebang when the time comes."

But the time would not come for another two-and-a-half weeks. More questions had to be answered: Where would the outhouse be plunked? What sort of foundation would it be plunked on? Who would build it? Lickety-split, the answers came.

I enlisted John Ducette, a fellow member of the GHS who was a civil engineer, to tell us where to site the two-holer and what sort of foundation should be built. He stopped by the schoolhouse en route home from working all day on a multi-million dollar project – a bridge spanning the Sakonnet River.

He glanced about, scratched his head, and pointed to a spot a few feet from the rear corner of the schoolhouse.

"There. Put it there. A four inch thick concrete pad should do. See you later."

Upcountry folk do not beat around the bush. In two work days, Tom and I had measured four times the length and width of the privy's sill, making sure we got the dimensions exact, shoveled the hole accordingly where John said to, and planked together the form for the foundation.

"Now the cement. I'll be damned if we'll mix it by hand!"

"I heard, Tom, Ken Lavoie and the owner of Barnes Concrete are pals. I'll talk to Ken about it."

Just like that, a Barnes mixer, passing through town from a job, poured its left over cement – for free! – into our hole. We waited a week for it to set and swung into action. On the evening of August 11th I made a call to Peter and Dick: Friday's moving day. The forecast looks perfect. Can you be at Mrs. Ryan's by nine in the morning?"

Pauline and I were the last to show up because the donut shop was busy. Peter was directing Dick who was backing his pickup and hitched up trailer across a shallow drainage ditch onto Mrs. Ryan's property. Tm and someone else were knotting ropes around the outhouse (that "someone else" turned out to be Dick's buddy – Wayne Carlow - whose size inspired Dick to include him in the moving gang).

The distance from Mrs. Ryan's yard to the cement slab in the rear of the schoolhouse was about 600 or so feet. But it took three hours for five men to move the privy. First, up and onto the trailer. Then across the drainage ditch and Dorr Drive. Finally up a grassy slope and onto the slab. Big Wayne, with a lot of common sense and experience in epical farm jobs, naturally became boss. It was a perilous journey:

At the count of three, grab hold of the ropes and lift. Ready? One, two, three lift! Watch it, Peter! Its leaning your way. Put your shoulder to it, Tom, and push . . . Whoa, my hand's caught in the rope . . . Okay, again push! . . . She's moving! . . . I've got this end tied, what about yours? . . . Easy as you go, Dick. Nice, nice . . . What the hell was that? We've hit some-thing . . . Quick, the thing's tipping! Get over here somebody and help me! . . . Swing the wheel, Dick . . . no, the other way, to the left . . . No, no, the other way, to the left . . . We're almost there . . . Stop! . . . Back her up real slow . . . Easy . . . Whoa! . . . We're home!

When the outhouse was hoisted off the trailer and down onto the foundation, Tom and I cheered to see that its sill precisely fit the dimensions of the slab. But the wonder of it all was the two-holer stayed together in one piece.

"The next time we do a job like this," I said, "we'll have it down pat."

"You must be crazy, man! What do you mean 'next time'?"

Talking around a mouthful of jelly donut, Wayne twanged, "An idea, guys. Let's go into the business of saving outhouses."

Dick laughed. "When you think of it, you can't take a shit in this thing."

"He's right," Tom giggled. "It did cross my mind. Did it yours, Harry?"

"Nope. My mind was other things."

"That so? Like what?"

"History."

"Don't laugh, guys," Wayne said, airing his sweat-soaked tee shirt and jutting his chin at the schoolhouse. "From the little I remember when I was in school, there's a lot of bull shit in history."

CAFÉ NUOVO, AN upscale restaurant smack in the center of Waterplace, attracts people who fancy menus graced with the likes of *garganelli* and *grana pedano*. Apparently, whoever picked the place to be the venue for Classical High School's Class of '53's golden reunion was one of those people. Then, too, the event planner probably thought that booking the restaurant on a September evening that coincided with a Water Fire gala might give a dash of romance to the reunion.

I abhor reunions. Most reluctantly, therefore, I knuckled under to Pauline's adamant intent to meet and greet her old classmates. The iota of goodwill I clung to on the drive into Providence dissipated in the snarl of traffic and evaporated completely when, to get to the front door of Café Nuovo, we had to bull through a throng of party-makers awaiting to board a gondola to get sculled past flaming braziers in the basin of Waterplace where the Providence, Woonasquatucket, and Moshassuck Rivers converged.

Cocktail hour was ending as we found two places at a table a room's length away from the bar. Although, considering the age of the Class of '53 and the time of day, attendance was good. But the conversations produced a low-volume hum – no boozy belly laughs, no startled exclamations like "My, you haven't changed a bit in fifty years!" The clicking of forks on the faux-china plates outsounded the voices.

I asked the server to bring Pauline a glass of wine.

"Yes, sir. And what might she prefer?"

She shrugged and said, "Something red."

Looking the paradigm of an esthete, the man across the table from her piped up, "If I may make a suggestion? Try the Sangioese. Buonissimo!"

She nodded to the server and squinted at the esthete's name tag.

"You're Sal Rossi! I . . . I . . ."

"You don't have to say it. I'm a craggy, old guy now. But look at you – as pretty as ever! I never thought I would see the shy Pauline Butler drink wine! Remember when we were sophomores and you helped me do Latin translations in study hall?"

They kept up a conversation all the way into the eating of a chocolate mousse. The three-course meal would have disappointed a trencherman, but I did learn something about the yellowish slivers in among the croutons and romaine lettuce that garnished the salad.

"Can anyone tell me what this is?" I asked to no one in particular.

Pauline's classmate – the one who once had had trouble with Cicero – dabbed his trimmed beard and answered, "Garganelli, a very expensive Italian cheese."

When Mrs. Rossi and Pauline excused themselves and headed for the ladies room, good-old-Sal and I sat in silence, he rotating the stem of a third glass of Sangiovese and I sipping a cup of black coffee. To ease my discomfort, I asked him what he did. That question put to a stranger, I had learned through the years, would invariably spark an eager answer. Sal did not disappoint me. His reply, tantamount to a resume, began with, "After Classical, I went on to Brown to get a degree in biology, Phi Beta Kappa to boot."

Yet not answering my question, he continued, "Then I earned a Master's and Ph.D. at Duke and took a teaching position at Auburn and stayed three years – or was it four years? Anyway, I moved on and was promoted to associate professor."

He paused, sipped his Sangiovese, and with a sleeve of his blue blazer wiped his brow. The professor was sweating.

"I was rapidly making a name for myself, pulling in substantial grants from the government to do genetic research and along the way publishing scholarly articles in the likes of *The International Journal of Applied Sciences and Biotechnology* and *The Journal of Theoretical Biology.*

"While on Sabbatical in Italy – Padua, to be exact – I met and married Filomena. That marriage didn't last long, unhappily. Both of us were too much into our careers. She, too, was a teacher, at the university there. Botany was her field. Her specialty was the *Spartium Junceum* plant indigenous to the Euganean Hills not far from Padua.

"Anyway, the short of it is when an opportunity arose at the University of New Orleans to head its Biology Department, I went for it and I'm still there – a full professor with tenure."

Pauline's prolonged absence annoyed me, and I searched the room for her, spotting her bent over a bald head and chatting. With nothing more coming from Professor Rossi, I turned to him. Our eyes met and he asked, "What about you? What do you do?"

"I restore outhouses."

I'm color blind. My guess was purple (or maybe red) flushed his cheeks. Without a hand shake or another word, he walked away and vanished. Tomorrow, I thought, I'll telephone Tom Samson and tell him about this. Perhaps he could explain this sudden, puzzling seizure of Sal Rossi. Who knows, maybe at this moment he needed an outhouse.

Let's play Twenty Questions.

STATE HOUSE

"MR. AND MRS. Harry Anderson!"

The basso voice of a Kentish Guardsman, announcing our arrival, reverberated in the rotunda of Rhode Island's State House. Pauline and I linked arms and followed the uniformed fellow up the grand marble stairway to one of the round tables placed along the corridor of the second floor. Momentarily halting their conversations, the four couples at the table glanced at us. I recognized no one.

I looked about. Beneath the leviathan granite dome – second in size to the Vatican's St. Paul Basilica's – light from wall sconces refracted off stem ware, silver place settings, ladies' diamonds and sequined gowns. Pauline nudged me and whispered, "Oh, oh . . . you're the only man not wearing a tux." I looked again to check that out. Yes, every gentleman was handsomely attired in black tie and tuxedo.

I discreetly took from my tweed sports jacket the invitation and read, "Governor and Mrs. Edward DiPrete cordially invite you to attend the Inaugaral Banquet . . .", followed by the date, time, and place. But no mention of a dress code. Never having been to such an event, I gave no thought to what to wear. Beside that, no tuxedo hung in my closet.

I whispered back to Pauline, "I'll just grin and bear it."

The off-white marble walls of the rotunda gave back the hum of conversations. We were clearly outsiders. It seemed that our table mates knew each other – quite well, in fact.

"The buzz downtown, Judge, has it you're thinking of retirement.

Any truth in that?"

"I'm no spring chicken, after all."

"Those young Turks fresh out of law school already have begun to scramble for position. Where do they get their brass? My God, some of them look like they're still supping on mother's milk!"

"But I spotted you, Judge, at the club last week. How's your game going?"

"Let's just say this, Ralphie. I bogeyed the twelfth hole at Alpine – and we all know what a bitch of a hole that is! I said to myself, 'JJ, you ain't going out to pasture anytime soon.'"

The one named "Ralphie" raised his champagne glass and, with a perfect Rhode Island accent, called for a toast: "Let's hear it for the judge, ladies and gentlemen!"

The woman in a high-neck purple gown, a strand of pearls the size of olives looping down to her bosom, touched my hand as I reached to the ice bucket.

"Sadly I say *tout de parti, pauvre homme*. But the boy will be bringing more champagne, I'm sure."

I tapped Pauline's shoulder to tell her the bad news, but she hushed me and turned back to the woman, who apologized for her terrible French accent.

"I'm practicing my French because next month Nick and I are flying to Paris. Anyway, what were we saying?"

"Sorry for the interruption, but my husband didn't realize we were talking. You were telling me about your daughter."

"Oh, yes, right. Caitlin's very much into the visual arts. She's a communications major at CCRI and hopes to get into film making. She's quite attractive, if I may say so myself, and it wouldn't surprise me if she someday becomes an actress. Wouldn't you say so, Dear?"

"Quite definitely"

He winked at Pauline and behind his hand said, "What's she asking me? Makes no difference, really, because I always agree with her."

I looked past the woman into the eyes of her husband who resembled Stewart Granger: his isosceles-ian nose was the centerpiece of a face that held a Caribbean tan. He seemed puzzled and asked, "Who are you, may I ask?"

"That was to be my question to you."

"You don't know?" His wife sounded incredulous.

"I honestly do not know."

Struck with a sudden impulse to be impish, I added, "I've an idea. You know how boring these affairs can be. So, suppose we liven things up a bit and play Twenty Questions. Is that okay with you?"

He sniffed his champagne, swallowed a sip, and said, "You're on! I'll ask the first question. Are you independently wealthy?"

Pauline laughed.

"I take it the answer's 'no'. Okay, it's your turn."

I asked, "What book are you presently reading?"

His wife laughed.

He came back with, "Are you self-employed?"

"No, I'm not. My second question is are you a politician?"

From below a drum roll sounded and someone boomed, Ladies and Gentlemen, the Governor and Mrs. Edward DiPrete!"

Chairs scraped, everyone stood, and an orchestra played *Hail to the Chief.* With that done, the same booming voice echoed off the marble walls: "Please remain standing as Father Cicone says Grace. At the "amen", chairs again scraped, conversations resumed, and a platoon of white-shirted-black-bow-tied waiters swooped to the tables to deliver the first course: four jumbo shrimps on a bed of lettuce with a side of red sauce.

"Hold on there!" Stewart Granger's look-alike ordered our waiter. "Two more bottles of bubbly, ASAP! And as for you, Mr. What's-Your-Name, you asked if I was a politician. My answer's negative."

I bit into a shrimp, awaiting his next question, but he fixed his attention on Ralphie.

"Yo, Ralph, I hear that the rep from North Kingstown's going to introduce a bill to convert those twenty-two-plus acres of state property down by Davisville into a park. Christ, just what we need, another damn park! I'm interested in that property. Think you can persuade the Speaker to bury the bill in committee?"

"Tell you what . . . we'll talk later about it. Anyway, you know what's to be done. So, eat up! Enjoy the shrimp."

With the arrival of the entrée – a sizzling medallion of filet mignon – came two bottles of champagne, one of which my Twenty-Question companion quickly snatched and popped the cork.

"Dear, Pauline and her husband haven't had anything to drink yet. Be a gentleman and pass them the bottle."

As I poured champagne into her glass, Pauline asked if the Twenty Questions had ended. Dabbing her lips with a damask napkin, the lady with the pearl necklace poked her husband.

"I believe, Sweetheart, it's your turn."

"My turn? For what?"

"To ask a question"

He frowned and without looking at me asked if I had any kids. Immediately, Pauline blurted, "He . . . we have seven."

"Christ, seven! At least I know what your husband does."

His wife's 18K diamond ring clinked her glass.

I had often witnessed Pauline's waiting for the chance to boast about our kids. This was her moment.

"Mark's our oldest. He's the free spirit of the family. Kristen graduated from Smith. Kim's a senior at Brown. Heidi's a sophomore at Wheaton. Nathan just started at University of New Haven, and Seth will go to Union in the fall. Our youngest, Rachel, is still in high school."

"And you say you're not independently wealthy? That's BS," the mystery man spluttered.

"Ah, there's my next question! Are *you* independently wealthy?

"You bet your ass I am!"

He drew from his tux's pocket a money roll held together with a gold clip.

"See this? Forty C notes. And they're yours if you can find me a good manager."

I looked around the table. By now all eyes were on us. Conversations had stopped. The orchestra began playing *Star Dust,* and I said, "I bet Ed requested that."

Slipping the wad of bills back into his pocket, he asked, "Ed? Who's Ed?"

"The Governor. Once upon a time he played clarinet in my band, and *Star Dust* was his favorite song. Oh boy, every gig he played it, and the people loved it!"

He smirked. "Aha! You're a musician!"

"I count that as a question."

"Well, are you?"

"No."

He pushed away his plate and sneered, "Hell with it. I've had it with this nonsense. Does anyone at this table know who this guy is?"

Shrugs all around. The judge, looking incredulous, asked me, "You really do not know the man seated to your right?"

"Truthfully, sir, I do not."

"Well, seeing that your little game has ended, it's fair of me then to ask you to introduce yourself. Would you please?"

Pauline beat me to the answer. "My husband's name is Harry."

"Harry what?" Ralphie asked.

"Harry Anderson, spelled 'on', not 'en'."

"And what is it that you do, Mr. Anderson?" The judge clearly was interested.

"I'm a teacher, sir."

With a shout, the Stewart Granger look-alike sputtered, "A teacher?" His eyes narrowed. "A teacher! What in hell are you doing here?"

My hand quivered at the stem of the champagne glass. Pauline answered for me.

"For your information, Ed DiPrete was Harry's Best Man and we are his son Thomas' God parents. Harry and I are here because the Governor is our friend."

PAULINE AND I shivered under the portico of the State House, waiting for the valet to deliver our Chevy Nova. We took in the Gatsby-like scene: well dressed celebrants stepping into expensive automobiles on a cold January evening.

"Can you believe any of this?" she asked.

"All night I felt like a fish out of water."

"What about your friend with the money wad?"

I snuggled my chin into the woolen scarf that a girl in my senior English class had knitted and given me for Christmas and said into it, "You don't have to ask. You know what I was thinking. Holy Toledo, I never did get his name!"

"I know his name. When his wife went to the ladies room she told me."

"No kidding? Tell me, who is he?"

Headlights of our Nova caught her face buried inside the hood of her parka. She was smiling. I gave the valet a dollar and he held the car's door open for her. I shifted into first and maneuvered around an idling Audi and shouted over the whirr of the car's heater.

"Well, are you going to tell me the guy's name?"

She shouted back, "Let's play Twenty Questions."

*They are not long, the weeping and laughter/Love
and desire and hate.*

ROOM 201

"MY MIND'S MADE up, Harry. This is it for me. Forty years of teaching is more than enough. Come June and I'll be retiring."

"I wish I could go out with you, Dick. I just can't, not with a daughter still in college. She'll be finishing up in a couple of years, and then we'll see."

He pulled from his jacket pocket a well used briar pipe, sucked at its stem a couple of times, and returned it to his pocket, grousing, "Holy Toledo, a man can't enjoy a smoke around here any more! There've been too many changes and none worth a tinker's damn. Just think about it for a minute. How many of the men teachers wear a tie and jacket? I'll tell ya. You, me, and Pat Kelly. The principal even doesn't. And speaking of him, he came to my classroom yesterday and had the nerve to tell me to get with the times and ditch T-squares! Imagine a mechanical drawing class without T-squares! He says it's in next year's budget to purchase computers that'll replace them. The guy's insane!"

"I know what you mean, Dick, about change. Did you hear about the plan to convert that storage room down by the gym into a day care center?"

"Come on! What for?"

"Yeah, the Home Ec department's adding child care to its curriculum and you know why? Get this . . . to accommodate the female students who've had babies."

"Oh, man, I'm getting out of this business just in time."

"Think you can stick it out until June? Anyway, you have to excuse me, Dick. I have to run something off for the next class. Oops, there's the bell."

When he opened the door, the quietude of my office followed him down the noisy corridor. A hodgepodge of adolescents thronged its length, hustling to beat the bell that signaled the start of the last class of the day. Over the din of dozens of voices and slamming locker doors lisping Lillian's scream was prominent: "You b-b-bitch!".

I shoved aside some of the kids who had formed a circle outside room 201, my classroom, in time to clutch Lillian's hand that was about to grab the hair of Tonya. Many a fight between boys I had broken up and learned that they seemed relieved that I had, but only once I intervened in a squabble between two girls and vowed never again try to quell quarreling vixens.

As I shouldered myself between the girls, Tonya's nails dug into my flesh just below my wrist watch and blood oozed from the scratch.

"This has got to stop, girls! Now! Both of you, get into the room! Capisce?"

Seeing the blood shushed them – temporarily. I shooed away the onlookers who were hankering to see a fight and as the bell clanged walked into my room, sensing tension in the air. The eighteen kids, largely an incorrigible lot, somehow managed to make it to senior year, barely eking out passing grades. I had seen bright, young neophytes so dispirited by such a class that they quit teaching. But by staying the course for thirty-two years I had acquired a bag of tricks that tamed the likes of these kids. This batch of kids, in fact, particularly pleased me, for not only had I forged a rapport with them but also I had them writing coherent paragraphs.

Seeing them settled in their seats, I turned to the chalk board and printed "VITAE SUMMA BREVIS SPEM NOS VETAT INCOHARE LONGAM". Behind my back someone stage-whispered, "You ain't gonna let Tonya call you a whore, are you, Lillian?"

"No w-w-way!"

"You and nobody else can stop me from callin' you anything I want to. So there! You are a whore!"

"Y-y-you better shut your g-g-god damned mouth, you b-b-bitch, or else!"

I pivoted and saw in the nick of time Tonya on her feet about to hurl a notebook.

Teddy Kopeck, the massive lineman for the school's football team who sat between the two girls began to thump his desk and chant "fight . . . fight . . . fight . . .".

My scowl shut him up, and a finger pointed at Tonya sat her down.

"I'll get you yet," she screamed.

"G-g-go to hell!"

This outburst sparked vocal reactions among the entire class. The Lillian allies whooped it up for her, and the Tonya-ites booed. There was anarchy in the making, and what course it took depended solely on what I would say in the next one or two minutes. Confident that I had gained their respect, my strategy was to slowly walk from the chalkboard and stop at Teddy's desk, folding my arms and putting the question to the class: "Behind me on the board I've printed a Latin sentence. Who wants to take a guess at its meaning?"

But the class was implacable. High dudgeon had seized them. Red-faced with anger, Tonya yelled, "I'm gonna scratch your eyes out, you bitchy whore!" And her pals egged her on. In retaliation Lillian tossed a pencil, grazing Teddy's ear. He guarded his head with crossed arms and shouted, "Holy shit, it's war!"

I was losing control and could not push back anger. Trembling, I let loose with a fusillade of purple rhetoric.

"You and you . . . you've descended into a snake pit. You've become disgusting miscreants! You make me feel dirty. All year I've been coddling you, and what thanks do I get? I've been casting pearls before swine. Graduation is only three weeks away and you'll be out of here into the real world, and I wouldn't bet a bent nickel on your chances of getting by, not by the way you're behaving right now."

I paused for a breath. That little tirade had not diminished the anger still roiling in my gut. I had more to say. But what came from the back of the room muted me.

"Shut your fucking mouth, Anderson! You have no right to talk to those girls like that. God damn it to hell . . . shut your fucking mouth!"

That was more than Gary Wentz had said in at least a fortnight. Gary Wentz – the quiet boy, the loner in the last seat by the windows, the one with black curly hair and bad acne and a fixation on passing traffic on East Street. Had a mortar round exploded in our midst, it would not have been more shocking than what he had shouted at me.

The scene freeze-framed. All eyes were on the kid, including mine. The utter silence, the electricity in the air protracted time. A minute seemed an hour. Gary returned to his private thoughts and to the East Street traffic beyond the windows. A convoy of school buses was lining up in the driveway. Another day at school was ending.

Crack . . . crack. Teddy was pulling his knuckles. Hiding behind his broad back, Lillian fumbled with her hair. In front of him Tonya chewed a finger nail, her face now the color of tapioca pudding. Every kid was staring at me, and I knew what they were thinking: "Goodbye, Gary Wentz. You're a goner."

He had crossed the line. To swear at a teacher was an unforgivable sin. A cat fight between two girls could be ironed out, but not the cussing of a teacher. He would certainly be expelled. I knew that. Everyone knew that.

In all my years of teaching I had never sent a student out of my room. If Gary were the first, he would have to deal with dire consequences. He would not be walking in cap and gown in three weeks with his classmates. Standing silent before the class with trembling hands in my pockets, I made a decision.

I went to my desk, took from it the pages I had mimeographed an hour earlier, and walked the aisles, plunking a page on each desk. Not looking at me, Gary bent his head to the page. Finally, I broke the silence.

"Okay, I've given you a poem. It's written by a guy named Ernest Dawson. But look. Before he starts the poem, he gives us a line from another poem, one written by an ancient poet named Horace, who wrote in Latin. There it is on the board. Now, I want you to write down in your notebooks its English translation. Ready?"

Notebooks opened. The class had never been so attentive.

"Here goes. *The shortness of life.* Got that? *Prevents us from entertaining.* Okay? *Far-off hopes.* I'll repeat it. *The shortness of life prevents us from entertaining far-off hopes.* Tomorrow we'll discuss what that means to you. Let's read now Dawson's poem. I'll recite it and you follow along.

They are not long, the weeping and the laughter,
Love and desire and hate;
I think they have no portion in us after
We pass the gate.

They are not long, the days of wine and roses,
Out of a misty dream
Our path emerges for a while, then closes
Within a dream.

"And there you have it. Your final assignment for the year is two-fold. First, I'm asking you to memorize these eight lines. Second, in three paragraphs tell what you think this poem is saying. Any questions?"

The bell sounded, piercing the eerie silence in the classroom. The kids stood and like specters drifted to the door. Teddy handed Tonya the wayward pencil who returned it to Lillian, and they vanished into the crowded corridor. I erased the board, wondering if the class had caught the irony in the timing of my introducing them to Horace's melancholic view of life.

"Mr. Anderson . . .".

Startled, I turned and saw Gary Wenz standing at my desk. His face, his eyes were ghastly. Clearly, I was looking at a troubled youth.

"Yes, Gary?"

"Mr. Anderson, I'm sorry."

"Apology accepted."

"What I said was awful. Everything just built up in me, and out came the words. That's no alibi I know. But . . ."

"What's 'this everything'? Do you care to tell me?"

He glanced about the room before slouching onto a chair. I sat on the edge of my desk, waiting.

"Last night after supper, Dad called us all together. My sister and two brothers and Mom. 'I got some bad news to tell you,' he said. And he told us what happened that afternoon. His doctor said he has cancer, a brain tumor and there's nothing they can do for him. He's dieing."

The boy lowered his eyes, paused, and continued.

"Then, about an hour later my girl friend called. She said she was pregnant."

He stood and went to the windows. With his forehead against the glass he finished his story.

"I've enlisted in the Coast Guard, something I've wanted to do for a long time. They took me on the condition that I graduate high school and wouldn't get married before basic training."

He faced me, dragging fingers through his curly hair, and blurted, "I'm all messed up, Mr. Anderson!"

I tongued my lips, struggling with exhaustion to find the right words to help the kid.

"You're going to report me, right? You have to. I'll be expelled and won't graduate."

"Wrong, Gary. I'm not telling anyone what happened. You will graduate."

"But what about Lisa, my girl friend?"

"Marry her after you finish basic training. Look, I tell you the truth. You're a good young man, a gutsy one. It took a lot of guts for you to look me in the eye and apologize. And as for your father, you'll make him very proud to see you in a uniform. More than that, can you imagine his joy when he holds for the first time his grandchild?"

He bolted from the room, and I understood why. A gutsy kid won't cry in front of anyone.

It was the second week of a new school year, and like Sisyphus I was rolling uphill another bolder – another batch of adolescents who begrudgingly would be putting up with my efforts to persuade them to value literacy. At the board I was Xing ISSUE, APPROPRIATE, AT THE END OF THE DAY, MOVING FORWARD.

"Those are clichés, kids! Don't you dare use them, not in room 201!"

From the corner of my eye I spotted something white at the door. Brushing chalk dust off my jacket, I went over and saw a tall, handsome fellow in uniform.

"Remember me, Mr. Anderson? I'm Gary Wentz. Excuse the interruption, but I'm on my way to the West Coast and have to show you something first. Can you come?"

To leave a class unsupervised was breaking a golden rule. Nevertheless, after commanding the kids to sit tight I followed the ram-rod straight fellow in a dazzling white Coast Guard uniform down the stairs and out the front door to a parked car from which a smiling young woman handed him a baby.

"She's Lisa, my wife. Lisa, meet Mr. Anderson. Here, I want you to hold our son, Eric."

Just for a minute or two I cradled the child there on a sidewalk beneath a September sun. Speechless.

Returning Eric to his mother, Gary said that I was right. His Dad was happy to have a grandson.

"Listen, I remember and always will this line. *They are not long, the days of wine and roses.* But I'm going to stretch them out as long as I can."

Then Gary Wentz saluted me, got into his car, and drove off, and I trudged back to room 201, to where a clutch of kids and their teacher were trying to learn a way to fashion the end of an essay - a cogent, clear, logical finale to an enigma.

All in all, I was in a snake pit.

RHODE ISLAND HOSPITAL

THE DOCTORS NEVER determined why I had bled so copiously, enough to turn the water in the commode a brilliant red. Neither did they tell me that they deemed my condition critical. The initial blood test taken in the ER informed them that my hemoglobin count had dropped to 7. Normal is 14. I was close to going into shock or even worse – death.

Other than feeling weak and woozy, I had no pain, no other symptoms. Pauline had known better to heed my protestations. She phoned Rachel, who wooshed us to Rhode Island Hospital.

At about 10:00 p.m. – eleven hours after entering the ER – I was wearing a hospital Johnny and was being wheeled onto an elevator to the ICU. Pauline and Rachel stuck with me and would sleep the night in chairs outside the ICU. A nurse inserted an IV port into my hand and connected me to a couple of plastic tubes. When I was awakened well before dawn for a blood draw (all in all, during my hospitalization I would have thirty-one of them as well as several insertions of IV ports), I learned that I had been hooked up to a heart monitor.

Not until Pauline came into the cramped cubicle where I lay belly-up, hands clasped, and eyes fixed on droplets dripping downward through the transparent IV lines did I learn the day was Sunday.

"Rachel's getting the car from the parking garage and will wait for me at the main entrance. Hope I can find it. After church I'll change, have a sandwich or something, and come back to the hospital."

"It's Sunday, Love? I've lost track of time. What's going on? I've seen only a nurse, and she's not telling me much. Where's the doctor?"

"I've looked into that and was told Dr. Harbr's been informed and will see you tomorrow morning. In the meantime you just have to stay put and do what the nurses say. Okay?"

"Looks like I have no choice, damn it!"

"How are you feeling?"

"Not bad. Just weak, that's all."

We kissed and she vanished.

"WELL, MR. ANDERSON, it's Monday. It'll be a busy day at the office."

I liked this nurse. She was calm and caring. When asked how long she had been at the hospital, she said that two weeks earlier she had celebrated her thirtieth year: "Had a nice lobster dinner at the Crow's Nest with my niece and her husband. They're my only family."

She had taken my vitals and was sponging my back when three men and two women clad in white lab coats crowded into the cubicle.

"Your team has arrived, Mr. Anderson."

Because the hospital was affiliated with the Warren Alpert Medical School of Brown University, it used a team approach in caring for patients in order to give its students first hand experience; therefore, in lieu of a patient's doctor's overseeing treatment, a group consisting of a specialist, a resident physician, a student, and whoever else may be needed did the examining, diagnosing, decision making. Only the specialist, a gastroenterologist, introduced herself – a Dr. Ulmberg. All five of them pressed cold stethoscopes against my chest and warm fingers into my abdomen; they read my chart and questioned my nurse. They buzzed like flies at a piece of carrion. Then they left.

I did not know how much time had lapsed as I lay there, mesmerized by the beeping of the heart monitor. Time had no relevance. When the nurse uttered "Ow!", I opened my eyes. A table on wheels entered the cubicle and grazed her hip. Following the fellow who was pushing the thing with a computer and a snarl of cables aboard were three women clad in blue surgical gowns and white masks dangling from their necks.

"Good morning, Mr. Anderson. I'm your anesthesiologist. We're here to prep you for a couple of procedures. Any questions before we get started?"

"Yes, Doctor. What procedures?"

"You haven't been told?"

"I haven't been told anything."

"Well, it goes like this. According to your chart, you've had a GI bleed and we have to find out why. So, Dr. Harbr, who'll be coming shortly, will perform a colonoscopy and an endoscopy. Basically, that's the score. Okay?"

"Do what you will."

As a nurse searched for a vein in the arm without an IV port in which to stab another one, the other two women in blue fussed with the computer and its cables behind me. When Dr. Harbr arrived, the anesthesiologist and nurse were chatting about their Dachshunds. He looked me in the eye and asked how I was doing.

"Sorry to keep you waiting like this, Mr. Anderson. Normally, these procedures are done upstairs where everything's set up and ready to go, but it's policy not to transport patients from the ICU. So, all the equipment has to come here. Gets complicated."

"We're ready to go, Doctor," the nurse said.

He raised a mask to his nose and tugged on latex gloves and the anesthesiologist held my hand and poised a syringe over the port. Her eyes held a smile, and she asked me how many kids I have.

"Seven."

"Good! Starting with the oldest, name them. Before you get to the seventh, you'll be out like a light."

"Mark, Kristen . . ."

"Wait! Something's wrong!"

The shriek resounded in the cubicle. Dr. Harbr lowered his mask, revealing a stunned expression.

"What's the problem?"

Because whoever shrieked was behind me, I assumed it was the woman at the computer.

"There's no arrow! The mouse is dead! Quick, someone get me a double-A battery!"

WEDNESDAY, THE FIFTH day of my hospitalization. At some point during the night, with the help of the nurse who seemed never to go home, I had left the bed and, wheeling the IV contraption as I went, shuffled to the bathroom. Getting to my feet for the first time since being admitted hit me with the realization that I was terribly weak. Last Friday's grilled swordfish supper was the last solid food I had eaten.

Back in bed, when the overhead light came on, I blinked. I first saw a red tie and an unbuttoned white lab coat and then the shaved, cleft-chinned face of a handsome young man. Seeing that I was awake, he introduced himself.

"Good morning, Mr. Anderson. I just joined your team. The name's Dr. Whitman."

"What's the time, Doctor?"

"A little after five."

"And what, may I ask, are you going to do with me at this ungodly hour?"

"Not a thing, really. I'm a psychiatrist doing my residency requirement. My role is to see you each morning and to let you know what your team's game plan is for the day."

He checked my chart.

"All's looking good. Monday's tests went well. The three blood transfusions seem to be doing their thing. The last blood draw shows your hemoglobin count to be rising. Up to 9, but still some way to go. Today you'll be out of the ICU and transferred to the Jane Brown unit."

He was concise, unsmiling. I sensed that he might not have slept well. Yet empathy nuanced his voice. His eyes scanned me. He tapped my foot and walked out.

Whereas the ICU cubicle had given me the sensation of being encased in a box, my room on the second floor of the Jane Brown building had a window. Disconnected from IV's and a heart monitor, I sat in a chair by the window and delighted to a couple of squirrels cavorting in the branches of a maple tree whose leaves were yellowing. Some were falling.

"Has autumn officially come?" I asked Pauline. Rachel and she were examining the new bed that replaced the older version soon after I had been wheeled into the room.

"Tomorrow, Dad," Rachel answered.

Both were showing signs of fatigue after five days of coming to the hospital. Years of cranking hospital beds up and down, nurse Pauline was too fascinated with this state-of-the-art, high tech thing to heed my question.

"Look, Rachel, it has a built-in telephone!"

"The men who set it up this morning said it cost $32,000! Can you believe that? I can hardly wait to try it out. Hey, Love, do you think anyone would mind if you joined me?"

My visitors stayed until gloaming darkened the window and a male nurse checked my vitals and drew yet another vial of blood. I backed onto the new bed, not daring to touch any of the several buttons, and pulled the blanket to my chin. I must have been more done in than I thought because I dozed off at once, and I was dreaming:

My footfall echoed in the first-floor corridor, empty of neither students nor teachers. Classroom doors were shut. Somewhere in the building a class was waiting for me. I was late. I climbed the stairs at the end of the corridor to the second floor, but the top step was missing and I could not get onto the landing. I went back down, trotting the corridor, passing closed doors, looking through their vertical windows into classrooms. In one, kids sat at typewriters. In another, kids held test tubes over Bunsen burners. I came to another stairwell and tromped up to the second floor and ran to the only classroom with an open door. No one had put on the lights. I made out figures seated at desks, and, as my eyes adjusted to the dimness, I recognized Tom and Cheryl, Mary and Byron. I had found my class. But the mood was hostile.

I awoke to the chatter coming from the nurses' station just beyond my door. I was disoriented, upset, and thirsty. More than that, my right knee pained. I pressed the kneecap and winced and knew that gout had set in. I sat up, dangled both legs over the edge of the bed, and with the aid of gravity stood. The pain was excruciating. With nothing between the bed and the bathroom to hold onto, I lay belly down on the floor and crawled, roundtrip.

I backed onto the bed and moved my bum leg in various positions, but the pain persisted. A veteran of these attacks, I knew that I would have to soldier through for at least five days. I studied the controls of the new bed, looking for the one that would signal those chatterboxes out there that I needed help. I pressed one and the bed warmed under me. I pressed another and the overhead light came on. On the third try the corridor chatter stopped and a youngish woman in a flowery top and blue pants and sneakers stepped into my room.

"Is there a problem, Mr. Anderson?"

"Yes. Big time! I'm having an attack of gout and my leg hurts like hell! Can you give me something for it?"

"Sorry, only a doctor can do that. I'll make a note of it on your chart."

"At least you can give me something to drink, please. I'm very thirsty."

"Of course. First, though, we've got some business to do, now that you're awake."

"Not another blood draw!"

"You've got it! Doctor's order. Which arm tonight?"

I surrendered to the needle.

"There, that wasn't so bad, was it? Now, let's check your vitals."

As she undid the pressure cuff, she murmured, "A bit elevated."

"I'm having a bad night."

" Oh? What else is going on beside the pain in your knee?"

"Let's just say nothing anyone in this hospital can deal with. How about getting me that drink now? Please!"

The ginger ale hardly slaked my thirst. All in all I was in a snake pit. I propped my sore leg up over a pillow, longing for music – some jazz, maybe, like Satchmo's *It's a Wonderful World* or Natalie Cole's *Unforgettable*. Race Vaughan Williams and his ascending lark would do. But no radio, no CD player was at hand, not even one built in to the $35,000 bed.

So, as I had often done in the throes of crisis, I recited the Lord's prayer. That worked! Sleep came, but with it came a continuation of that awful dream.

Panic struck. I was sitting alone in the faculty room when I should have been with my AP composition class – the same class that yesterday I had had trouble finding. I dashed into the corridor, up the stairs, and stopped. The last step was missing. Back to the first floor, I reversed direction and halted at a solid steel door. I struggled to open it. I walked into a shop class. Kids at work benches hammered nails into blocks of wood. All eyes were on me. Then they laughed, their laughter following me as I ran frantically through the shop and out its rear door onto grass. I was out of the building! Again and again, over and over I ran the corridors. Then . . . I found my class! I stood before them. Their faces were distorted with disgust, with hatred.

"AH, YOU'RE AWAKE, Mr. Anderson. Good morning. When I came in a few minutes ago, you were zonked. I read your chart and see that you're in pain. Your right knee is it?"

"Yes, Dr. Whitman. I'm pretty sure it's gout."

"Here, I've brought you a Tylenol capsule. Because we haven't found the cause of your bleeding, we're hesitant to give you anything stronger."

As I washed down the capsule with a Dixie cup of apple juice, he summarized my team's thinking.

"You're making excellent progress what with no further episodes of bleeding and your hemoglobin count continues to rise. It's at 10 as of last check. The plan now is to see if you can take solid food. So, today you can order anything on the menu."

By now I was catching on to his style and expected the sustained silence that followed along with his unblinking eyes fixed on me. I took this to be a tacit invitation to dump at his feet some ghastly burden.

"Doctor," I blurted, "do you think stress – or maybe 'distress' is the better word – can bring on physical ailments? Like gout, for instance."

"Absolutely I do! In fact, that's exactly what I plan on doing, researching the connection between mind and body. Do you ask because you think your hospitalization has been stressful and, therefore, has caused your gout?"

"I suppose that's part of the problem. But there's more to it than that."

I told him of last night's dream. When he said nothing, I unburied my guilt.

"When I retired, I was at my peak. With utmost modesty, Doctor, I tell you people have said that I helped a lot of kids in important ways. I was terribly wrong to quit teaching so soon."

His eyes gleamed. He was aboard my psyche.

"Your chart lists your age to be 78. When did you leave teaching?"

"In 1992. I was 58 years old with plenty of zip to keep at it. But I quit!"

"My hunch is for these past twenty years you haven't been idle. Am I right?"

" 'Idle', Doctor? I don't know its meaning."

He looked at his watch and apologized for having to keep with a schedule.

"Have you considered that you had to do what you did? Maybe not consciously, but certainly somehow you knew it was time for you to move on. I say without qualification that your feeling guilty is without justification. Give thought to this little conversation. Now, you must excuse me."

He smiled, tapped my toe, and vanished.

A SQUALL COMING from nearby Narragansett Bay tore leaves from the trees that lined the walkway from the parking lot to the hospital's main entrance. I hobbled to the window to watch the wretched weather have its way with visitors whose umbrellas wee useless in the wind. I worried about Pauline's driving to Providence in the dark that comes early in late September. A voice behind me broke the room's silence.

"Mr. Anderson, are you up to a visit?"

The gentleman at the door was every inch professorial – an antediluvian figure quite like my college teachers: carefully trimmed salt-and-pepper hair, bow tie, tweed jacket. Two young men and a book-wormish young woman accompanied him.

"I'm Dr. MacIntosh, associate professor of internal medicine at Brown, and these three bright lights are my students. You've been recommended to me. It seems that you've a knack for gaining a rapport with students. May we spend a few minutes with you to get your story about what brought you to the hospital?"

I hobbled back to bed, sensing that my visitors were taking measure of me.

"There's my chart, Doctor. It should fill you in on things."

"We pretty much know what your chart says. It's what we don't know that intrigues us. The big mystery, of course, is what caused your rectal bleeding in the first place. By allowing us to ask questions will go a long way in helping us learn something important about diagnostics."

As I moved my eyes from face to face, I felt a surge of an old passion, and I wanted to animate the kids' expressionless features.

"If I may, Doctor, I would like to ask the first question."

"Go right ahead." He seemed surprisingly pleased.

"You with the red hair. That's a neat pony tail you got. Anyway, to the question. When I was first examined in the ER, I was asked a lot of things, things like my diet, bowel movements, family medical history. But never was I asked what, to me, would be an obvious first question. So . . . what's your name?"

"Eric, sir."

"Ha, Eric the Red! Well, Eric, what would you have asked?"

He glanced at his teacher and back at me.

"You mean other than your diet, etc.?"

"You're stalling, Eric. Come on, think!"

"Ah . . . ah, maybe I would ask if you've had an earlier bleeding episode?"

"Very good. But that's not it. Maybe your buddy knows. What's your name?"

"Arnold. And frankly I'm stymied."

I pointed to the young woman, whose eyes looked down at her shoes, and asked, "Have you ever had a colonoscopy? Oh, what's your name?"

"I'm Agnes and, no, I've never had a colonoscopy."

She blushed, and I added that I was hinting at what question no one ever asked me.

Eric's hand shot up and, like a grade school kid who eagerly wanted to impress his teacher, blurted, "I got it! They didn't think to ask if you had that procedure!"

"You almost hit the nail on the head, Eric. Almost."

Agnes' hand grazed her glasses as she raised it, and Arnold at the same time did a little dance step. These kids had come to life.

"Whoa!" I commanded. "Cool it for a sec. Eric's answer lacked a key word. Think. Now, together, what's that word?"

" 'When'!" the three of them shouted in unison.

"Yes, yes, yes! No one ever asked *when* I had had a colonoscopy. You see, just prior to my bleeding out I was scoped."

Dr. MacIntosh frowned. "Are you suggesting that something went awry during your procedure that caused your hemorrhaging?"

"No, Doctor. I'm simply speculating."

The visit was over. Eric was last to leave the room. At the door he

RHODE ISLAND HOSPITAL ✝

paused, looked at me, and decided not to say what was on his mind. But a smile and a nod sufficed.

DR. WHITMAN, PROMPTLY at 5:00 a.m., stood at the foot of my bed. My ninth day at Rhode Island Hospital was beginning. As usual, a calm came with him into the room.

"How is everything with you this morning?"

"Not bad at all, Doctor. The pain's letting up in my knee. The truth is I'm feeling pretty darn good."

"Any more bad dreams?"

"None! Amen! I thank you for that."

"What I'm about to tell you will really perk you up. Your team has decided that you're fit to be discharged today."

All sorts of emotions roiled me. I could not speak. In the silence we stared at each other. Then, inexplicably, I asked a question.

"Doctor, do you believe in Providence?"

In a sudden his face darkened and he whacked the bed's table. An empty Dixie cup toppled to the floor.

"No, I do not!" he fulminated.

Silence.

"Is that so?" I whispered. "Well, from my point of view there's a lot of Providence in you."

He pulled at his tie, tapped my toe, and turned.

"You've made my day, Mr. Anderson."

I WAITED UNTIL I had eaten scrambled eggs and toast and exchanged my hospital Johnny for street clothes before telephoning Pauline. She was not an early riser.

"Would you please come get me, Love? They're letting me go home."

Old timers' best buddies are themselves.

TYRINGHAM

WE HAD TO stop. There it was – true to life – a cottage like the evil witch's gingerbread house in Grimm's *Hansel and Gretel:* a thatched, undulating roof, sugar-white walls, arched windows, a heavy plank door, and a bed of multi-colored nasturtiums swaying to an audience of three built-by-fairies stone columns reaching to the eaves.

When Pauline and I left our tent at the October Mountain campground in Lee to explore the Berkshires, I expected to see – and did see – quiet hills, idyllic dales, birch bowers (vistas that had enchanted Melville, Hawthorne, Edith Wharton). But never did I expect to come upon such a cottage. We stopped in the gravel driveway, spotted a sign that read ART MUSEUM, and moseyed to the entrance.

"Should we knock?" she wondered. "Maybe this isn't open to the public."

"Hey, the sign says it's a museum, right? If the door's not locked, we're going in."

I pressed the brass handle and the heavy door opened, and we stepped into a great room. Had I knocked, no one would have been there to greet us. The preternatural silence of the room transfixed us. We paused in a rectangle of light cast through an arched window by a July sun now above the firs that ascended the hills that circled Tyringham, a hamlet of 327 citizens in western Massachusetts, a stone throw from the New York line.

"Now what?" Pauline whispered.

"We'll look about."

Paintings hung on the white walls: oils, water colors, charcoal and pencil drawings, a potpourri of subjects – old men doing what old men do, cute pets, nudes, optically teasing abstracts, but by and large Berkshire inspired landscapes like Stockbridge Bowl at sunset or the snow capped twin humps of Mt. Greylock.

We strolled through a maze of rooms, eyeing the paintings, seeing no one. The utter silence was spooky. Our passage dead-ended in a small room. A couple of sculptured pieces stood guard on either side of a French door. We either had to retrace our steps or chance going outside through that door. Outside we went.

"Oh, this is beautiful!" Pauline, a devotee of gardens, gushed. The back yard of the gingerbread house – at least an acre in all – was ablaze with day lilies, fox gloves, heather, and zinnias. We kept to a gravel, serpentine path, crossed over a rill on an arched, stone bridge, and rested on a garden bench beside a bronze statue of an angel holding a dove.

"This is paradise," she sighed, reverently.

"That it is, Love. But look at the time! Can you believe we've been here going on two hours? I'm getting hungry, aren't you?"

Up we stood and followed the path that lead to another stone bridge and to a bed of gay marigolds and beyond to a blue door. We had no choice but to go back inside. There, on a sofa, sat a man and a woman, he with his head on her breast and she with an arm around him. They had to be at least eighty. Startled to come upon them, I blurted, "Oops, sorry! I should've knocked. We're trespassing, aren't we?"

"That's quite all right. There was a time when we had to post a "Private Entrance" sign on the door because so many visitors were coming. But these days hardly anyone shows up. Frankly, my husband here and I miss the old days. Don't we, Dear?"

When she pinched his cheek, his eyes opened and he muttered, "It's in the shed under . . . under that green thing. You know that green thing? Well, it's there, under it."

He raised his head, and I was looking into eyes that were leaking their color.

"Have you come to shoot the rabbits?" he asked me.

With a hanky, his wife dabbed away spittle bubbling at the corners of his thin lips. She glanced at us and whispered one word: "Alzheimer's".

Pauline squeezed my arm and gave me a let's-go look, and I apologized for intruding and turned to the door. But the plaintive tone of the old woman's plea to stay halted me.

"Please sit down for a bit. If you're not in a hurry, I'd welcome a little chat."

We sat in the two Windsor chairs across from them – the owners of the gingerbread house I presumed. She introduced her husband as "Mr. Davis" and herself as "Mrs. Davis", and our little chat began. Had not Mr. Davis's peeing his pants an hour into her monologue, we very well might have tarried an hour longer, for she had much to tell us.

"Of course you're familiar with the famous Minuteman statue in Lexington. Who isn't? Well, the gentleman who sculpted it – Henry Hudson Kitson, an Englishman – designed this house and used it and the adjacent silo for his studio. It's truly a unique building, wouldn't you say? The roof alone makes it so. It looks like a thatched roof, doesn't it? But it isn't. Mr. Kitson employed three men who cut literally tons of asphalt shingles and layered them just so to look like a thatched roof. Took them nearly four years. When all was said and done and Mr. Kitson moved into Santarella – that's what he named it – he was broke."

She paused and shifted her attention to Mr. Davis when he groaned and tugged at the top button of his shirt

"What is it, Dear? Oh, look at you sweat! It's warm in here, isn't it?"

She dabbed his brow with a hankie and scowled at us.

"Shame on me. I never asked for your names."

"I'm Pauline and he's Harry."

"Look, Pauline, would you please be so kind to fetch something to drink? Through that door you'll find the kitchen and in the refrigerator a pitcher of iced tea. Glasses are in the cupboard over the counter."

When Pauline returned and placed a tray with four glasses and a half-empty pitcher on the coffee table, I was answering questions Mrs. Davis was putting to me. The old woman seemed truly interested in us.

"Do tell me more about yourself after I get Mr. Davis squared away here. Careful, Dear! You almost tripped. Come now, you have to sit up. That's it! Pauline, will you please hand me a glass?"

The old man grasped it with both hands and slurped a mouthful of tea, and he smiled. All eyes were on him until he had emptied the glass.

"It's so hard to see this man like this. So totally dependent and all." She smoothed his hair, thick as a lion's mane and as white as the morning glories twisting up a trellis beyond the window. "Of course you had to notice the gardens out back as you came along the pathway. That was his doing, every last bit of it. When we purchased the property back in 1947, a year after he came home from the war, the yard was a disaster. Mr. Kitson had let go to ruin. My husband worked his fingers to the bone, designing the layout, digging the fish pond, cutting away the brambles . . . everything!

"We bought Santarella to fill a huge need. You see, there are a lot of talented artists in the Berkshires, but they had no place to exhibit their work. So, we gave them a place."

She put his glass on the tray, clasped his fingers and kissed them.

"All that's ended now. The time's come to rest, hasn't it, Dear?"

The old man's lips parted and he gargled, "The fish . . . did they go home?"

She sniffled and reached for a glass. With her eyes fixed on the side window, she softly announced that Santarella was for sale.

"We've turned down several offers because we're not going to let it go to just anyone."

Turning to me, she most earnestly asked, "Harry, would you be interested in buying Santarella?"

I swallowed hard the last of my tea and looked at Pauline, who seemed nonplused.

"Mrs. Davis, I . . . I'm flabbergasted, really! You honor me to ask, but . . ."

"Ah, there's the 'but'. It's as I thought. So be it. Oh my, Mr. Davis, you're wetting yourself! You young people must excuse me. I've got to attend to him."

She scooted him away, and Pauline rounded up the four glasses. I followed her to the kitchen where we deliberated whether or not to stay. Deciding not to stay, we shouted an unanswered farewell and exited through a side door and faced two raised beds of herbs. Weeds fought with sage, rosemary, parsley, mint for space. Compulsively, I clawed into the soil and tore at the spreading, thready roots of clover. Foolishly, I angered at their lack of conscience, the nerve of them to invade an old man's garden with impunity when he couldn't fight back.

I stood at the car door and, with a small pocket knife, uncaked dirt under my fingernails. The sun had sauntered farther west, bringing shade to the nasturtiums, and I suppressed the urge to pull up the horseweed among them that earlier I had noticed.

As I coasted out of the driveway, I gave the gingerbread house a final glance and vented my melancholy.

"Oh boy, the ancients got it right."

"What are you talking about?"

"*Ars longa, vita brevis* . . . that's what I'm talking about."

MY PLAN FOR the day included gathering butternut squashes, still at-tached to the vines. They lay plump and ripe on the straw I had spread about the hills last June to smother the weeds. But uprooting the five rows of corn stalks and piling them for burning at the far edge of the garden and raking the hills and holes smooth, I had spent my strength. There was no need to fret about a killer frost yet. We were only two days into fall and September's sun encouraged the tree toads to continue their mating call.

I rested on a boulder too big to roll out of the garden and tapped a cigarette from its crushed pack and scolded myself for not taking it out of my pants pocket as I worked to put the garden to sleep for the coming winter. Joeie, the nurse practitioner whom I had chosen to be my primary person, would be much pleased were I to quit smoking. Both of us had down pat the grand finale of every office visit: stethoscope to chest, deep breath, hold it . . . exhale.

"Sounds good," she says, and, before she asks, I say, "Yes, I'm still smoking."

A couple of grackles cawed back and forth in the top boughs of an old oak tree whose leaves never returned after early summer's infestation of gypsy moths.

"I've got to nail that sucker. Should get a good cord of firewood out of it."

I had begun to talk to myself, not always out loud. Usually only when Maisie came around for a belly rub. My father talked to himself in his latter days. At his lathe in his cellar workshop, I had once overheard him pondering calibrations as I came down the stairs: "Another sixteenth of an inch should do." Old timers' best buddies are themselves.

"Maisie, come! Where are you? Come!"

Our four-year-old Dachshund sprinted from a thicket of raspberry stems and reared on her leprechaunic legs, her crayon-thin tail lashing my boots.

"Joeie just doesn't get it . . . right, Maisie? Crazy Maisie . . . you want your tummy rubbed, don't you?"

She flopped, belly up, and I rubbed.

"As I was saying, Joeie doesn't understand the pleasure of a smoke after a job's been done. Nothing like it, to sit back and light up and look at what you've accomplished. You're a good girl. No back talk from you."

From somewhere up the road a dog barked and she rolled to her feet and ran off, yipping. I backed up onto the boulder and put a match to a cigarette (three matches, actually, because the breeze had become gusty). Forgetting that I had plunked today's mail on the boulder to save steps rather than taking it into the house, I accidentally nudged a stone off the envelopes and a gust scattered them. Annoyed by my carelessness, I chased the mail about the garden and returned to the boulder, tearing open the envelope with the Citizens Financial Services return address. I was curious to learn what interest my municipal bonds had earned since June.

"A lousy two hundred bucks! In with the junk mail you go."

I regretted looking at that quarterly report because it brought to mind a nagging problem. Now, when it's not needed, having some money and a proper yard was a problem. What a joke! Years and years the opposite was the case. We aren't travelers, gamblers, or into consumerism. How would we dispose of this money when the time came? If we first ended up in a nursing home, though. . ."

To blot out black thoughts, I got busy again. But when I pried up a root of a corn stalk, the spade's handle snapped.

"Damn it!" I yelled and looked up at the house to see if Pauline had heard. She was at the hose, filling her father's banged up, galvanized watering can. Maisie had heard my cussing and whizzed down the slope toward me, her ears flapping like a fledgling's wings.

"See what happens, Maisie, when you leave tools outside? The rain rots them and they go kaput."

I swear it was amusement I saw in her brown, button-like eyes.

"Now I have to go to the hardware store for a new spade. These interruptions bug me, like tomorrow's appointment with my urologist. There's a lot to get done before the snows come. Right, Maisie?"

She begged to be lifted. I must have bent her leg or something when I hugged her, for she yipped and leapt from the boulder.

"Sorry, sweetie."

She looked back at me and rolled in the freshly mowed grass beneath the Joshua tree – the red maple that I had planted the week of our first grandchild's birth twenty-four years ago. I reckoned that I had held Josh for the first time about when we had been to Tyringham and the gingerbread house. The tree was only a stick with one tiny leaf then. Now it stood a sturdy twenty or so feet high. And look at him! A college graduate!

"My God, I must be as old as Mr. Davis was back then!"

Maisie, thinking I was speaking to a visitor, picked up her ears and barked.

"Cool it, sweetie. No one else here but you and me."

I thought it odd that that day in the Berkshires so long ago had come to mind. It got me remembering . . . the spittle bubbling at the corners of the old man's mouth, the stain of piss on his pants, confusion brimming in his eyes. But most of all, his hands that twitched on Mrs. Davis' lap, veins like wadies crisscrossing them. Hands of a laborer: cracked nails, a two-inch scar on the left one that ran parallel with gnarled knuckles, white hairs sprigging from tautly drawn skin, the color of adobe, over bones. And I remembered Mrs. Davis' testimony to the man: "He worked from sunup to sundown doing everything. Everything!"

"God meant it when he kicked Adam and Eve out of Eden and condemned them and all of us to a life of toil. Paradise was lost and with it went our immortality. You, Mr. Davis, bashed up your hands converting God's curse into a passion . . . until that day when you called to Mrs. Davis for help, when you had strayed from the path and gotten lost in your garden." I was talking to myself again.

Last May, Mrs. Beaudin accepted Pauline's invitation to come see our flowering azaleas and rhododendrons. "Your yard . . . it's beautiful!" she raved. "It's Xanadu!"

Her allusion to Coleridge's dream vision of paradise went a long way to make me feel that all those years of work maybe were not a quixotic pursuit after my own dream vision.

THE YEAR WAS 1959 – fifteen months into marriage. Mom and Dad gave us $500 for down payment on a "fixer upper" with four acres of uncared for land. The sellers let Nature have her own way. A snarl of wild grape vines, brambles, poison ivy had advanced to the kitchen door.

Pauline had no place to park the baby carriage. Determined to see our son creep on grass on his first birthday, I began my battle with Nature at the outset of spring thaw, and on April 13th Mark's grandparents sat on kitchen chairs plunked in a swath of cleared land and sang "Happy Birthday" to the lad.

Fifty-six years later I was still whacking away with a Maddox at tough rhizomes of ferns and the underground network of roots, prying up rocks and muscling them one atop another to build stone walls.

Pauline's shout broke my thoughts. "Do you know what time it is? We'll have to leave in an hour, you know."

"I'm coming, Love. I was about to quit anyway. I've had it!"

With Maisie at my heels, I went to the trash bin and tossed the broken spade into it and then, as was my custom, before going into the house at day's end, I lit a cigarette and ran my eyes over the property.

"The Feather Reedgrass looks great! And I'm glad I put in that raised bed for the herbs by the back door. Everything's looking nice, don't you think so, Maisie?"

I knelt and rubbed her muzzle, her tail thwacking my shin.

"You're a good girl. You love the yard, too, don't you? If you could push a lawn mower or swing an ax, I'd leave all this to you. Yes, I would! There would be no problem then. Cripes, Maisie, I don't know what to do."

It was good to feel the warm life of someone.

"Are you coming or not? It's getting late! Who are you talking to?"

Pauline's head was at the kitchen window. I pinched the lit end of the cigarette and put the butt in my shirt pocket.

"To Maisie."

"You're wasting time. You know how Vivian likes to start the meeting on the dot of seven."

I unlaced my boots and banged them together to loosen the mud from the soles. Maisie pounced to the door, awaiting me to open it.

"Are you still there, Love?" I asked to the screened window.

"I hear you. Do you have to shave?"

"I've been thinking. Do you remember the Davises, that old couple we met years ago in Tyringham?"

"Vaguely. What about them?"

"I wonder what ever happened to their gingerbread house."

"That was a long time ago. They have to be dead now."

"That's why I'm wondering about the gingerbread house."

"Who knows? And honestly, I really don't care. What matters here and now is I don't want to be late for the meeting. So, would you plea-se hurry up!"

Shoeless, I went to the herb garden and yanked up a horseweed that was horning in on the parsley. I just had to do it.

I too had had the wont to tell my story.

AUTHOR'S AFTERWORD

IN MY READING, I came upon an account of an illiterate South Carolina slave who, heeding the wont to tell her story, did so by fashioning a quilt. The finished work – twenty-four blocks, each fabricating with strips of cloth a depiction of a seminal event in her life – was a visual compendium of what went into the making of her identity.

"That's it!" I nearly shouted aloud. I, too, had had the wont to tell my story, but put off doing it for lack of ambition among other reasons such as having no idea of how to go about structuring it. Learning about story quilts, however, prompted me to consider replicating that slave's novel idea. Rather then using fabric and thread, though, I would use words, something that she could not do. I would select twenty-four seminal moments in my life - envisioning the narration of each to be as a block in a story quilt - that, when "stitched" together, would reveal enough of the essence of who I am in order to slake the curiosity of those who have wondered.

To complement my narration, I thought it a good idea to craft an actual quilt, something that I could not do. Enter serendipity. On a Saturday morning when I had accompanied Pauline to her weekly rug-braiding session at the Greene Library I was introduced to Peg Facker, a quilter. The more we chatted, the more apparent became her acumen, her simpatico with my idea. When I left for home, I had myself a quilter.

The lay-out of this book is, among other things, the result of our – Peg's and mine – learning quite quickly our compatibility. For two years, we stayed true to a process that seemed to come easily, naturally from our time-honed – shall I say – wisdom: I emailed her, one by one, a revised chapter; she chose an archetypal quilt pattern – its fabric, color, and design – and variously fashioned a block that symbolically depicted each chapter's theme. And beneath each she wrote a brief interpretation.

Again serendipity entered as I sought for a title, something that would tie together quilting and recollecting. Months passed without success. But while idling away an Indian summer afternoon by browsing through unread magazines, I came upon an article about commercial flying and learned the meaning of "block time": how a plane's flight time is measured. The clock begins ticking when the ground crew removes the chocks at the departure gate and stops ticking when, at the arrival gate, the crew slides them into place beneath the plane's wheels.

I had my title. Those two monosyllabic words, "block" and "time" not only united quilting with recollecting but also dished up a feast of connotations. For example, isn't the writing of one's life – indeed, the living of that life – tantamount to a journey or flight? Isn't the living of a life episodic that ultimately validates the axiom that the whole is the sum of its parts? And doesn't "block", seen as a transitive verb, invite speculation on what this author's intent is by structuring his memoir through the eyes of a quilter?

Peg Facker's stunning quilt hangs in my living room. You, my reader, are holding its counterpart, my book. Together they tell my story, or at least blocks of it. Like that illiterate 19th century South Carolina slave woman who passionately wanted her story told I, too, have felt that passion.

ACKNOWLEDGMENTS

THANK YOU, PEG Facker, for your courage to take on the formidable task of reading my manuscript and then transposing it into a story quilt of exquisite design. And to Albert Tavakalov goes my praise for your skill in photographing each of the quilt's blocks. Most desperately I needed the computer skills of grandson Tim Horton and Professor Donald Paquette, both of whom came through for me. As for my wife, Pauline, and all those others who people the episodes of my life that I have chosen to narrate, without you I would have no stories to tell. My love and gratitude for you are ineffable.

CPSIA information can be obtained
at www.ICGtesting.com
Printed in the USA
LVHW020927110221
678898LV00010B/1008